In Search of a
National
Morality

In Search of a National Morality

A Manifesto for Evangelicals and Catholics

Edited by William Bentley Ball

Baker Book House
Grand Rapids, Michigan

Ignatius Press
San Francisco, California

Copyright © 1992 by Baker Book House
Baker Book House Company

Baker Book House ISBN: 0-8010-1029-2
Ignatius Press ISBN: 0-89870-423-5

Scripture citations are taken from the following translations:
KJV: King James Version
NASB: New American Standard Bible, copyright © 1960, 1962, 1963, 1968, 1971, 1972, 1973, 1975, 1977 by the Lockman Foundation.
NIV: New International Version, copyright © 1973, 1978, 1984 by theInternational Bible Society.
NJB: New Jerusalem Bible, copyright © 1985 by Darton, Longman & Todd, Ltd. and Doubleday, a division of Bantam Doubleday Dell Publishing Group, Inc.
RSV: Revised Standard Version, copyright © 1946, 1952, 1972 by Division of Christian Education of the National Council of the Churches of Christ in the United States of America.

Printed in the United States of America

Contents

PREFACE

William Bentley Ball

William Bentley Ball is a constitutional lawyer who has been lead counsel in First and Fourteenth Amendment litigations in 22 states and in many cases in the Supreme Court of the United States, including the landmark decision in the Amish case *Wisconsin v. Yoder*. He has also written and lectured widely on religious liberty issues and has been honored by both Catholic and evangelical organizations. For the past quarter of a century he has been associated with the law firm of Ball, Skelly, Murren & Connell in Harrisburg, Pennsylvania.

Life in an Occupied Country

William Bentley Ball

"New Breed of Activist Travels U.S. Pitching Issues, Not Candidates." This headline on page 1 of the November 4, 1991, *Wall Street Journal* topped a marvelously upbeat article describing one Jeannette Fruen Turk—"part agitator, part organizer . . . the canny leader of the new breed of political strategists . . . brilliant, astute." And she's crusading throughout the land over an issue that has "really got her blood boiling." What's this exciting person crusading for? Abortion rights, which she calls "the very core and essence of everything in a woman's life—for young women, for older women, for people who have families and for people who don't." The right to kill the unborn, that is.

A headline in a recent "TV Weekend" column in the *New York Times* praises an ABC movie offering "an impassioned and dignified argument on behalf of—*what*? A daughter helping kill her mother.

And as I write this, New York City's Board of Education is considering a curriculum that will promote the use of condoms by children and acquaint them with "all forms of intercourse—vaginal, oral and anal."

A famous feature of the military occupation of various countries in past decades has been the political use of media to distort reality, to propagandize points of view, and so to manipulate the popular mind for support of these. Few things were more outrageous to the captured populations than these daily affronts to truth. And, as George Orwell pointed out, language as a tool of reason was made to serve deception by masking truth. So it is now, when American propagandists speak of "termination of pregnancy," "sexual preference," and "death with dignity."

We are assaulted by media (and, widely, through our educational institutions) in ways no less distressing to Christians than political propaganda was to people of occupied countries. Many Christians attend theaters or use television less and less. They cannot endure the blanching experience of watching sexual acts, hearing lewd or blasphemous speech, witnessing direct attacks on Christian beliefs, or viewing scenes of unspeakable violence and horror. The Christian nature cries out with pain over this drenching in evil, and Christians well understand the effect on the general public of this drenching:

> Vice is a monster of so frightful mien,
> As to be hated, needs but to be seen;
> Yet too oft familiar with her face.
> We first endure, then pity, then embrace.[1]

Discerning Christians rightly note the ongoing success of the media in *normalizing* evil—perhaps the best current example is the nationwide campaign to obtain a consensus, not of charity to homosexual persons, but of acceptance of homosexuality as a natural part of our social fabric.

"Christians?" A "Christian manifesto"? What "Christians" are we talking about? Surely all this talk about "life in an occupied country" is, if not false, grossly exaggerated or paranoid. Should we be concerned over the fears of single-issue zealots? Aren't the "Christians" who are imagining themselves victims of media conspiracies better described as religious fanatics? Aren't they trying to live in a long-dead past? Do we want to see an evangelical Religious Right gaining charge of our affairs? Or the reactionary Catholic hierarchy?

Surely that will be the response of militant secularists to this book, but it could also be the response of a majority of our people. They have church affiliation. They rely on the media as their chief source of entertainment and information. They go along with what they hear. Their modest level of social concern does not often impel them to speak out on public issues, yet they tend to resent the Christian neighbor who protests what people in the media describe as normal, good, or, in any event, to be accepted.

But I believe that only when the concerns spoken of in this *Manifesto* become truly manifest in the lives of the majority—in the form of worse violence on the streets, more ruined children and families, more failed marriages and businesses, less and less belief that the public servant's word is his bond—will the now complacent start to ask whether the Christian protesters had points worth pondering. The members of a society too dangerous to live in will eventually cry out for order and get themselves a Hobbesian police state. But perhaps they will perceive, before it is too late, the realities of their times and learn that order, tranquility, and freedom are possible only in a society that embraces Christian values.

To discuss this possibility, the thoughts of eighteen seasoned observers are brought together in this volume.

A MANIFESTO

Writing the curious poem "Clarel" in 1876, Herman Melville, attempting to view the future, had an Anglican priest predict:

> Rome and the Atheist have gained:
> These two shall fight it out—these two;
> Protestantism being retained
> For base of operations sly
> By Atheism.

While I put aside Melville's dire comment on Protestantism, I did not doubt, until the early 1970s, that the sole force in the world against atheism would be the Catholic Church. Through the twentieth century she had been of all religions the most unremitting antagonist of world communism. The strength of the high moral code that she enjoined upon her faithful, especially in respect to sexual matters, was attested to by the hatred it inspired among secularists. Everywhere she could, she maintained schools. Having been educated at one of these, under the guidance of sisters who gave their lives to help us, I know how wonderful that endeavor was. But in the 1970s I, along with many other Catholics, shared in the appalling experience that many evangelicals had earlier experienced—the entry of modernism into the church, the rise of dissidents within its body who boldly attacked the fundamental teachings of the faith and, indeed, the very teaching authority of the church. Confusion was sown. Providentially, within my church today is a strong surge toward orthodoxy and, in the words of James Hitchcock, "the recovery of the sacred."

11

Also in the 1970s I had my first contact with the evangelical school movement and thereafter, widely, with the kinds of evangelicals who support that movement.

In 1990 I tried to state in an article[2] in *Christianity Today* what these experiences had meant to me:

> As they [Catholics visiting an evangelical school] became familiar with this community of believers . . . they would experience the joy of finding people ever so much like their brother and sister orthodox Catholics—people of prayer and unshakable belief in Christ. They would realize, too, that Catholics need not go it alone in resisting materialism and hedonism in our society, but that here are cultivators of the soil of society, at the root level, as contrasted with the statist-minded, who would cover society's fertile earth with lifeless pavement. Moral courage, too, that most unfashionable virtue, the visitors would find—a love of freedom, with a despising of license.

My article argued that "orthodox" Catholics and "orthodox" evangelical Protestants should work together in the battle against rampant secularism. I defined "orthodox" as those who hold belief in God, the Trinity, the divinity of Christ as our personal Savior, the Virgin Birth, the Holy Spirit, the inerrancy of Scripture, the existence of Satan, man as created by God in His image and likeness, man's salvation through Christ. From these common beliefs, many Catholics and evangelicals have arrived at clear and identical positions on many issues of law and public policy—especially in opposition to the secularizing of our society and in the areas of the freedom of religion and morality. Avoiding the often misused term "conservative" I nicknamed these "orthodox" evangelicals "OE's" and their Catholic counterparts "OC's."

Among the responses my article generated was a letter from Mr. Allan Fisher, the distinguished editor of Baker Books, who asked me:

> Would it not greatly encourage cooperative effort between orthodox evangelicals and orthodox Catholics if a book existed that developed clear positions on issues of law and public policy based on the beliefs common to OC's and OE's?

He suggested that we make a list of such issues and assemble evangelical and Catholic scholars to address them. I agreed emphatically and began the job of enlisting the authors. What surprised me (but should not have) was the enthusiasm the occasion produced.

The book centers on nine topics. Under each are two chapters, one by an evangelical and another by a Catholic. Chapters were not exchanged; there was no dialogue between the participants. I preferred that each address the topic at hand on his own.

I do not believe it will be Rome alone fighting it out with the atheist; it will be the orthodox among both Catholics and Protestants. This does not suggest an ecumenical endeavor. The OE's and OC's, each convinced of their own religious professions, do not care to have these picked over by others. Rather, it suggests two things: acting together upon significant occasion and showing respect for one another. We are already acting together. I think of such things as the annual March for Life and our common resistance to socialized child care. But as to "respect," we pretty much ignore each other in our publications—almost as though identifying and speaking well of the other might give scandal to our own flock. We ought not practice such foolhardy exclusions but rather express happiness that we have allies in the great moral crisis that is upon us all.

A joy I have had in assembling our authors has been to find out how deeply each understands the spiritual significance of our times and how each, in his chapter, seeks to bring Christian witness to bear publicly on issues he addresses.

In every chapter I have found encouragement and hope.

Chapter 1

SECULARIZATION

Carl F. H. Henry

Carl F. H. Henry was, before retirement, World Vision's lecturer-at-large, a position that he held for thirteen years and that took him to all parts of the world. He was editor of *Christianity Today* from 1956 to 1968, before which he was professor of theology at Fuller Theological Seminary. Henry has written and edited more than thirty books, including his magnum opus, *God, Revelation, and Authority,* a four-volume statement of evangelical theology. He holds the Th.D. from Northern Theological Seminary and the Ph.D. from Boston University.

James Hitchcock

James Hitchcock is professor of law in history at St. Louis University. The former president of the Fellowship of Catholic Scholars, he has published numerous articles and books, including *Catholicism and Modernity, What Is Secular Humanism?* and *Years of Crisis, 1970–1984.*

Dismantling a Noble Heritage

Carl F. H. Henry

The diffusion of cultural naturalism throughout the West and much of the world beyond has precipitated a crisis in religion and culture of unprecedented dimensions. Our society is the first in the history of humanity that, while forsaking the supernatural and discarding fixed truth and the good, expects nonetheless to preserve civilization.

For many centuries most Europeans, and later most Anglo-Americans as well, considered the universe a unified sphere whose ultimate significance derived from God, the sovereign creator and judge of all. One need not rewrite Western history in millennial terms to establish the superior moral and spiritual power of Christianity. Christianity offered the masses a supernatural and moral salvation effective for this lifetime and for eternity. It also offered cultural transformation. The Western sense of reality and awareness of public duty embraced, to be sure, certain Graeco-Roman elements alongside biblical principles, but it was Christianity that lifted society above its pagan mires. The long-entrenched cultural vices were precisely those that Christian sanctification spiritedly challenged and those to which it offered ethical alternatives.

The scriptural canon affirms that a sovereign, transcendent God created the universe and controls it, thus giving human history meaning, purpose, and a goal. Apart from God, the cosmos and the historical process have no inherent purpose or sense. God rules nature and history through a providential moral order that leads toward his kingdom and its end-time manifestation.

17

Some three centuries ago a cadre of intellectuals projected naturalistic views of the universe and history, and these alternative concepts gradually permeated Western society. This intellectual movement, known as the Enlightenment, soon despiritualized and secularized the sense of purposive history that the West had inherited from biblical Christianity. Once the transcendent God was swept out of purview, the conviction that nature and history had no independent inherent meaning gave way easily to speculations about their meaning and worth. The Enlightenment nurtured a new faith—one in an exhaustive scientific explanation of nature and in history's inevitable progress. The door was thus open to human self-deification and to man's manipulation of the outer world for his own preferences.

Not all influential participants in the Enlightenment agreed on a preferred alternative to theism, nor were all hostile to biblical theism. Yet the Enlightenment, as Willis B. Glover remarked, "was a seedbed of modern culture."[1] What distinguished the Enlightenment from earlier intellectual struggles was that despite its confidence in reason and science it found no anchor in the speculative waters of new ideas. "The repudiation of Christianity by an influential minority eliminated that as a common ground. This was accompanied by a growing contempt for tradition as a guide to action."[2]

Soon no option was subject to greater distrust than "the Great Tradition," as scholars characterized the Western heritage. Today the voices of modernity more and more demean the Great Tradition as essentially mythical.

Secularization is doubtless an apt term to depict what has happened to western society. It is well to note, however, that the terms *secular* and *secularization* have accumulated a variety of meanings. Another term, *desacralization*, is now customarily applied to a turning away from pagan and philosophical cosmic myths about nature and history in the interest of "objectively factual" views, as modernity perceives this. Secularization may be used to refer to man's proper and necessary devotion of interest to the temporal world in contrast to other-worldly preoccupation. Yet the term secularization is more routinely applied to a decline in religious orientation, or the process by which religious authorities lose control of space and time and personnel and resources, so that society is supposedly detached from theological assumptions and pursues human affairs autonomously.

Secularism denounces supernaturalism and promotes a nonreligious or antireligious basis of social organization and morality. Eastern European countries were officially secularist before the recent collapse of Marxism, while secularism remains the voluntary stance of much of Western European society. The secularization of society has confounded Western culture with unprecedented uncertainties. "We are experiencing a crisis of faith," Willis B. Glover commented, "more complex and profound than anything known in the West since its origin in the early Middle Ages."[3]

Contemporary Western society, Lesslie Newbigin remarked, is pluralist not "merely . . . in the variety of cultures, religions, and lifestyles which it embraces," but pluralist in that it celebrates this plurality as something "to be approved and cherished."[4]

"Religious pluralism . . . is the belief that the differences between religions are not a matter of truth and falsehood, but of different perceptions of the one truth; that to speak of religious beliefs as true or false is inadmissible."[5]

By contrast, Christianity in earlier generations shaped a public consensus that provided the norm of belief and conduct. "The great thinkers whose work heralded the dawn of the modern world were Christian believers and took it for granted that theology belonged no less than physics or mathematics to the one seamless robe of truth," noted Newbigin.[6]

"In a pluralist society such as ours, any confident statement of ultimate belief, any claim to announce the truth about God and his purpose for the world, is liable to be dismissed as ignorant, arrogant, dogmatic."[7]

The current reductionist theories of reality have placed on the pedagogical defensive not only ancient classical idealism, which on the basis of philosophical reasoning affirmed the priority of an eternal and unchanging supernatural realm, but also medieval revelatory Christianity, which championed the holy Creator-Redeemer God, and Reformation Christianity, which promoted a spiritual recovery of New Testament principles. The socially cultural centers of contemporary society now widely consider irrelevant the central thesis of the Judeo-Christian heritage, that a living, personal, sovereign, and moral deity created and judges the universe and has verbally revealed himself and his redemptive will in Scripture. The currently reigning outlook perceives all existence as temporal, changing, and perishable. No conceptual framework is considered final; no moral verdict beyond revision; no historical event of absolute significance. This judgment in effect nullifies the mainline conviction of about 2,500 years of the history of thought from the pre-Christian Greeks and Romans through the Christian era, which probably ended at the forepart of the twentieth century. Since then theism and naturalism have been locked in a cultural death-strife.

It is nothing less than astounding that Western society—which to its past ethical and spiritual affirmations has added almost incredible industrial and technological achievements—should in our century have experienced a loss of confidence and a crisis of identity. Shortly after the dawn of this century, Protestant modernism speculatively restated Christianity as a gospel of social transformation premised on man's essential goodness and history's inevitable progress to utopia. But Freudian psychology's preoccupation with the dark recesses of the human psyche, the devastating world wars that were optimistically linked to an expectation of global democracy, and the reorientation of much Christian social concern to bureaucratic socialism, precipitated growing doubts over a politicized Christianity. Modernism's "social gospel" forsook transcendent divine creation and supernatural redemption and eliminated the Christ of the creeds from the Christian message. Focusing on unjust social structures while ignoring man's sinful predicament and need of supernatural moral renewal, it was consumed by the vision of a just society in present history. As modernism dominated Protestant ecumenism, not a few of its Marxist enthusiasts ventured even to declare non-Western culture superior to Western culture.

Meanwhile Euro-American morality declined, loosed as it was from its revelatory and regenerative biblical anchor. Ever more prestigious, scientism usurped the explanation of ultimate reality in terms of impersonal processes and events. The self-styled intellectual elite hailed atheistic scientism as a trustworthy guide to the ultimately real world. The goal of learning became the explanation of all reality in terms of physics and chemistry, while human life in turn was regarded as an outcome of random physical happenings.

The modern Western mind-set, Huston Smith affirmed, involves an epistemology that aims relentlessly at control of all existence, and in principle rules out the possibility of personal transcendence.[8] Smith saw little slowing of reductionist momentum in current scientific theory, whether in psychology, biology, or sociology and sociobiology. In his volume *Living Faith, Belief and Doubt in a*

Perilous World, Jacques Ellul too warned that "Science carries no built-in guarantee of respect for people, for human freedom, autonomy, or individuality. As science expands, it continues to look upon people as objects. All sorts of investigators train their instruments on these objects to get to know them better and, of course, to bring out their special features, but that's no safeguard against exploitation."[9] The scientific mentality dehumanizes life and existence; it nurtures a humanity knowledgeable about nature but ignorant of who man himself essentially is. The scientifically-literate masses today are unsure of the meaning and value of man's own existence.

The rise of European neo-orthodoxy—paced mainly by theologians of paradox who disowned reason as a test of truth and denied the objectifiability of God—stimulated little academic interest in theism in the influential public universities. Instead, secular humanism emerged as the masked metaphysics of liberal arts learning. The "death of God" stir especially entranced the religion departments. Not only was the American student mind harnessed to naturalism—qualified only by a slim agenda of social concern on which secular humanists insisted—but also to antisupernatural emphases, which deluged many of the 400,000 international students pursuing mainly graduate studies in scientific fields in the United States. Scientism promoted skepticism about their own cultural heritage, and in effect undermined also the credibility of creedal Christianity that Western missionaries had carried to distant developing nations.

The forfeiture of Christ-centered education, to which Harvard, Duke, Vanderbilt, and a dozen other universities were originally dedicated, has led on to the loss of any abiding center whatever in polytechnic and liberal arts learning. Enlightenment philosophy had made the imperious claim that human beings, if they are just properly educated, can know the ultimate world apart from transcendent divine disclosure, and that empirical knowledge is superior to the truth claims of the scriptural heritage. Mediating theology, both dialectical and existential, was also much to blame, for it disengaged "Christ the center" from a comprehensive world view and concentrated instead upon internal considerations. Postmodernism currently denies ultimate coherence.

The question arises whether in the present interim between modernity and post-modernity the gospel can any longer be effectively proclaimed as public truth. Must we concede to the post-modern view that all rational commitment is historically and

21

community-related and thus present the gospel in a way that stresses contingent happenings at the expense of propositionally revealed truth and assured historical factuality? The post-modern revolt is in some ways a revolt against the Enlightenment model of truth, which tributed reason unaided by transcendent revelation as fully adequate and ambiguously defined experience as its source of truth. Current expositions of narrative theology emphasize the historical and contingent character of divine revelation, yet in doing so they tend to minimize propositional revelation and the objectively historical nature of divine disclosure.

If some social critics blame the present state of human fragmentation on preoccupation with science and technology, others like Alasdair MacIntyre focus more directly on "the moral bankruptcy of our culture" and identify the "enlightenment experiment" as its blameworthy cause.[10] The reason for this refocusing is apparent: Western culture has made a quantum leap in its view of indecency and immorality.

In 1942 Pitirim A. Sorokin, professor of sociology at Harvard University, wrote the book *The Crisis of Our Age* in which he took a dim view of Western civilization.[11] It had become, he affirmed, essentially sensate—that is, the masses were now prone to believe only what they feel, taste, smell, hear and see. Some six years later the Federal Bureau of Investigation reported that a third of the national population was given to reading pornographic sex magazines, a million babies annually were born illegitimately, a million girls had social diseases, and one in five marriages ended in divorce. There was one murder every 40 minutes and 100,000 unapprehended murderers were walking the streets. Sorokin's bleak verdict was confirmed—Western society was "progressively becoming mentally deranged and morally unbalanced."[12]

If Sorokin considered America at mid-century in moral crisis, the statistics of decline since then are anything but reassuring. To be sure, one must qualify comparative statistics, for the population of the United States has grown from 132,164,569 in 1940 to 226,545,805 in 1980 and 251,400,000 in 1990. Yet the latest available figures leave no doubt of striking moral decline.

While at mid-century abortions were morally and legally discountenanced, in 1991, following legalization, there were 1.5 million abortions performed in the United States. The right-to-life movement clearly has not made spectacular statistical headway against crusaders for freedom of choice. In 1989 the number of unmarried couples living together was estimated at 2,764,000. In addition, lesbians and other homosexuals have promoted redefinition of the traditional concept of the family. Today the social cohesion of the monogamously grounded home, the basic unit of society, is under unprecedented pressure.

The present cultural deterioration reeks with radical naturalism's putrification of contemporary life and its institutions. Its spoiling influences are apparent in all the power centers of present-day living, whether one thinks of public education, the political arena, the mass media, or literature and the arts.

Secular humanism, which for a generation has covertly supplied liberal arts learning with its governing metaphysics, while securing its own favored position by emphasizing tolerance of all views except theistic alternatives, is now giving way to unabashed naturalism. Moreover, even the nation's large doctorate-granting universities now reflect the academic pressures for "political correctness" in feminist and racial views in their course offerings, lecture content, and invited campus speakers. *Newsweek* magazine has commented that this new liberal orthodoxy—which some critics depict as illiberal education—could alter "the consciousness of the entire generation of university students." British educators have deplored as unthinkable such exclusion of a qualified professor simply on the basis of a differing academic viewpoint. Yet the routine ostracizing of competent evangelical scholars by some American religion departments and by university divinity schools has been a standing complaint that is now inviting deeper scrutiny through the debate over "political correctness."

Never has the call for the academic excellence of Christian scholars been more imperative to confirm the conviction that the rejection of revelatory theism rests less on reason than on emotive rationalization. The main complaints against American education today, from elementary to graduate learning, are its prejudicial exclusion of the Christian world view, the promulgation of which was the primary reason for which many great universities were founded, and its ready misunderstanding of the doctrine of church and state as an occasion for secular naturalistic reductionism.

The mass media, with their brilliant use of graphic arts and cinematic skills, sustain the interest in swift-paced materialistic lifestyles and unstable family patterns that subtly place mind and conscience at moral risk. Instead of enriching the intellect, the media impoverish the soul through a steady diet of sex-oriented, violence-prone, and trivia-weighted entertainment. Scientists who have researched the effects of exposure to present-day television say that it promotes a 20 percent decline in creativity, reduces persistence in problem solving, increases sex-role stereotyping, and accelerates aggressive behavior.[13]

Public television, moreover, seems more interested in novel modern religious fads than in the constructive impact of historic evangelical Christianity. Religion editors—some of them agnostics—more eagerly publicize radical protest movements than depict the ministries sustained by traditional churches about which they sometimes know very little. It is noteworthy that commercial television and many daily newspapers as well now face a declining audience despite the notable media tilt toward a *Playboy* mentality and exposure.

The sorry fate of literature and the arts in our time likewise gives great reason for cultural concern. The early twentieth century, to be sure, produced some outstanding architecture, art, and literature. To this day the Bible remains the world's bestseller. It has often been commended as "great literature," nothing more. Some portions may indeed rank with or even outrank Shakespeare. But Christianity honors the Book primarily as the revealed Word of God. Some of the world's great literature owes much to the Bible. Even in the recent past numerous authors who wrote from a consciously Christian stance have gained prominence, among them W. H. Auden, T. S. Eliot, Graham Greene, C. S. Lewis, Francois Mauriac, Flannery O'Connor, Alan Paton, J. R. R. Tolkien, Thornton Wilder, and Charles Williams. Some of the best literature since World War I has been penetratingly critical of Western culture, especially of its loss of community and experience of alienation, and its meaninglessness and unrelatedness to ultimate reality. The humanistic faiths and their ideological progeny are losing credibility, as the collapse of Marxism in Eastern Europe now attests.

Catholics have been more successful than evangelicals in writing significant novels; they also far outnumber evangelicals as syndicated newspaper columnists. This may in part reflect the price of an excessive evangelical withdrawal from the culture. The fields of journalism and literature remain to be fully pursued as evangelical vocations. Some sensitive parents now commendably postpone their children's access to television until their reading and learning habits are first established. Once that is done, writing for the masses may well become a lifelong ambition.

The drift of political institutions away from their earlier predominantly Christian outlook, and their loss of biblical imperatives, is perhaps the most disconcerting of all. To be sure, the United States towers above totalitarian or dictatorial powers with its emphasis on democratic self-determination, its leadership role in respect to human equality and rights, its affirmation of religious liberty, and its commitment to a free market economy and private property. In such matters the oppressed Eastern European multitudes and inhabitants of most developing nations have understandably looked with envy toward the United States.

The Christian view is that God has created and preserves a law-ordered universe, that God promotes respect for his role of law through civil government, and that law convicts human beings not only of civic wrongs but of sin, and thus prepares them to accept Jesus Christ the Redeemer. Indeed, it is not civil government's role to deal with the spiritual realities of sin and redemption; the state is not to adjudicate theological differences. Yet the highest glory of the American Revolution, said John Quincy Adams, was that "it connected in one indissoluble bond the principles of civil government with the principles of Christianity."[14] The Declaration of Independence affirms explicitly that God the creator has endowed all human beings with inalienable rights. The emphasis on church-state separation has been made to support secular applications that the nation's founding fathers never intended. The result has been a gradual eclipse of some of the very principles that the founders considered distinctive. David A. Noebel commented on the supreme irony of "Creator/creation concepts being generally outlawed in America's public school systems and most American law schools ignoring Christian law concepts."[15]

A disturbing aspect of modern political activity is the increasing disjunction between personal and public life. The fact that a philanderer or a homosexual can be elected to some of the highest offices in the land reflects not only a deterioration of constituency morality, but the indulgence of the secular media, and a secularizing of political theory that would exempt politics from ethical demands. The American public is being increasingly sensitized to accept homosexual relations and to view any moral criticism of the gay community as needless bashing and intolerance. The notion that morality cannot be legislated—true enough in the sense that legislation cannot transform character—overlooks the fact that almost all legislation concerns moral action.

Ready tolerance of the gargantuan national deficit (estimated at $70.8 billion for 1991) may be viewed as an extension of this segregation of personal and public morality, for personal bankruptcy is still widely looked on with disdain. The total public debt outstanding on August 13, 1991, was $3,578,842,179,492.37. National insolvency is a disgraceful witness to developing countries which have a crippling indebtedness. The budget process—which almost routinely exceeds authorized expenditures—the savings-and-loan and banking crisis, the Senate's self-gratifying salary increase voted almost covertly, the cumbersome tensions between highly centralized legislative committees and some 300 study committees, select committees, and subcommittees, and some 12,000 congressional staff members who recommend positions on pending legislation, are precipitating a call for reform. This comes at a time when newly emerging national democratic experiments abroad look to the United States for structural guidance. True though it may be that no better system of government than democracy has been devised by a sinful society, political self-determination not only is a great blessing but also holds great potential for miscarriage of justice. The system does, however, include a capacity for self-correction, provided that it comes before an errant nation glides off the map. The balancing of the transnational good, of national justice, of constituency interest, and of political self-interest calls for a level of statesmanship that only a morally dedicated leadership and citizenry can promote.

A special vice of our media age is its accommodation of new possibilities for promoting political image at the expense of reality. A candidate who wins nomination and is elected to office by moral posturing and media distortion can be expected to perpetuate himself or herself in office by further deception. When enough successful aspirants do this, true representative government cannot exist.

If American society is to reach a propitious conclusion of the present search for personal meaning and national purpose, it must recognize that reality comprises more than the here and now, and it must recover a concern for conscience, love for neighbor, and public justice. The decline of belief in humanity's own intrinsic worth is latent already in the loss of the reality of God and of the expectation of final moral judgment.

It should be patently clear that neither education nor the mass media nor the political process can on their present course arrest the nation's further decline. The United States spends $212,900,000,000 on elementary and secondary education; it enrolls 12,935,000 students in colleges and universities (1990 statistics). It has 1,362 television stations and 9,087 radio stations. An estimated 90,000,000 homes have television sets and 47,800,000 persons are cable television subscribers. The nation offers the world's most advanced education in science and technology, and there is every reason to think that more spectacular achievements of science still lie ahead of us. Only since World War II have commercial air transportation and commercial television been available. Atomic fission and fusion, space flights, men walking on the moon, transistors, computers, and laser technology all belong to our generation. Yet the sentiment increasingly emerges that everyone has a right to do whatever he or she prefers, and that science or government has the task—or shall I say the "duty"—of insulating us all from the adverse consequences of our preferences. Infallible condoms are considered the answer to the crisis of sexual morality; safe abortions, the answer to unwanted pregnancies. Perhaps such rationalization of conduct provides a clue as to why the number of arrests for crimes has surpassed 14 million annually, why households annually touched by crime now number over 22 million, and why violent crimes number 1,566,000 (1988 figures).

What clues can we offer for a recovery of moral and social wholeness? Surely those who deny fixed truth and good, and explain all moral distinctions as historical relativism and cultural conditioning, are not hopeful contributors to the solution; they are part of the problem. The flagging faith in government as a protector of public interest, and the growing sense of the irrelevance of political solutions to many of the nation's crucial domestic problems, call for comprehensive confrontation. So too education and technocratic science are no longer viewed as solvents of cultural disintegration. Any notion that the media are to be identified as "channels of blessing," moreover, needs great qualification.

So dire is the need for transformation that a keen observer can scarcely fail to see the relevance of the biblical call for individual regeneration as a universal necessity. However equitable social structures may be, an unregenerate disposition is prone to yield to inordinate self-interest. Even in our time one's relation to Jesus Christ remains more important than one's relation to the ballot box, for it will shape the quality of one's political engagement. Yet Christians who rely on personal evangelism alone to rectify social injustices forget that the Bible gives no assurance of universal salvation, and that in this life even God's redeemed people lack final perfection. Christians and non-Christians alike need legal constraints on volitions that have yet to fully escape their rebel propensities. God is, to be sure, in the business of surprising atheists, both in this life and in the next, and evangelism is indeed a necessary way of inviting them to be stunned by grace. But humans—whether or not they are believers in Christ's gospel—are obligated, one and all, to exemplary personal godliness and to public justice.

The Bible is the inspired text on human duties and human rights. It publishes the standards by which God will judge mankind and the nations. It addresses disagreements over specific rights and the basis on which rights rest. The very urgent social problems for which naturalism has no real solution—among them the burgeoning population, destitution of the poor, ecology, nuclear weaponry—all gain immense illumination from scriptural principles. Emergence of a movement like Prison Fellowship Ministries, which brings the concerns of justice and grace to bear on one of the nation's main social problems, indicates that even in our time the potential for transformation has not yet been completely eroded, and gives hope that the nation as a whole can be renewed and revived in the enduring ethical principles and legal imperatives that modernity has obscured.

Yet so serious is the moral decline of the West that some social critics wonder whether Christians now, as in the darkening decades of the declining Roman Empire, should again probe the possibilities of new community alternatives to replace existing social structures. The easy assumption that a moral majority can, with little more than a sudden burst of energy, recapture the nation for social justice and for spiritual priorities would be a gross misreading of the American condition. Nor can any propitious turn be summarized merely in terms of a fortuitous "Catholic moment" or "Evangelical moment" in contemporary American history. A significant turn in national life will require a spiritual recovery of what it means that regenerate Christians are "*the* new society," a return to persistent prayer in the pews and to principled preaching in the pulpits, and to evangelism in urban and rural centers. It will require no less than civic engagement that begins at the precinct level and involves political participation to the limit of our ability and competence. It calls for co-affirmation and co-belligerency.

The ethical indignation of morally concerned people must crest in a network that takes strenuous public initiatives, at local, state, and national levels, for truth, goodness, and justice. The critical question is not whether one is religiously a Catholic, evangelical, or Jew. It is whether one affirms the legal propriety and superiority of certain statutes and personally honors them, encourages neighbors and responsible communities of morality and faith to share them, and promotes and votes for candidates who stand tall for political renewal and social justice. These terms, to be sure, are not self-defining, and the founding fathers encouraged in town hall meetings and local assemblies a means of discussion and debate that preserves respect for dissenting opinions without permitting radical minorities to reshape our political fortunes.

Concerned Protestants can cooperate with concerned Catholics in the public order without subscribing to a natural law theory and without forsaking the principles of the Reformation, and Catholics can cooperate with Protestants despite the agreement of many of the latter with Willis Glover's verdict that attempts "to reestablish a natural law basis of morality . . . have not been successful."[16] The viability of natural law is not what we are deciding at the ballot box; it is, rather, the specific content of statute law.

The avant-garde would have us believe that monogamous marriage is a medieval residuum, that a virgin co-ed is a social misfit, that the media mirror the updated morality of an elite new generation, that permissive investigative reporters are licensed monitors of national conscience while their own conduct is nobody's business. Some of these avant-gardists had no god before the recent rise of a new Madonna, and they seldom see the inside of a church. If we do not act promptly, they will triumphally thrust their pagan gods and hollow creeds on us, and then assure us that it is for the well-being of mankind that these lustful barbarians dismantle the noble heritage of the West.

Two Roads to Secularization

James Hitchcock

Whether or not the United States is a secularized society is itself at issue. A quarter of a century ago, standard sociological accounts assumed that religion was essentially a "pre-modern" phenomenon destined to wither away with the gradual triumph of distinctively modern attitudes. In this view all signs of vital religion, such as Protestant evangelicalism, or Roman Catholicism before the Second Vatican Council of 1962–1965, were essentially mere atavisms that had survived as anomalies but could not do so for much longer. The celebrated book *The Secular City* by the liberal Baptist theologian Harvey Cox assumed this was the case and prescribed accordingly.

But the 1970s saw a major religious revival, particularly in a resurgent evangelicalism or fundamentalism. While in part this may have been merely the public unveiling of groups that had remained inconspicuous, the conservative churches were in fact measurably growing by the late 1960s, and unexpected kinds of people—entertainers, professional athletes, and politicians—began to proclaim themselves "born again" as they would not have done a decade earlier. Although some observers still regard this as merely a final burst of brilliance before extinction, most think that traditional religion is a permanent feature of modernity, with unexpected powers of survival and even growth.

But the resurgence of traditional religion also owes much to the deepening sense of pessimism about the culture that many people now feel. Those who have been believers all their lives sense that they must live their faith much more aggressively if culture is to be saved, and some non-believers have been drawn to faith also by the realization that their culture is in radical need of salvation.

The United States is arguably the most religious society in the Western world, based on the findings of a Gallup Poll. More Americans profess belief in God, in the divine inspiration of the scriptures, in miracles, and in life after death than peoples from other Western cultures.[1] Those who spend time in countries comparable to the United States—Canada or Australia, for example—at once sense how religiosity permeates the United States in ways it does not elsewhere. None of this, however, necessarily alters the judgment that the United States also is a highly secular society, and is becoming more so.

The roots of modern secularization are not well understood. Standard sociological theory holds that industrialization is the ultimate cause—wherever heavy industry, and the accompanying urbanization, is found, religion loses its power and credibility.[2] Such a judgment, however, seems to hold for Europe, and possibly parts of the Third World, but not for the United States. There is no reason to suppose that Pittsburgh in 1960, for example, was a particularly secular place. The rate of church membership there was probably as high as in most other parts of the country, and there is no support for thinking that the secularization now occurring is more precipitous in the "rust belt" than anyplace else.

Indeed, the reverse may be true. Pastoral New England and the forested Pacific Northwest now have a more secular "feel" about them than do the large industrial cities such as Chicago or Cleveland. California, where experiments in secularization have perhaps been carried the farthest, is only partially industrialized, and its secularity is not necessarily centered in those parts.

Throughout most of the twentieth century Roman Catholic, Baptist, and Lutheran churches have remained strong, and have even grown, though their members have largely been from the white working class. Meanwhile the black working class has also been extraordinarily religious.

Possibly the tenacious faith of the working class survived because industrialization was already well under way before whites arrived from Europe and blacks from the rural South. Whereas massive moves in Europe from country to city disrupted a way of life, including making religion a part of a defunct past, in America

31

immigrants found a well-developed urban religious system, and religion was usually a major help in coping with disruptive changes.

In ways which are perhaps not sufficiently appreciated, the Calvinist origins of the American Northeast seem to have stamped a permanent religiosity on the American soul, a reality already noticed as early as the 1830s by Alexis de Tocqueville and others. Classical Puritanism disappeared in time, and New England eventually became (apart from its Catholic immigrants) one of the more secular parts of the country. But the Puritan spirit spread westward, so that revivals, bible-reading, crusades for moral reform, and numerous other pious practices became familiar even on the wild frontier. Expressive religiosity seems to come easy to Americans even now, as it always has in the past. This popular Protestantism may sometimes appear moribund, as it did during the 1960s, but it is like petroleum hidden deep in the ground, liable to ooze forth or erupt powerfully when and where least expected.

Sociologists, for reasons that seem inherent to their discipline, simply assume that the causes of secularization must lie outside the churches themselves, which are thought to be passively shaped by larger social forces. However, the real causes of the decline of religion probably lie within those churches, and especially with their spiritual leaders.

Carried to extreme, both Catholicism and Protestantism bear the seeds of secularization within themselves, though based on different concepts of religion.

Catholicism, virtually from its beginnings, chose to bless the world as far as possible, to insist that "grace builds on nature," to attempt to create a Christian culture in which what is worldly (art, philosophy, politics, economics) is integrated with what is supernatural. Thus everything worldly can lead to God if properly ordered. There are such truths as natural law, natural human virture, even natural theology. God regards the lives of his creatures and rewards them for their good works. (Thomism exemplifies this.)

The inherent danger in this is the ease with which what is merely worldly can be invested with a false religious significance that ultimately renders explicit faith almost superfluous. Particularly since the Second Vatican Council, many Catholics have chosen the broad and amorphous concept of "social justice" as the genuine meaning of their faith and regard everything else as at best tangential. (It is not uncommon in Catholic circles to hear people say that the purpose of formal worship is merely to fortify and inspire people for more strenuous efforts at political reform.) Some Catholics are no longer able to distinguish truth from falsehood, glory from baseness, in art, literature, and philosophy because of a conviction that everything that has been stamped "creative" must be intrinsically worthy.

Against this, classical Protestantism, culminating in Barth, rejects "religion" as a merely human invention that is a counterfeit of the faith to which God summons his people. Such faith is a radical response to God who is declared to be "wholly other" and is no way dependent on any worldly supports. There is a radical disjunction between human life in the world and the transformed life of the believer.

When this theology is carried to its extreme, the gulf between God and man appears unbridgeable. Robbed of any religious significance, worldly activity simply proceeds by its own rules and its own logic, and the Christian becomes someone whose faith is intensely private, without public manifestation.

The leading exponents of these two approaches never intended such results, but the results have occurred nonetheless.

Ultimately secularization in the West stems from the brutal intellectual assault on belief that was mounted beginning in the seventeenth century and culminating in the Enlightenment of the eighteenth. This assault asserted quite bluntly that religious belief in the traditional sense was based not only on illusion, but also on lies, and was not even a benign falsehood—it destroyed human freedom and dignity and retarded genuine progress.

The popular basis of belief survived those onslaughts relatively well, but it did so largely without the aid of vigorous intellectual defense. Movements such as Pietism and Methodism rekindled Protestant fervor, but mainly on the personal, emotional level, which was also true of most forms of popular Catholic piety. (Perhaps the most vital kind of eighteenth century Catholicism was the quasi-Calvinist movement called Jansenism).

When the shock of the Enlightenment assault was over, some believers (John Henry Newman, Søren Kierkegaard) began the task of picking up the intellectual pieces, attempting to give faith an adequate intellectual foundation. But in many ways believers now found themselves nervously looking over their shoulders to see what their "cultured despisers" (in the words of the early Protestant liberal Friedrich Schleiermacher) thought of them. Religious believers in the West since about 1700 have suffered from a permanent inferiority complex.

Sometimes those with inferiority complexes can genuinely confess to a sense of inadequacy, but often they mask self-doubt by over-compensating through bold and triumphant claims. Even when they may appear vibrant and untouched by external criticism (as Catholics appeared to be prior to 1960), forces of dissolution may be gnawing at their inner spirit.

Catholicism in the United States has suffered under a double inferiority complex—the general one that affects Christians in the modern world, plus the specific one of alienation in a dominantly Protestant society.

Huge beasts are most vulnerable in their brains, as the Catholic historian Christopher Dawson pointed out, and the loss of vitality within modern Christianity has been due more to the doubts and uncertainties of its own spiritual and intellectual leaders than to impersonal forces like industrialization. Most believers since the seventeenth century have been rather vaguely aware of the untiring intellectual assaults on the legitimacy of faith. Clergy, theologians, and others in positions of importance have usually been much more aware; and while some have taken up the gauntlet, many others have accommodated the enemies of the faith.

From the early nineteenth century, liberal Protestantism, as it came to be known, disregarded its traditions and the authority of Scripture and primarily found its bearings in the writings of secular intellectuals, usually university professors. This pattern continues to this day and has grown even stronger. Until the time of the Second Vatican Council the Catholic Church had been remarkably successful in resisting those secularizing forces, partly by engaging them in intermittent battle and partly by devising a practical pattern of religious living that made the supernatural vividly real for the masses. Fundamentalist Protestantism did much more the latter than the former.

The liberal churches themselves, including liberal Catholics, are now perhaps the major secularizing forces in the United States because their leaders understand one of their principal tasks to be that of "demythologizing" traditional faith wherever it appears. Many religious liberals regard all forms of "fundamentalism" (a term they extend to orthodox Catholics now as well as conservative Protestants) as far worse than outright unbelief. They are capable of warmer "ecumenical" relations with Jews, Buddhists, agnostics,

Marxists, and Freudians than they are with many members of their own denominations.

Anyone seeking spiritual guidance in liberal religious circles today is likely to imbibe a theology somewhat as follows: "God is the name we give some mysterious power that we sense is both within us and within the larger universe. To place one's entire faith in Jesus is to be overly narrow and smug. Jesus was a great teacher, but there are other great teachers in the world's other great religions. The Bible is to be read respectfully and, wherever possible, profitably, but it is finally the product of the evolving human religious sense. What have been called miracles are things that the human mind does not as yet understand. Religion can provide people with general moral guidelines, but specific moral actions are ultimately subject only to conscience and individual judgment. No one can be certain what happens after death, and it is better to ameliorate the state of this world than to think about the next."

The 1970s were, contrary to Harvey Cox and others' predictions, a religious tropical jungle in which no plant was so exotic (or so archaic) that it could not bloom—Eastern religions, American Indian religions, astrology, witchcraft, pantheism, etc. In one sense there was not a lack of belief but a surfeit of it. This, confirmed by the Gallup Poll and other studies, shows that American culture is almost drowning in an inchoate, unfocused, unsystematic religiosity that could become the basis for massive Christian evangelization. Instead some of the most insistent "Christian" voices deny the very beliefs that sincere searchers might find meaningful, a denial that hastens the stampede towards what is sometimes called New Age spirituality. Were it not for the liberal churches, America would probably be a far more genuinely religious society than it now is.

In the words of the liberal Lutheran sociologist Peter Berger, believers today constitute a "cognitive minority," meaning that they formally espouse beliefs that the majority of the surrounding culture seems to regard as false or unfathomable. As Berger pointed out, this minority status in and of itself says nothing about the validity of such beliefs, but it does render the minority faith more difficult to espouse.[3]

Religious believers in fact seem to be a large majority of the society, however unsophisticated and eclectic their beliefs may be. But the major organs of communication—the mass media, popular entertainment, the educational system from kindergarten through the universities—in effect conspire to proclaim that such belief is at best a purely private and subjective "preference," and quite possibly a sign of personal disorder.

Although the forces of secularization have been in motion for over three centuries, this intellectual conspiracy was not operative as recently as thirty years ago, except at the university level. Even at that time institutions of higher learning had been for some decades places of refuge for people who felt alienated from the surrounding culture and especially from its pervasive religiosity. Many professors as early as the 1920s prided themselves on their skepticism, their iconoclasm, their "liberation" from traditional dogma. Only after 1960 did these attitudes begin to trickle down in noticeable ways into more popular organs of communication. As late as 1960 much of music, films, and television supported traditional moral beliefs, as did major news organs, while public education was probably in the hands, in most parts of the country, of devout believers who saw themselves as inculcating their students with essentially religious values.

As conservative Protestantism was girding itself for a spectacular revival, Catholicism in 1960 at last found itself overtaken by the full force of corrosive modernism. The decrees of the Second Vatican Council were subtle and highly nuanced, a delicate balance between fidelity to tradition and cautious openness to the new. But they were presented to the public (including most of the clergy) as representing in effect the Church's confession of past error and its tardy capitulation to the world. Very quickly Catholic leaders, beginning with the Pope, lost control of the process that called itself "renewal."

In the United States this runaway movement fed the Catholic hunger for social acceptance. The election of John F. Kennedy to the presidency in 1960 seemed to show that Catholics had indeed been accepted into the mainstream of American society, but his success was built on a generalized humanitarianism with a thin religious gloss. This trade of religious principles for political and social acceptability is accepted by perhaps a majority of American Catholics, including many priests and even some bishops.

Sociologists also argue that the reality of religious pluralism itself undermines belief—the visibility of numerous competing "sects" makes it difficult to assert the truth of any particular one. However, Catholics did so successfully through almost two centuries of American history. But the ability to relativize one's beliefs about inessential things, for the sake of social harmony, without compromising their essence, requires a profundity and a delicacy that most American Catholics appear now to lack. Ecumenism has become for many merely an act of capitulation to liberal Protestantism, which is thought to have already "solved" the problems Catholics face (sexual morality and the role of women in the church, for example).

The reality of pluralism has been a major reason for the liberalization of Protestantism, which is now about to relativize itself radically with regard to the various non-Christian religions. Only conservative Protestantism, for reasons not altogether clear, has been able to sustain its sense of uncompromising truth in the midst of a dizzyingly varied religious landscape.

The phenomenon called "the Sixties" (roughly the period from 1965–1975) marked the final working out of the corrosive potential of modernity. The reasons why this acidic spirit spread through society so suddenly are also mysterious. The New Left and the Counterculture were fanatically set against all forms of authority, and religion is by its very nature the most authoritarian of all. Many of the ideas of the radicals of 1970s have simply become a part of the mainstream of American culture, accepted as conventional wisdom by educators, journalists, and professionals of all kinds.

The assault was also motivated by the estimate, correct as far as it went, that the Catholic Church that had seemed to be an implacable bulwark against secularization, had now abandoned the fight. The secularist assault has predictably, however, brought forth a renewed militant Catholicism, as on the abortion issue. This militantness has led many liberal Catholics to complain that the church is reverting to its old identity. Had it not been for the sudden institutional weakening of the Catholic Church around 1965, it is unlikely that the secularist assault on religion would have been nearly as intense or successful as it has been.

The chief task in the struggle against secularization is to build strong and vital Christian communities at both the local and the national levels. Only very rare people can sustain their commitments indefinitely without strong communal support, which alone alleviates the sense of being a "cognitive minority."

The culture today favors highly personal, expressive religion over what is structured and formal. Thus the most effective form of Catholicism in the past quarter century has been the charismatic movement, which at its best has found the key to combining tradition and innovation, discipline and spontaneity, dogma and piety, in effective and creative ways. So also on the Protestant side the most effective groups have not been the liturgical churches but often those from such a "low church" tradition as to be almost anarchical.

All the churches, even the most conservative, face massive tasks of education. They must not only inform their members about the larger issues and instruct them in the fundamentals of their faith but also teach professed believers to think like people of faith, not merely like secular people for whom religion is one compartment of their lives. Even those who adhere to traditional positions on matters like sexual behavior often lack a genuine understanding of how the Christian view of life is profoundly different from that of the good pagan.

The religious tropical jungle of the 1970s itself promoted secularization in that it reinforced a popular religiosity that seeks for personal fulfillment only and does not understand that faith imposes dread responsibilities on the believer. New Age spirituality, in the broadest sense, is simply an attempt to ransack the religions of the world to find whatever is spiritually tasty, whatever will enhance the individual's egotistical hedonism. Traditional religion is rejected and despised precisely to the degree that it makes demands on people rather than simply offering them shallow comfort.

This condition can sometimes affect even ostensibly orthodox people who, in an age of highly expressive personal piety, can fall into the trap of appreciating their faith to the degree that it heightens their feelings. Even the conservative churches face a major task in disciplining their members actively to live as Christians, difficult as that sometimes is. Many otherwise devout people have imbibed prevailing secular attitudes (about money, for example) without even realizing that they are doing so.

Strong, self-consciously orthodox churches are essential for the Christian witness to be heard in the larger society, and for that task both the Catholic and the Protestant approaches are necessary.

Protestantism here stands for the unadorned proclamation of the gospel, without concession to human culture. Paradoxically, there may actually be more of this now than there was thirty years ago, as various public figures talk about having "found the Lord" as they would not have done in a more settled time with its fixed notions of what was or was not proper to say in public.

By tirelessly proclaiming the gospel in public and demonstrating the power that it has in people's lives, Christians force the larger culture, even against its will, to concede that reality, to tolerate and even respect it. It makes it impossible to pretend either that such a faith does not exist or that it does not deserve a hearing. Persistence here counts for a great deal, as does fearlessness.

But unadorned proclamations of the gospel, especially on disputed public questions, also invite the response that the individual is simply stating a subjective preference. The Catholic approach is to find what in the culture can serve as a scaffold on which the Christian message can be hung. People can be brought to faith through innumerable intermediate steps. (In the public sphere abortion is a crucial instance. Arguing against it solely on the grounds that the Bible forbids it permits non-believers to dismiss the claims against it out of hand; concentrating on the inherent dignity of human life itself, without any necessary reference to religion, forces every sincere person at least to consider the argument.)

Conservative Protestantism has begun to show a greater degree of intellectual sophistication than was apparent thirty years ago, and it is essential that believers of all persuasions begin to engage in systematic dialogue with the secular culture on every significant point, practical and theoretical. Dialogue implies careful listening to the other side, but does it imply capitulation? Believers must in effect force themselves into the continuing discussion, even if their presence is not welcome.

Genuine dialogue is also not incompatible with what some people view as coercion, since practical decisions, often political in nature, have to be made every day. Thus religious believers are well within their rights in agitating for the outlawing of abortion, for example, even if they fail to persuade the whole society of the correctness of their position.

To this end the churches should make much more strenuous efforts to hold public figures to their professed principles. Now Catholics (Mario Cuomo), Protestants (Paul Simon), and Eastern Orthodox (Michael Dukakis) on the one hand profess their piety when it seems suitable to do so, and on the other hand rarely miss an opportunity to demonstrate that it in no way influences their political behavior. For the most part the churches do very little to inform their people of these discrepancies, much less to urge those same members to champion their beliefs in the public sphere.

Any success in the struggle against secularization rests on the assumption that at bottom the United States still is a basically religious nation that mainly needs adequate religious leadership to rediscover that reality. Paradoxically, pluralism may now aid that process rather than retard it.

As Peter Berger has argued, the relativizers themselves should now be relativized.[4] For two centuries they have argued the case for unlimited tolerance but have shown themselves in practice to be intolerant of religion in the traditional sense. Relativism can now tolerate everything except absolutism, and those who believe in absolutes must now demand they too be included under the broad tent of tolerance, that their legitimate concerns about family, education, the mass media, and, other things be respectfully heard and accommodated.

To the degree that the United States is becoming even more religiously pluralistic than it already is, this may result in a move away from religious liberalism rather than strengthening it. Orthodox Judaism seems more potent and healthy now than it did thirty years ago. Islam, which scarcely existed in the United States in the time of John F. Kennedy, is an absolutist faith when it is true to itself, and devout Muslims might find much common ground with devout Christians and Jews on practical moral issues. Many of the new immigrants from Asia and Latin America manifest a strong sense of family, of personal discipline, and of self-reliance, which, if not necessarily religious in nature, nevertheless goes against the prevailing hedonism of the culture.

Mother Teresa of Calcutta is famous for saying, "I am called by God to be, not successful, but faithful." Perhaps the process of secularization is so far gone as to be irreversible, but this surmise does not excuse Christians from trying to stop the process. Perhaps the best advice is a popular Catholic maxim attributed to the seventeenth-century bishop St. Francis de Sales, "Pray as though everything depends on God. Work as though everything depends on you."

Chapter 2

MORALITY

Paul C. Vitz

Paul C. Vitz has been professor of psychology for more than twenty years at New York University. Since his conversion to Christianity, his professional interests have focused primarily on the relationships between Christian thought and such topics as personality theory, psychotherapy, and moral development. Among his books are *Psychology as Religion*, *Sigmund Freud's Christian Unconscious*, and *Censorship*. He earned his Ph.D. from Stanford University.

Harold O. J. Brown

Harold O. J. Brown, an ordained Congregational minister, holds the Franklin Forman chair of ethics in theology at Trinity Evangelical Divinity School. He also serves in the summer school of the International Institute of Human Rights in Strasbourg, France. He is a contributing editor for *Christianity Today* and remains active in the Christian Action Council, a Washington-based national prolife group that he cofounded. He earned his Ph.D. at Harvard University and has also studied at the universities of Marburg and Vienna.

An American Disaster: Moral Relativity

Paul C. Vitz

One of the major characteristics of moral decline in the United States in recent decades has been the rapid growth of moral relativism.[1] The idea is now widespread that each individual has some kind of a sovereign right to create, develop, and express whatever values he or she happens to prefer. This kind of personal relativism is far more serious and extreme than even cultural relativism. America's moral crisis would be much less severe if America's own traditional values were reliably upheld in our media, educational system, and in the economic sphere. But hard work, self-reliance, self-control, the delaying of gratification, sexual restraint, an active concern for democracy and patriotism have all fallen on hard times. Unfortunately, America has now reached the point where it permits almost everything and stands for almost nothing—except a flabby relativism.

One of the places in which this relativism has been self-consciously and actively advocated to great effect is in our public school system in the past three decades. The most influential model of moral education during these decades is officially known as Values Clarification (VC). And the major part of my contribution to this chapter is a critique of this model, which was first developed in the 1960s. Values Clarification became standard operating procedure in the 1970s and early '80s. However, as a result of some of the criticisms noted here, this system is now officially shunned, but its fundamental logic is still widely found in many curricula throughout the nation.

Very generally, Values Clarification is a set of related procedures
designed to engage students and teachers in the active formula-
tion and examination of values. It does not teach a particular set
of values. There is no sermonizing or moralizing. The goal is to
involve students in practical experiences, making them aware of
their own feelings, *their own* ideas, and *their own* beliefs, so that
the choices and decisions they make are conscious and deliberate, based on *their own* value systems [emphasis in original].[2]

Values Clarification must be contrasted with the traditional
view of explicit praise for virtue and strong condemnation of
wrong-doing. Those who espouse Values Clarification would pejo-
ratively characterize the traditional approach as "sermonizing"
and consider any form of "inculcation" of values as hopelessly
outdated.[3] Direct teaching of values is outdated, they say, because
today's complex society presents so many inconsistent sources
of values.

Thus, it is argued, "Parents offer one set of should and should
nots. The church often suggests another. The peer group offers a
third view of values. Hollywood and the popular magazines, a
fourth. . . . The spokesman for the new Left and counterculture an
eighth; and on and on."[4]

In the context of this confusing contemporary scene the devel-
opers of Values Clarification reject the direct teaching of morality.
They also reject indifference to the problem of values, since a
laissez faire position just ignores the problem and leaves students
vulnerable to unexamined influences from the popular culture.
Instead proponents such as L. E. Raths and S. B. Simon argue that
what students need to know is a process. By using this process,
students will be able to select the best and reject the worst in terms
of their own values and special circumstances.[5]

To enable young people to "build their own values system" the
Values Clarification system focuses on what is conceived as the
"valuing process."[6] Valuing, according to VC, is composed of three
basic processes, each with subcategories, which are presented in
the following order:

CHOOSING one's beliefs and behaviors[7]
- choosing from alternatives
- choosing after consideration of consequences
- choosing freely

PRIZING one's beliefs and behaviors
- prizing and cherishing
- publicly affirming, when appropriate

ACTING on one's beliefs
- acting
- acting with a pattern consistency and repetition[8]

Instead of teaching particular values, the goal is to help students apply the seven elements of valuing to already formed beliefs and behavior patterns and to those still emerging. The Values Clarification theorists then propose classroom exercises designed to implement their process. The exercises, called "strategies," represent the major contribution of their recent writings. Before we can investigate these strategies, an analysis of their model and philosophy is needed.

A PSYCHOLOGICAL CRITIQUE

The psychological and, one should add, educational assumptions of the Values Clarification theorists are rarely presented and, to my knowledge, never explicitly defended. But their premises are essential to the approach, and their basic assumptions about human nature and education can easily be inferred from a Values Clarification model. At the center is the concept of *the self*, with a corresponding emphasis on self-expression and self-realization. Philosopher Nicholas Wolterstorff nicely captured the way in which this psychological notion of the self is related to the educational theory of Values Clarification. Here is his description:

> The fundamental thesis is that each *self* comes with various innate desires and interests . . . that mental health and happiness will be achieved if these innate desires are allowed to find their satisfaction within the natural and social environment, and that an individual's mental health and happiness constitute the ultimate good for him. Such self-theorists characteristically stress the malleability of the natural and social environments . . . What must be avoided at all costs, is imposing the wishes and expectations of others onto the self. Down the road lies unhappiness and disease.
>
> The proper goal of the educator, then, is to provide the child with an environment which is *permissive*, in that there is no

> attempt to impose the rules of others onto the child, and which is *nourishing* in that the environment provides for the satisfaction of the child's desires and interests.
>
> According to some, a permissive and nourishing school environment is all the child needs. Others, however, argue that persons characteristically develop internal blockages or inhibitions of their natural desires and interests, with the result that they fall into mental disease and unhappiness . . . The school should not only provide a permissive nourishing environment, but also work to remove inhibitions on self-expression.[9]

The advocates of Values Clarification aim to remove any inhibitions in the realm of values (all inhibitions are negative) that students might have picked up from home, church, or elsewhere. Exactly how this takes place will be discussed later.

The view that the self is intrinsically good, that corruption comes only from one's parents and from society, arose at least in modern times with Rousseau, continued through the nineteenth century, and has culminated in the twentieth century, especially in the United States. In the recent past this self-expression or actualization theory of human nature has dominated much of American psychotherapy, popular psychology, and educational theory. From Carl Rogers' psychotherapy to open classrooms and Values Clarification, "self" therapists and educators have sought to promote mental health and happiness through the magic door of "self-expression." If we develop unconditional trust among students (and between students and teachers), remove inhibitions, support moral relativism, and let each do his own thing, then all will be well.[10]

The Values Clarification theorists specifically note[11] the similarity of their basic orientation to that of Carl Rogers, one of the major theorists committed to the innate goodness of the self. Values Clarification theorists simply don't accept evil—that is, anything naturally negative—as a part of human nature. Indeed they don't even discuss the issue. They avoid discussion because to do so raises the issue of objective values, as well as the question of how to deal with the intrinsically flawed self—a self that is given absolute power in the Values Clarification model.

In spite of the popularity of this self-theory, psychologists of almost all "schools" have been consistently critical of this position. In fact, criticisms have been especially strong. The central thrust of these critiques has been twofold. First, there is substantial objective evidence that human beings are not entirely good by nature. Instead, they come into this world with a significant natural component of selfishness and aggressiveness.

The clinical evidence assembled over many years from a large and heterogeneous group of people reveals the persistent recurrence of such behaviors as sadism, destructiveness, narcissism, and violent fantasies and dreams without any apparent societal cause.

If human beings are so naturally good, how did they happen to set up such bad societies? Where did this badness in society come from? It is simpler, more in accord with accumulated evidence, and more economical from a theoretical point of view to accept the idea that humans are both good and bad.

Other arguments about human selfishness steadily gaining ground are those of scientists such as Nobel laureates Konrad Lorenz and Niko Tinbergen.[12] Such scientists fully accept aggression as one of the basic characteristics of animals, especially of the primates and of humans in particular. They see aggression as usually quite functional in maintaining social organization and in keeping other groups of the same species at a reasonable distance. Warding off predators also has obvious benefits. To biologists, aggression, like all traits, can be either "good"—that is, functional or "bad"—that is, dysfunctional, depending on the circumstance in which it is being displayed. The claim that man is naturally without aggression is preposterous; indeed, our very success and dominance as a species strongly suggest we have too much of it. Both Lorenz and Tinbergen believe man's aggressive capacity is now out of balance with recent cultural changes. As a result a lively debate has developed over the exact nature of our aggression and how to control it.[13]

It is not just scientific evidence and theoretical discussion that discredit the "total intrinsic goodness" assumption. The demise of our supposedly neurotic inhibitions in our classrooms has not served to bring a great increase in student happiness and mental health—if anything, as already noted, the opposite seems to have occurred.[14] In short, the assumption about the complete natural goodness of the self, which stands at the heart of the Values Clarification theory, is false. This weakness alone is enough to remove it as a sensible candidate for a theory of moral education.

A PHILOSOPHICAL CRITIQUE

Values Clarification usually espouses personal relativism: what is good or bad is so only for a given person. It follows that blaming and praising anyone's values or behavior is to be avoided. The problem is that the relativist position involves Values Clarification in a number of very basic contradictions. Taken as a whole, these contradictions completely undermine the coherence of the system. The first basic contradiction is that, in spite of the personal relativity of all values, the theorists clearly believe that Values Clarification is good. That is, relativity aside, students *should* prize their model of how to clarify values. Raths and Simon attack the inculcation of traditional values by teachers, but they simultaneously urge teachers to inculcate Values Clarification. Indeed when they argue for their system they moralize and sermonize like anyone else. They criticize traditional teaching of values as "selling," "pushing," and "forcing one's own pet values" on children at the price of free inquiry and reason.[15] But when it comes to the value of their position, relativism has conveniently disappeared.

The second major contradiction in Values Clarification derives from the basic absurdity of personal moral relativism. This is clearly identified by Wolterstorff,[16] whose analysis we will present.

When Raths and his colleagues bring up the question of whether children in the classroom should be allowed to choose anything they wish, they answer no.[17] Parents and teachers have the right to set some "choices" as off-limits. But they don't have this right because the choices are wrong. Instead, they say that they have this right because certain choices would be intolerable to parents or teachers. As Wolterstorff cogently concluded, Values Clarification turns into arbitrary authority.[18] How personal relativity turns into arbitrary authority is instructively portrayed by the Values Clarification theorists themselves in the following example:

> Teacher: So some of you think it is best to be honest on tests, is that right? (Some heads nod affirmatively.) And some of you think dishonesty is all right? (A few hesitant and slight nods.) And I guess some of you are not certain. (Heads nod.) . . .
>
> Ginger: Does that mean that we can decide for ourselves whether we should be honest on tests here?
>
> Teacher: No, that means that you can decide on the value. I personally value honesty; and although you may choose to be dishonest, I shall insist that we be honest on our tests here. In

other areas of your life, you may have more freedom to be dishonest, but one can't do anything any time, and in this class I shall
expect honesty on tests.

Ginger: But then how can we decide for ourselves? Aren't you
telling us what to value?

Sam: Sure you're telling us what we should do and believe in.

Teacher: Not exactly, I don't mean to tell you what you should
value. That's up to you. But I do mean that in this class, not
elsewhere necessarily, you have to be honest on tests or suffer
certain consequences. I merely mean that I cannot give tests
without the rule of honesty. All of you who choose dishonesty as
a value may not practice it here, that's all I'm saying. Further
questions anyone?[19]

From this startling example we might suggest as analogies: "You
may or may not steal in other stores, but I shall expect and insist
on honesty in my store." Likewise, "you are not be a racist in my
class, but elsewhere that is up to you." You may have "more
freedom" somewhere else!

The only reason for the forbidding of a particular choice in the
classroom is that the teacher or parent finds the choice personally
offensive or inconvenient. And, of course, teachers and parents
(usually!) also have the power to enforce their will. That is, students
don't have enough freedom to do what they value in the classroom!

Values Clarification theorists explicitly support the position
that morality is relative to each individual. The advocates of Values
Clarification should acknowledge, although they don't, that as a
result their system pushes and indoctrinates one particular interpretation of morality. Out of all the many different approaches to
morality, to personal values, only personal moral relativity is sin-
gled out for approval.

The central problem raised by Values Clarification (and similar
approaches) is that it rejects all absolute or non-relativist interpretations of the moral life. In particular, Values Clarification represents a direct attack on traditional religious morality. For example,
orthodox Jews and traditional Protestants and Catholics would all
reject Values Clarification. For that matter the morality of Aristotle
or any contemporary representative of such a "noble pagan" view
is rejected by those advocating Values Clarification. There is a
serious political issue here. The public schools in recent years have
given Values Clarification much support, and in so doing the

schools have given the morality of personal relativism a *privileged position*. That is, the public schools have used tax money to systematically attack the values of those students and parents who believe certain values are true, especially those who have a traditional religious position. Such a policy is a serious injustice to those taxpayers who expect that in the public school classroom their values will be treated with respect or at least left alone.

A CRITIQUE OF PROCEDURES AND STRATEGIES

The classroom exercises are a major part of Values Clarification. These exercises are called "strategies," and they are easily used vehicles for discussing and clarifying values within the framework of the Values Clarification philosophy. They have been a major reason for the popularity of the approach. Even those educators aware of the relativistic philosophy of Values Clarification have often used the exercises under the assumption that they are neutral tools with which to approach the topic of moral education.[20]

I have not carefully evaluated each of the published 79 strategies in the handbook;[21] however, it is possible to make some generalizations. First, the actual questions asked of the students (plus the supporting text) are filled with the social ideology of a small segment of American society. This segment is secular, relativistic, very permissive, openly anti-religious, and generally ultra-liberal.[22] This is, of course, a perfectly legitimate position in American society—however it has no right to the special status given it by so many schools.

To begin, the procedures in Values Clarification always focus on the isolated individual making choices based on the clarity and personal appeal of each alternative value. Such a procedure, as Bennett and DeLattre[23] point out, strongly encourages the student to narcissistic self-gratification.

It is also important to keep in mind that many questions even if neutrally worded carry strong ideological overtones. That is, to control what questions are asked, even to get a question on the agenda, is in many instances to inevitably reflect ideology, as most politicians know quite well. The major reason for this is that even to raise a question about something that was previously considered settled or unimportant is in itself an ideological activity. It unsettles a previous answer or gives importance to a previously unimportant issue. Typical of those recommended for secondary students and adults include the following *do-you* or *would-you* questions:

Think giving grades in school inhibits meaningful learning?

Approve of premarital sex for boys?

Approve of premarital sex for girls?

Think sex education instruction in schools should include techniques [!] for lovemaking, contraception?

Think that teachers should discuss their personal lives with students?

Would approve of a marriage between homosexuals being sanctioned by a priest, minister, or rabbi?

Would approve of a young couple trying out marriage by living together for six months before actually getting married?

Would encourage legal abortion for an unwed daughter?

Would take your children to religious services even if they don't want to?

Would approve of contract marriages in which the marriage would come up for renewal every few years?

Would be upset if your daughter were living with a man who had no intentions of marriage? If your son were living with a woman?. . .

Would be upset if organized religion disappeared?

Think the government should help support day care centers for working mothers?

Think that parents should be subsidized to pick any school they want for their children?

Think we should legalize mercy killings?[24]

The very wording of these questions often suggests a favored response, one in line with the author's philosophy. For example, when they want a positive answer they start a question with "approve" or "would approve"; when they want a negative answer, they begin the question negatively, e.g., "Would be upset if organized religion disappeared?" The word *upset* suggests something negative. It subtly implies that one would not be upset. Of course, they don't ask such questions as, "Would be upset if public schools disappeared?" Two other questions make this point in another way. Consider the item "Think the government should *help support* day care centers for working mothers?" Here the bias is toward "yes." "Think that parents should be *subsidized* to pick any school they want for their children?" Here the bias is toward "no." In the first question tax money "helps support," but in the second question tax money is called a "subsidy." For example, why not ask the question this way: "think the government should restrict children to the public school rather than the school the student freely chooses?" In short, in spite of claims to neutrality, the above questions show much bias including the simple political one of supporting the growth of anti-religious, state-controlled education while attacking any threat to this position.

The common procedures of Values Clarification have other negative consequences. The procedural goal of increasing the number of alternative positions on a given issue reinforces the idea that values are relative. Each of the potential different values about premarital chastity, for example, is likely to be embodied by at least one of the students' peers. This makes it psychologically very hard to maintain a firm belief in any absolute value without experiencing painful peer rejection. It is very difficult even for adults to reject a belief without seeming to reject also the person who holds the belief.

Another type of bias in a Values Clarification strategy for use with adults is quoted from an article by Bennett and Delattre:

> In Priorities, Simon "asks you and your family at the dinner table, or your friends across the lunch table, to rank choices and to defend those choices in friendly discussion." One example of Simon's "delightful possibilities" for mealtime discussion is this:
>
> Your husband or wife is a very attractive person. Your best friend is very attracted to him or her. How would you want them to behave?
>
> - Maintain a clandestine relationship so you wouldn't know about it.
> - Be honest and accept the reality of the relationship.
> - Proceed with a divorce.[25]
>
> [This] exercise asks the student how he would want his spouse and best friend to behave if they were attracted to each

other. Typically, the spouse and best friend are presented as having desires they will eventually satisfy anyway; the student is offered only choices that presuppose their relationship. All possibilities for self-restraint, fidelity, regard for others, or respect for mutual relationships and commitments are ignored.[26]

This example, with its biased and limited options, speaks for itself about the Values Clarification system.

A VIOLATION OF PRIVACY CRITIQUE

The techniques and strategies of Values Clarification often very seriously violate the privacy of the student and the student's family. In fact parents disturbed by the loss of personal privacy have been some of the most vocal and effective critics of Values Clarification and related procedures as used in the schools. The exact nature of this important criticism has been spelled out by Professor Alan L. Lockwood, and his analysis will be summarized here.[27]

All Americans consider personal privacy to be something of great value and a general right to such privacy is assumed. Reasons for this are worth mentioning. Privacy protects us from public embarrassment or ridicule. "For example, consider the probable hazing were it known that the captain of the football team slept with a tattered, old teddy bear. Similarly we could predict adverse social reaction if a person, currently living in a racist community, came to believe in racial integration."[28]

Privacy also helps to maintain our psychological well-being. We need privacy to get rest from the pressures and demands of life. We need time to reflect privately about our life. It is hard to imagine how this reflection could function if we were under frequent pressure to reveal our feelings, thoughts, and plans—often when they are only tentative and partially formed. Even more crucial to psychological well-being is the very private inner core of beliefs, hopes, faith, and ultimate secrets that everyone has at the center of their personality. To be forced to expose these to the public view is for most people to threaten basic psychological integrity.

Lockwood also noted that "privacy is . . . essential for preserving liberties characteristic of a political democracy."[29] Secret ballots, the right to assembly, and many of our other liberties are only possible if social and government surveillance is limited and our privacy is maintained.

The right to privacy is, as Lockwood mentioned, not an absolute right since there are many kinds of information that the state, the schools, and other public institutions need to function properly. Nevertheless, the right to privacy is a very important one and invasions of it should never be allowed except when fully justified.

In order to maintain our privacy we must be able to control information about ourselves. This means that when information is requested one must be informed about what information is being requested and what it will be used for. That is, there must be informed consent. Certain ways of getting information undermine a person's informed consent. First, informed consent requires a mature judgment—something no child is likely to have. Second, the information being requested must be clearly specified. However, many psychological tests—i.e., projective tests—elicit information that the person doesn't know is being asked for, such as sentence completion and Rorschach inkblot tests. In these situations people may reveal information about themselves of which they are quite unaware. Of course, if the person is doing this within the context of psychotherapy, there is no violation of privacy since the person has sought out psychological help; the therapist is trained in the use of such information and is legally bound to secrecy. But when a teacher requests such information in a class setting, a violation of privacy is very likely.

Another way in which informed consent is violated occurs when the person giving the information is under strong group pressure to be especially open with personal information. (Again, if the individual in question has chosen to go into group therapy and knows this pressure is going to develop, there is normally no violation of the right to privacy.)

With this analysis in mind look at how Values Clarification often operates. As Lockwood has made clear, many of the questions that are used in Values Clarification violate the students' right to privacy. In particular, questions about the interpersonal dynamics of family life and about personal, emotional life, and general world views are all almost certain to invade one's personal life. From the VC handbook here are questions noted by Lockwood.

> *Family dynamics:* What does your mother do? Does she like it? Is she home a lot? What disturbs you most about your parents? Reveal who in your family brings you the greatest sadness, and why?

Personal behavior and emotions: Recall the last ten times you have cried. What was each about? Is there something you once did that you are ashamed of? What do you dream at night? The subject I would be most reluctant to discuss here is . . .

General world views: How many of you think that parents should teach their children to masturbate? If your parents were in constant conflict, which would you rather have them do: get divorced and your father leave home, stay together and hide their feelings for the sake of the children, get divorced and you stay with your father?[30]

Clearly, the above questions are likely to directly violate the privacy of the child or the parents or both. Keep in mind that there is strong group pressure in the classroom where the questions are asked, that the answers will often become public knowledge in the school and community, that the children are too young to give truly informed consent, that the teachers or facilitators are untrained in psychology, and that the students, much less the parents, have never agreed to participate in such a process.

To further undermine privacy, Values Clarification questions are often open-ended in a way that makes them a projective technique. Here are some Values Clarification sentences that students are to complete, given by Lockwood:

Secretly I wish . . .
I'd like to tell my best friend . . .
My parents are usually . . .
I often find myself . . .[31]

Lockwood concluded from his analysis that "a substantial proportion of the content and methods of Values Clarification constitute a threat to the privacy rights of students and their families."[32]

The strength and clarity of Lockwood's analysis should make it clear that this criticism alone is enough to reject the Values Clarification approach to morality in any school where informed student and parent consent has not been obtained.

WHY HAS VALUES CLARIFICATION BEEN POPULAR?

Given the obvious and serious problems with Values Clarification, a natural question arises: why has it been so popular? And it has been very popular indeed. Values Clarification theorists were enthusiastically received speakers at scores of education conferences. Their books sold hundreds of thousands of copies. Workshops showing teachers how to use Values Clarification in the classroom were common at countless national and regional meetings of teachers and educators. Tens of thousands of teachers were trained to use it. As a result Values Clarification spread quickly throughout the country in the 1970s, and many aspects of it are still prevalent in school courses, especially those dealing with values or value-laden topics such as drug and sex education programs.

The major reasons for the popularity of Values Clarification apparently are the following:

- For the students the many strategies required no prior preparation; they were easily grasped and led to spirited classroom discussion.
- The teacher was only a facilitator—not a true teacher since there was no actual knowledge to be passed on. As a result little preparation was required of the teacher and exams were usually unnecessary. After all there were no right or wrong answers. The spirited or active discussions implied that the class had been a success.
- The entire philosophy of letting each student pick his or her own values fitted in easily with our consumer society. People picked value systems rather like they picked a magazine to read, a movie to see, or a brand of soap to use.
- The alternative seemed to be the direct teaching of particular values and this seemed almost impossible to do. This seemed impossible because the reasons justifying many values were no longer familiar to teachers or students or seemed easily rebutted. Such a process required prior training and knowledge justifying particular values, but most teachers had never received this training or the appropriate knowledge. The only way to teach such values seemed to involve heavy doses of lecturing, or sermonizing. This kind of teaching was hard to do and was often rightly unpopular with students.
- Finally, many teachers had come to believe that in a pluralistic society teaching any particular value might be illegal. That is, a parent might complain or

even sue if a teacher taught a value rejected by some parent. Along with this fear was the belief, at least at first, that Values Clarification was the answer because it was value free or neutral as its proponents claimed.

WHY VALUES CLARIFICATION MUST BE REJECTED

In spite of the immediate appeal of letting each student pick his or her own values (personal relativism), the Values Clarification approach must be firmly rejected. The major reasons are that individual relativism leads to arbitrary authority and social anarchy, and it flies in the face of simple common sense.

The issue of social anarchy may sound abstract and distant, but it is already in each citizen's backyard. For example, racism is perfectly okay in the Value Clarification system. Hating people because of their race or religion or ethnic background is fine as long as the student chooses it. To reject school itself, to say yes to drugs, to cheat on exams, to steal from your schoolmates—all these are okay if values are up to each person. These behaviors cannot be rejected by Values Clarification advocates.

It is a common observation that certain values (or virtues) are regularly admired and accepted as obviously valid all around the world. Everywhere such traits as honesty, altruism, heroism, hard work, and loyalty are admired. And the liar, the thief, the coward, the lazy, the selfish, and the traitor are rejected. In short, there are common cross-cultural values and character traits that go with them.

Furthermore, the other criticisms mentioned put the final nails in the coffin of Values Clarification. Recall that Values Clarification assumes the self is entirely good with not even a slight tendency to harm or exploit others; yet the strategies and exercises often contain serious political and ideological biases, and the Values Clarification questions often violate the privacy of the student and the student's family.

The contradictions and incoherence of Values Clarification demonstrate that it is an intellectually absurd system. Because of parental protest, most school systems have abandoned or downplayed Values Clarification;[33] nevertheless, its widespread success reveals the disturbing prevalence of a confused moral relativism in much of American education.

Unfortunately this moral relativism remains even now in the 1990s as part of many programs—especially in health and sex and drug education. The name "Values Clarification" is gone, but the concept under other names continues to undermine the moral life of our children.

A RETURN TO CONTENT—CHARACTER AND VIRTUE

Philosophers and theologians disagree over various abstract principles of the moral life. But they are in general agreement about personal characteristics which are "good"—characteristics usually called virtues—such as courage, self-control, altruism, hard work, honesty, patience, and so on. There can be disagreement about which are the highest virtues and about difficulties that occur when one virtue conflicts with another, but these occasional difficulties should not blind us to the basic positive significance of such character traits.

In the legal world it is generally acknowledged that "hard cases make bad law." It is equally true in the moral life that painful dilemmas produce confused moral systems. Simple prudence, therefore, strongly implies that in teaching basic morality to children, one should avoid complex, ambiguous, conflicting, and anguished moral dilemmas and paradoxes. Such a pragmatic rule also acknowledges the simple fact that most moral issues in real life *are* fairly straightforward and do not involve head-on collisions between different virtues or moral principles. Let's face it: if the moral life is difficult, it is rarely because we do not know what to do but because it is hard to do what we know we should.

There is today in American education a slowly developing consensus that we need to return to a traditional understanding of the moral life.[34] This approach is very roughly known as character education. Its opponents in the past have derided this as the "bag of virtues" approach, but surely, better a bag of virtues than a bag of tricks, better good character than smart thinking, better right behavior than cognitive dilemmas!

But how are we to teach character in view of the widespread relativism found in contemporary American society? Are there virtues that most Americans will agree upon? Here I think the answer is yes. Who would dare seriously to argue in public that courage, honesty, altruism, and self-control are "bad" things and should not be taught to our children? The question still remains, however: how are these virtues to be taught? Here again I think the answer is now fairly clear—use stories. This traditional approach, found in all cultures at all times, is easy for the teacher and delights students; and, as evidence indicates, affects behavior. Of course, stories by themselves are not enough. It is necessary for the students actually to practice the virtue and for the school and home environment to support good character.

Fortunately there is recent evidence that concerned parents and reflective educators have already begun to implement a return to character education[35] as an antidote to relativism and as a major step toward America's recovery of moral sanity.

The Decline of Morality

Harold O. J. Brown

Plus que ça change, plus que c'est la même chose.
–French proverb

TWO VIEWS OF CHANGE—OR THREE

The late Henry Luce called the twentieth century the American century, displaying the optimism, widely seen in the United States: "Things are getting better and better. This is an age of constant and continual Progress." The First World War shattered most of Europe's faith in unbroken progress and human perfectability. America's own optimism was largely suppressed by the Vietnam War. The many economic, social, and political setbacks since then have added to the malaise.

Nevertheless, while our own society wrestles with problems that were unexpected and unexpectedly large, there is news from elsewhere in the world that could help us to recover our traditional American trust in progress and help to reinforce our national superstition that changes are always for the better. The former prime minister of Great Britain, Margaret Thatcher, warned in her Clare Boothe Luce Lecture on September 23, 1991, that recent changes have not meant progress at all but rather totalitarianism, collectivism, mass murder, wars, and refugees. Writing in 1937, sociologist Pitirim A. Sorokin observed that the twentieth century had already become bloodier than the previous nineteen combined—and that was *before* World War II. But Mrs. Thatcher wanted to look on the bright side: "Only now do we dare to trust, as this Twentieth Century is coming to an end, both in years and in philosophy, that the cause of liberty *will* prevail throughout the world; and that the coming century *will* be the American century—because people everywhere are turning to what have become American ideas—ideas of liberty, democracy, free markets, free trade, and limited government."[1]

Is Mrs. Thatcher right? Are things going to get better and better and more "American"?

It is certainly true that there are hopeful signs in formerly enslaved societies such as those of Eastern Europe and the Soviet Union. However, in our nation, the United States, where we have enjoyed a measure of freedom that verges on license, we are beginning to experience what Sorokin called the "moment when the expansion of the wishes outruns the available means for their satisfaction."[2] In lines written in 1937 and reaffirmed in 1957, the late Russian-born Harvard sociologist wrote:

> Persons with an overdeveloped wish for sensate freedom are likely to become the oversensual seekers for perverse pleasures that soon debilitate body and mind; or the egotists who do not want to reckon with or respect any value except their own fancy or volition. Through their scandals, indecencies, erratic exploits, and through the actions of robbery, murder, sacrilege, and the like, they ruin themselves and the society of which they are a part.
>
> A society with a considerable proportion of these overfree members cannot exist for a long time, with such lunatics at large. It will either disintegrate, or must take measures to bridle them: bridling them means a limitation, sometimes even an elimination, of the greater part of sensate liberty.[3]

Who is right—former Prime Minister Thatcher with her optimistic hope that the future will be an American century, meaning a century of political and economic freedom and personal responsibility, or Sorokin who warns of "lunatics at large"? Both are doubtless correct in affirming that changes are coming. There are two questions to answer: (1) Do the changes into which we are heading mean hope or distress? (2) Is there anything that we can do to influence and direct them?

Mr. Toffler told us that vast and dramatic changes were upon us; Mrs. Thatcher claimed they would be beneficial; and Professor Sorokin was less optimistic, yet held out a prospect of hope on the condition that we manage to overcome the crisis by the sequence that he called catharsis-charisma-resurrection. However, Sorokin

61

was absolutely sure that if we did not pass through purification and spiritual renewal—which he conceived in generally Christian terms—there would be no resurrection for our society, only debacle and disaster.

One does not have to be particularly astute to see signs that there are indeed "lunatics at large" among us. There are the "lunatics" in Sorokin's sense, who are the "oversensual seekers for perverse pleasures," and there those who, in St. Paul's words, "approve of those who practice them" (Rom. 1:32 NIV). It is unfortunate not to have the Russian scholar's gift for heaping up invectives, for the pages of the entertainment section of any major metropolitan newspaper consists largely of fawning upon the most extreme abusers of sensate freedom.

In a recent sensational and macabre trial in Chicago, a couple were accused of murdering their seven-year-old daughter. The original trial judge dismissed the charges against the mother, but the father was found guilty of murder by the trial jury. An appellate court reversed the conviction (a reversal which is being appealed to the Illinois Supreme Court). In bizarre fashion, Chicago papers published photos of the man's wife, mother-in-law, and preschool daughter wearing t-shirts with the legend, "STOP INJUSTICE/FREE (*name*)," and exulting rather as one would expect Chicago Bears fans to exult over a victory in the Superbowl.[4] Even murder trials, false charges, and escape from lifelong injustice become entertainment, as it were, for the very participants themselves (except, of course, the dead girl). To be cleared of such an accusation is surely a reason to rejoice, but somehow the fact that this verdict was published on Halloween, which is becoming an ever more ghoulish celebration in *fin-de-siècle* America, makes the whole affair look like one more illustration of Sorokin's "lunacy at large."

Will we progress to more freedom worldwide, on the "American plan," as Mrs. Thatcher hopes, or will our plunge into lunacy force one of Sorokin's alternatives, namely, either social disintegration or the elimination of the greater part of liberty? Inasmuch as our society shows hardly any wish to limit sensate liberty, despite warning signs of all kinds, one is more inclined to expect disintegration rather than repression.

In addition to the optimists who rejoice in change and the pessimists who deplore it, there is a third group, which is telling us that things really aren't changing all that much at all: "*Plus que ça change, plus que c'est la même chose.*" Is divorce on the increase?

Indeed it is, but previously there was marital unhappiness and infidelity. More divorce may sound bad, but it is actually a good thing, as it means that people are placing higher expectations on marriage. Is there an increase in pregnancy among unmarried teenagers and an epidemic of abortion in women of all ages and conditions? Indeed there is, but this is a sign of greater sexual freedom and of the liberation of women from the unfair conditions of "biology as destiny." Has homosexuality become rampant, leading to the rise and spread of an epidemic disease that could conceivably wipe out a large part of the population, and that under conditions of the most extreme misery and degradation? Indeed it has, but homosexuality has always been practiced; it is only that now it is open, free, and somehow better. In addition, it is genetically predetermined, and so those who practice it do so by nature, or, alternatively, they choose it as an expression of the fundamental human freedom of choice. If indeed it does spread AIDS, it is an unfortunate development, but it would hardly be appropriate to reproach those who suffer from and propagate that plague for doing what for them— supposedly—is perfectly natural.

In other words, don't worry about apparent changes and the evidence of social disintegration, for nothing important is being lost. The apostle Peter seemed aware of the tendency to reason thus, for he cited those he called "scoffers of the last days" as saying: "Since the fathers fell asleep, all things continue as they were from the beginning of creation" (2 Peter 3:4 KJV). It is not evident whether or not we are living in the "last days" of the human race, but from the calendar it is apparent that we are in the last days of the second millennium. It is easy to recognize the numbers at the top of the calendar; it is harder to analyze what they mean and to predict where we are all being taken.

We encounter paradoxically conflicting descriptions of our era. On the one hand, some—such as Alvin Toffler—do not merely admit but trumpet abroad their conviction that change in every area of life has become incredibly rapid, leaving bewildered, spiritually uprooted multitudes in its wake, incapable of digesting and coping with it. Toffler published *Future Shock* in 1970. None of the trends he found "shocking" (although generally in a positive sense) has slowed since then. Toffler saw them all as positive, exciting, hopeful, the wave of a brave new future. Perhaps so, but I'm reminded of a comment by Professor John H. Finley, Jr., as he looked out of the windows of Harvard's Widener Library in the early 1970s and observed the colorful chaos in the Harvard Yard: "If only it weren't all so sordid."

Thus, on the other hand, many writers see the West, if not the whole world, not as on the verge of something wonderfully new, but rather as mired in the decline that accompanies the aging of a culture, viewed as a sort of biological organism. Every living thing comes into being, grows, matures, ages, and ultimately dies. Society, like any biological organism, must decline and die after it has flourished as long as it is able. Who is right, the Tofflers and Thatchers or the Sorokins and Finleys? Are we in the effervescence of fresh life, or are we experiencing how a society can lose its reason as it declines into senescence and extinction? Which is correct?

DUSK OR DAWN?

The most celebrated of those who took up the biological model of society and proclaimed that society was in decline was certainly Oswald Spengler (1880–1936), whose *Decline of the West* appeared in its first German edition in 1918. What both camps—optimists in Toffler's and pessimists in Spengler's—have in common is that they see the present age, with its values and its traditions, being rapidly brushed off of the stage of world history. The late Christian philosopher Herman Dooyweerd wrote of "the Twilight of Western Thought," and the dean of evangelical thinkers, Carl F. H. Henry, has spoken of "the Twilight of a Great Civilization." They apparently were not thinking of a new beginning. But the very astute analyst, Pitirim Sorokin nevertheless hoped for "a new magnificent era," provided, however that "the Apocalyptic catastrophe can be avoided," and the Austrian Roman Catholic sociologist Hans Millendorfer said that the world "will renew itself"—provided, however, that Christians are active as "salt that does not lose its savor." We do not want to underestimate the degree of moral degeneracy that now prevails in our society nor minimize its potential for causing total chaos, but we must not throw up our hands as though there were no longer any task for "salt" in the world.

Spengler spoke of "Decline," James Burnham of "the Suicide of the West," Dooyweerd and Henry of "Twilight." One is moved to ask: Is this really the end? Or is the twilight possibly the prelude to a new dawn? From a Christian perspective, we know that there will be a great "tribulation," or a time of troubles, before Christ returns and wraps up world history, but we cannot know how close we are to that development or whether we are actually entering it.

In a way it would be wonderful if we could say, "These are the signs of the end: only a little longer to wait." However, Jesus admonished his disciples that they were not to know the day or the hour when the Last Day would break in like a thief. If we knew that a particular patient was to be executed tomorrow, we would hardly have the incentive to perform a life-saving operation today. But since we cannot know when the end will come, it is up to us as Christians to do all that we can to understand the situation that exists today—to diagnose the patient's condition, if we may put it thus—and to determine, as best as we can, what kind of treatment might be most helpful.

THE EXTENT OF OUR PROBLEM

Are we dealing with changes in the United States only, in the West generally, or worldwide? Spengler wrote of the West, but in universal terms; Toffler took his data chiefly from the West. The transformations certainly affect the entire "Christian" (or "post-Christian") West, and most of the rest of the world as well. However, since the essays in this book are written primarily by Americans for American readers, we will direct our attention chiefly to what is happening in North America.

TWO CHARACTERISTICS

The transformation of American society reveals two increasingly strong developments: a loss of fixed standards of moral value and an incredibly narcissistic fascination with ourselves. The two things go together. Because for so many of us self-centeredness is taken for granted as the normal orientation in life, we have no objective standards of value against which to measure ourselves and our conduct. Nothing external matters, only, as Sorokin said, our own fancy or will. Thus we increasingly act on the assumption that whatever we desire to do or to have must be right. This self-centeredness extends to society as a whole, both individually and collectively: most of us think first if not solely of ourselves, and as a nation we think so singly of ourselves that we are very ignorant of the impression we make on the surrounding world and the legacy we leave to history.

One illustration is our trivialization of life; our news and enter-tainment media abound with reports of so many disasters both great and small that a sense of proportion and scale seems to vanish. The confirmation hearings held in September and October 1991 on the nomination of Judge Clarence Thomas to the United States Supreme Court are a case in point. Trivia took on gigantesque proportions. Lewd remarks allegedly made in a Washington office ten years ago preoccupied the Senate, the media, and the general public for weeks and furnished an occasion, or a pretext, for the further debasement of public discourse and for habituating the general public more and more fully to life in what Sorokin called "the social sewers."[5]

Allegations were made against Judge Thomas which, from their very nature, were totally incapable of verification and hence were without evident value. The Senate hearings were more reminiscent of Communist or Nazi show trials than of anything that has a legitimate place in American law or politics. A great deal more could be said about them, but what is relevant to our interest is the fact that the highest legislative body in the land staged a spectacle of this nature. What they attempted, or at least purported, to investi-gate was not in fact a crime nor, even at the time it was alleged to have happened, a cause for civil action. It did not consist in deeds, but only of speech. Speech is in general entirely free in the United States, and a speech that took place a decade ago is very hard to precisely recall, much less prove its actual occurrence. But what appeared to be at stake was the "sensate liberty" that is the highest value of modern society, namely the right to unbridled sexual liberty, requiring in turn abortion on demand, which the (now successful) nomination of Judge Thomas appeared to imperil. Thus for the sake of that sensate liberty, a new offense was tacitly discovered and ranked as heinous, "speechcrime" (to borrow an idea from the late George Orwell), and it seemed for a moment as though no proof were necessary. Objectivity and truth were of no consideration. The fact that the chosen procedure had no chance of even approaching them, much less of achieving them, demon-strates that they were not the focus of the Senate's true concern.

Even though the full Senate subsequently confirmed the nomi-nation of Thomas, the fact remains that America's highest legisla-tive body, the great television networks, and much of the general public wallowed in denunciation and prurient dialogue for days on end. A society in which the legislatures, the media, and the general public have lost a sense for the importance of objectivity and truth is a seriously disoriented one.

IS CHANGE IMPROVEMENT?

The paradoxical contrast continues: if we recognize change, we are told that however unsettling it may be it is good and it would be foolish, reactionary, and obscurantist to criticize it, not to speak of resisting it. In the words of the hymn, "time makes ancient good uncouth." We are told that tradition has created oppressive structures that must be abolished, but note what has happened: dramatically rising statistics for divorce, poverty, child abuse (including sexual abuse), abortion, venereal ("sexually transmitted") diseases, homelessness, illegitimate births, homosexuality, mental disturbances, adolescent suicide, alcohol and drug abuse, pornography, violence against women, and transformation of universities and colleges from centers of learning to centers of debauchery. When we predictably deplore these changes, we are told that nothing really important has changed—unless possibly for the better, in terms of greater openness, freedom, and sensate liberty—those very things that Sorokin saw as producing "lunatics at large."

If we complain, we are told that these things that we deplore have always been with us. The statistical deterioration is only apparent, the result of more openness and better record-keeping. If anything, we are now more fortunate than before, in that before we were ignorant of the true nature of human society and tended to condemn as abuses things that in a more liberal and enlightened age we must recognize as natural and fully justifiable expressions of liberty and choice, if not altogether desirable in themselves. Now we are better informed. "*Tout comprendre, c'est tout pardonner*," but in this case we do not merely pardon—for that would imply that something was actually *wrong*—but rather admire.

With respect to most of the phenomena mentioned above such as abortion, divorce, homosexuality, homelessness, they have indeed always been with us. Yet it is evident to anyone with even the slightest familiarity with social statistics that those phenomena for which accurate statistics exist have indeed increased dramatically— divorce and homelessness are the easiest phenomena about which this can be asserted, inasmuch as marriages and divorces have been matters of public record for centuries and homelessness is generally visible. What is striking about the extent of homelessness—whether one takes the lowest figure offered or the highest, which may exceed it by a factor of ten—is the fact that it is much greater now, in what must still be called an age of affluence, than it ever became during the Great Depression of the 1930s.

The reason behind the fact that many people have no home is the fact that homes in the old sense are ceasing to exist because families in the old sense are breaking up, or not coming into being at all.

It is fashionable for "experts," such as those who are called to Washington from time to time to discuss the family, to deplore the nuclear family, which was of course inherently patriarchal, wicked, destructive, and dysfunctional and to rhapsodize over its replacement by imaginative new ways of living together, called "non-traditional families," which are created by "alternate life-styles." Unfortunately, the non-traditional families that come from the alternate life-styles are leaving vast numbers of miserable, homeless people strewn about the cities of this rich land. Is this so surprising? By what logic should a society care for its old, its sick, its less productive, its marginally useful or entirely useless members, when it readily accepts a situation in which one-third of every new generation of potentially healthy, happy, hard-working, and creative children can be "safely and legally" exterminated before birth, with no chance to develop the potential with which God endowed them and which their parents transmitted to them—however briefly—in their genes? All these things spring from a common outlook and constitute in Hans Millendorfer's expression *ein Block des Bösen*, "a bloc of evil."

ABORTION: A CASE IN POINT

Abortion has increased dramatically throughout the developed countries of the world where it has been legalized in varying degrees and where comprehensive records are kept. The United "States" probably hold the world record in abortion, at least in abortion for trivial or frivolous reasons, with the total running at about one-and-a-half million per year, or close to one abortion for every two live births. Even if one were to accept the legitimacy of abortion when the mother-to-be finds herself in extremely difficult circumstances, can anyone suppose that the circumstances of American women are so difficult, in one out of three cases, to warrant the "termination" of pregnancy or, to put it more clearly if less soothingly, the killing of the baby? Can anyone in his or her right mind think that the prenatal extermination of one-third of the future generation is a social boon? That people *do* think so was apparent from the immense furor that arose when Supreme Court nominees Robert Bork (unsuccessful) and Clarence Thomas appeared likely to be inclined, if confirmed, to do something to limit abortion. (Whether their impassioned critics are in any meaningful sense in a right mind is another question.)

In what appears to be the earliest scholarly study of the abortion phenomenon, dating from 1888, Raffaelo Baelstrini has written about ancient society:

> Abortion, elevated to the degree of a social custom, is in sum nothing but the apparent manifestation of a state of decadence of a people, which has very deep roots and which can only be cured with far-reaching remedies, not with the attempt to suppress the manifestation itself.[6]

A VIRTUE OF NECESSITY?

Prior to the extreme liberalization of abortion in the early 1970s virtually everyone, even advocates of liberalized laws, agreed that every abortion is a personal tragedy and that abortion should be avoided as much as possible. In his standard work *Jurisprudence,* Edgar Bodenheimer unsuspectingly cited the generalized prohibition of abortion in all civilized countries to illustrate his contention that the killing of innocent human beings is universally regarded as evil in every human society.[7]

Even while contending that it should be available to all who actually "need" it and allowing the pregnant woman to be the sole judge of her need, virtually everyone who discussed abortion prior to *Roe v. Wade* called it a solution of last resort. Psychologist Magda Denes, who had one of her own pregnancies aborted, expressed her view about abortion sadly but clearly in her 1976 book, *In Necessity and Sorrow: Life and Death in an Abortion Hospital.*[8]

After liberalization, however (*Roe v. Wade* dates from 1973) abortion advocates increasingly began to view abortion in a positive light, so much so that even before *Roe*, on the basis of the liberalized laws in several states, Lawrence Lader could call the rapid increase in abortion figures "a triumph of the human spirit," exulting that "an act of faith can become a revolution."[9] Illustrations abound in which abortion advocates now speak of abortion not only as a right but also as virtually a morally good deed—for example Union Theological Seminary Professor Beverly A. Harrison in *Our Right to Choose*.[10] In what might seem a contrary development, while some people praise abortion as a moral act, others seek to avoid the word entirely. As columnist Steven Chapman pointed out in the *Chicago Tribune*, the term "abortion" is increasingly avoided in favor of "choice."[11]

If it really *is* a highly moral act, why should we avoid calling it by its name? But we do not so call it; virtually no one wants to be cited as being in favor of abortion, at least not of abortion as such. One is merely for "choice," an ideal that, if it is taken for granted, will appeal to all democratically-minded Americans. The media have even reached the point where they not only describe abortion advocates as "pro-choice," but often call abortion opponents "anti-choice." Both of these trends have in common that they change something that has always been perceived as an evil, even if sometimes tolerated as a necessary evil, into something good, either good in itself because it "permits women to be moral agents" (so Professor Harrison) or good because it is subsumed under the heading of choice.

It ought to be self-evident to anyone capable of logical thought that the "right to choose" is defensible as a general right only if the area within which it is to be exercised is defined. For example, whatever the relative merits of gun control versus gun ownership may be, the gun lobby could not carry its case, as the abortion lobby has done, by calling for "freedom of choice." (Should one allow one's business or sports rivals to live, or murder them? "We believe in freedom of choice." Surely not.) The fundamental conviction of the anti-abortionists is that, as in the killing of one's rivals, each abortion involves the taking of human life. In such a debate it is morally and ethically fraudulent to defend the right to abort with the slogan "freedom of choice."

The fact that so many in the media simply accept this language of "choice" as a matter of course—although they would reject it as ridiculous if it were brought forward by the gun lobby—reveals that the pro-abortionists are permitted to define the terms of the discussion, which in turn implies that our moral consciousness nationwide is sorely impaired. It is tantamount to allowing slaveholders to reduce the discussion of the morality of slave-owning to one of the right to private property, and to call the abolitionists "anti-property." What would be unexamined in such a case is the fact that the "property" to which one claims ownership is arguably, even demonstrably, a human being. This is precisely the case with the fetus that many claim the right to choose to "terminate." The intellectual dishonesty that characterizes most reporting and discussion of the abortion question represents an affront to human values that is indeed different in kind from the violence of abortion, but that, like abortion, is "the apparent manifestation of the state of decadence of a people."

AND HOMOSEXUALITY?

The situation with regard to homosexuality is hardly different: the incidence of homosexual practice, to the extent that it can be quantified, has risen dramatically; and with the increase in the practice, its acceptability increases as rapidly as the problems it causes.

It is often argued that homosexuality has always been present in human society, and no doubt this is true. It is also alleged that because homosexual acts were illegal in most societies until recently, their true frequency was concealed. There is no doubt also a measure of truth in this assertion. Nevertheless, a superficial consideration of the phenomena connected with homosexuality in our day indicates a substantial increase, even though it is hard to evaluate statistically. Major cities have not only whole streets but large areas filled with gay bars.

The homosexual bathhouse phenomenon, which reached a high point before the nature of the AIDS epidemic was recognized, is now, after a period of decline, again on the rise in a somewhat altered form. Such facilities cannot exist except where there is a high level of demand. "Speakeasies" existed during Prohibition, for many people wanted to drink alcohol and insisted that it was their right, regardless of the law; the existence of such speakeasies was an open secret throughout American society. Where facilities do not exist in any visible form, legally or illegally, it is reasonable to assume that the demand is not intense.

When we observe that homosexual bathhouses were unknown if not altogether nonexistent prior to the 1960s but began to proliferate because of the "gay rights" movement, it is reasonable to assume that more homosexuality began to be practiced, just as we

71

can assume that more people are exercising when large numbers of health and exercise clubs spring up and prosper.

With respect to this component of the "bloc" homosexuality— it is increasingly politically correct to consider this phenomenon merely a legitimate variation of human conduct, whether it is to be interpreted as a so-called creation variant and part of the homosexual's genetic makeup, or as an entirely proper and justifiable expression of freedom of choice. Consequently, if one were to point to the increase in homosexual behavior as the sign of a decline in morality, this would be vigorously contested by all "correct" thinkers.

Instead of acknowledging widespread patterns of homosexuality as a sign of decadence, it is now widely claimed not only by homosexual activists but also by a substantial part of the intellectual elite that homosexuality is at least as legitimate as heterosexuality. Another fashionable, politically correct prejudice plays into this view: people are a burden on the environment, and zero (or negative) population growth is a moral imperative. Indeed, since it is not entirely possible to separate heterosexuality from human procreation, in other words from population growth, homosexuality appears almost superior to heterosexuality. The atrocious and horrible fatal disease known as AIDS is still spread primarily by homosexual conduct, as every new set of statistics from the Communicable Disease Center in Atlanta shows, but in a paradoxical way AIDS has contributed to making homosexuality socially more acceptable. AIDS patients are called not only "victims" but "martyrs," condemned by an unsympathetic nature if not by an unjust deity to suffer for their blameless, perhaps even praiseworthy, exercise of a legitimate right of choice and entitlement to sexual fulfillment.

Abortion on demand and open acceptance of homosexual conduct have not been with us long—only since the later 1960s or the early 1970s—but in a sense they are already passing as big-time issues. The next item on the agenda is euthanasia. Derek Humphrey's *Final Exit* became a best-seller, after much free publicity from the *New York Times* and other important media. Humphrey described how he assisted in the death of his first wife when she was in a late stage of cancer. When his second wife, who co-founded their euthanasia organization, developed the same illness, he divorced her. She too is now dead, apparently having taken her own life. Like abortion, euthanasia, in Professor Millendorfer's words, is "a method in which killing represents a solution."

All these evils hang together. Abortion separates human sexuality from any natural connection with reproduction. The numerous court decisions which decree, in the name of "reproductive freedom," that a father, whether married or not, has absolutely nothing to say about a decision to abort his child, clearly deny to the male any rights with respect to a child that he has begotten, although of course his *obligations*, in case the mother does not exercise her "constitutional right" to abort, are extensive. This clearly implies the breakup of the old social covenants of marriage and family to a child and thus makes homosexuality no longer appear unnatural, but simply an "alternate sexual orientation."

UNCERTAIN SOUNDS

The Roman Christian jurist Tertullian lived in the second half of the second century and during the first decades of the third, a time when the great Roman Empire appeared to be at the height of its power and wealth, but when widespread corruption, sexual license, cruelty, disregard for human life, greed, and dishonesty were rampant. Many of Rome's rulers and officials were involved in the degeneracy and could hardly be expected to combat it, but even those who were not involved seemed somehow unaware of what their society was doing to itself and its members. The "good emperors" such as Antoninus Pius and Marcus Aurelius, who were competent administrators and valiant soldiers, were impotent to check the internal rot of society. It remained to the Christians, as Tertullian pointed out in his *Apology*, first to take a stand against the prevalence of immorality of all kinds and ultimately to bring about changes. Rome's traditional religious leaders did nothing effective, even when they themselves were not part of the problem.

What about America's religious leaders? In the space of only thirty or forty years we seem to be attaining a degree of moral degeneracy to which it took ancient Rome two centuries to sink. Are they offering a solution, or are they too part of the problem? Some—fortunately not all—are making themselves part of the problem.

Major denominations support abortion on demand, "value-free" sex education, and virtually every other evil of which our society is capable except environmental pollution and the bludgeoning of baby seals. Several leading denominations participated in the formation of the Religious Coalition for Abortion Rights, which is certainly no less a moral atrocity than a Religious Coalition for the Establishment of Slavery would be. And significant parts of the religious establishment promote the decline in other ways, rather than opposing it.

An example of how supposedly spiritual and moral leaders, both Jewish and Christian, have allied themselves with the forces of social disintegration is the removal of sexual conduct from the area of moral concerns. Historically both Judaism and Christianity were extremely committed to high standards of sexual morality— no sexual relations before marriage, fidelity in marriage, and no homosexuality. In the last two years, however, a number of religious bodies have in effect declared that the Lord is not concerned with the sexual morality of his servants. In the early 1990s a number of religious ministries have opened their ranks to practicing homosexuals. Among them are the Reform Jewish rabbinate, the priesthood and perhaps the episcopate of the Episcopal Church, and the ministry of the Unitarian Universalist Association and subsequently of the United Church of Christ. Early in 1991 the Presbyterian Church in the U.S.A., which has its roots in the Calvinist tradition, produced a study of human sexuality that explicitly approved of sexual relations of most kinds, though it had little to say for marriage. Early that summer, the church's General Assembly roundly rejected the study, but it or something like it will certainly soon be put forward again. Among the groups that generally claim the name Christian—for the Unitarian Universalists no longer do— it is the United Church of Christ that has gone farthest, for it has resolved that even practicing bisexuals should be admitted to the ranks of its nominally Christian clergy. Inasmuch as no one can be bisexual without having at least two different sex partners, what this means is that, for all practical purposes, the U.C.C. has abandoned the idea of marriage as a monogamous covenant. It either no longer considers sexual behavior a matter of moral concern, or else no longer considers personal morality something to be desired in and expected of its clergy.

QUO VADIS, AMERICA?

The recent end of the Cold War seems to remove, for a moment, the danger that our nation and our world will be engulfed in a nuclear disaster of apocalyptic proportions. However, the continuing increase of what Sorokin called "sensate liberty," which we might express with the slogan, "Anything goes!" is almost certain to result in internal disintegration. Tertullian called the Christian minority in pagan Rome the "soul" of society. Indeed, it did prove to be so for several centuries. The sensate liberty that ran wild in Rome had to end, but thanks to the rise of Christianity, it resulted in a new beginning, which we used to call fondly "Christian civilization."

The "freedom of a Christian man," which Martin Luther extolled, in terms of responsibility to God rather than to ecclesiastical and civil preceptors, has now degenerated, with the widespread loss of faith in God, into chaotic sensate freedom, which unfortunately is all too often abetted by those who pose as religious leaders. Can we recover values and experience a "resurrection" in society? There are no better words with which to end this essay than Hans Millendorfer's: "As long as there are real Christians, this world will always renew itself. As long as the salt of the earth does not lose its savor, this world will not be lost."

Chapter 3

WITNESS-BEARING

Richard D. Land

Richard D. Land is executive director of the Christian Life Commission, which is the moral and social concerns, public policy, and religious liberty agency of the Southern Baptist Convention, which is the nation's largest Protestant denomination. Previously he served as vice-president for academic affairs at Criswell College in Dallas for fourteen years. During a leave of absence from the college, he served as administrative assistant to the Governor of Texas in 1987–88. He is a graduate of Princeton University and New Orleans Baptist Theological Seminary, and he received his Ph.D. from Oxford University in England.

Henry J. Hyde

Congressman Henry J. Hyde has represented the Sixth District of Illinois since 1974. He is a member of the House Judiciary and Foreign Affairs committees, and he is author of the Hyde Amendment, which has prevented the use of federal funds to pay for abortions since 1976.

The Right and Duty to Speak Out

Richard D. Land

Christians are citizens of two kingdoms—the earthly and the spiritual—and they have *rights* and *responsibilities* in both realms.

THE RESPONSIBILITY

As citizens of heaven (Phil. 3:20),[1] Christians are commanded to be obedient to the Lord God (Ex. 20:1–5). Jesus' instruction to "render therefore unto Caesar the things which be Caesar's, and unto God the things which be God's" (Luke 20:25 KJV) means giving ultimate allegiance only to God. It does mean paying your taxes. It also means much, much more.

The apostle Paul instructed Christians of their responsibility to be good citizens of the state "for conscience' sake" because God has ordained government to punish and restrict evildoers and to reward and protect moral behavior (Rom. 13:1–7 KJV). Christians are to support the civil government unless the authorities require believers to support or to do evil in direct contradiction to their ultimate allegiance to their heavenly Father.

Christians are also commanded by Jesus to be the "salt" of the earth and the "light" of the world (Matt. 5:13–16 KJV). Obedience to this commandment necessarily involves Christians in active engagement with the world, preserving as "salt" and illuminating as "light." Thus, the citizenship responsibilities of Christians include not just obedience to and support of the civil government but also active involvement and interaction in society.

THE RIGHT

When Christians bring their religious and moral convictions into the public marketplace of ideas and involve themselves in the public and political arenas, they are not only practicing obedience to Jesus' command to be "salt" and "light," but they are also standing solidly on the ground of the best of both the Christian and American traditions.

Far too often in recent decades Christians have allowed themselves to be driven from the arena of public debate by false understandings and misleading applications of church-state separation and religious liberty.

President John F. Kennedy once said, "The great enemy of truth is very often not the lie, deliberate, contrived, and dishonest, but the myth, persistent, persuasive and unrealistic." One persistent, persuasive, and unrealistic myth deceiving America is the belief, under the rubric of a false understanding of church-state separation, that you cannot, or at least should not, legislate morality.

Nothing could be more false. As a practical matter, all governments legislate morality. If there were no laws against theft, property losses would soar. If we had no laws against rape, its incidence would explode. If we did not have laws against murder, the morgues would overflow. Government *must* legislate morality in order to fulfill its God-ordained purpose in society (Rom. 13:1–7). God requires that Christians hold government responsible to fulfill its purpose of punishing evil and protecting its citizens. And in so doing, they are not so much imposing their morality on the thief, the rapist, and the murderer as they are preventing them from imposing their immorality on their victims.

SEPARATION OF CHURCH AND STATE

A total separation of church and state—of morality and politics—will debilitate moral values and public virtue as much as a state-dominated religion or a religion-dominated state will thwart personal and religious freedom. Our forbears intended—and the Constitution of the United States provided—a balance between morality and public virtue and a separation of the institutions of church and state. This delicate constitutional balance, solidified and anchored by the First Amendment, is endangered at present, and it will not cease to be imperiled unless people of faith act with dispatch and insist upon their First Amendment rights to "the free exercise" of their religion.

The mistaken idea that separation of church and state means that Christians and other people of faith are banned from the arena of public debate and that religious ethical values and moral convictions cannot be discussed in forming public policy is a terribly distorted, false understanding of our forbears' intent. It is also a revisionist understanding of only relatively recent vintage. Indeed, much of America's history is unintelligible apart from the participation of people of faith in the epochal events and great social movements that have shaped the nation. The words and deeds of our political and spiritual ancestors amply demonstrate this truth.

THE DECLARATION OF INDEPENDENCE

The great *sine qua non* of the American nation, the Declaration of Independence, explains that

> When in the course of human events, it becomes necessary for one people to dissolve the political bands, which have connected them to another, and to assume among the powers of the earth, the separate and equal station to which the Laws of Nature and of Nature's God entitle them, a decent respect to the opinions of mankind requires that they should declare the causes which impel them to the separation.

In declaring their independence from Great Britain, our forbears asserted their firm belief in such moral and political convictions as that all human beings are "endowed by their Creator with certain unalienable rights" such as "life, liberty and the pursuit of happiness." They declared their appeal for independence "to the Supreme Judge of the World for the rectitude of our intentions" with "a firm reliance on the protection of divine providence."

One Declaration signatory, Samuel Adams, said, "We have this day restored the Sovereign to Whom all men ought to be obedient, and from the rising to the setting of the sun, let His kingdom come." Another signatory, John Adams, destined to become the new nation's second president, wrote to his wife when the final draft of the Declaration was finished, and predicted

> the fourth day of July will become the most memorable epic in the history of America. I believe that it will be celebrated by

succeeding generations as the great anniversary festival. It ought to be commemorated as the day of deliverance by solemn acts of devotion to God.

When they issued the Declaration of Independence, they never intended to declare their independence from God, only from Great Britain.

THE ROLE OF RELIGION AND MORAL VALUES — THE EIGHTEENTH CENTURY

Indeed, the Declaration's main author, Thomas Jefferson, a deist, and certainly no believer, at least in any orthodox way, never intended to divorce religious convictions, Christian or otherwise, from public policy issues.

In 1781 Jefferson, commenting on the paradox of Americans fighting for their independence while maintaining the institution of slavery, which he found so morally repugnant, said

> And can the liberties of a nation be thought secure when we have removed their only firm basis, a conviction in the minds of the people that their liberties are of the gift of God—that they are not to be violated but with His wrath? Indeed, I tremble for my country when I reflect that God is just; that his justice cannot sleep forever. . . .[2]

These words echo the Declaration of Independence's acceptance of and belief in divinely endowed, unalienable rights that human beings possess as an essential part of their having been created as human beings. "Unalienable" rights are rights that cannot be taken away, given away, surrendered, or seized. They can only be acknowledged, accepted, and assured by government.

In his "Farewell Address," George Washington, our nation's first president, declared:

> Of all the suppositions and habits which lead to political prosperity, religion and morality are indispensable supports. In vain would that man claim the tribute of Patriotism, who should labour to subvert these great Pillars of human happiness, these firmest props of the duties of Men and citizens. The mere Politician, equally with the pious man ought to respect and cherish them. A volume could not trace all their connections with private and public felicity. Let it simply be asked where is the security for

property, for reputation, for life, if the sense of religious obligation desert the oaths, which are the instruments of investigation in Courts of Justice? And let us with caution indulge the supposition, that morality can be maintained without religion. Whatever may be conceded to the influence of refined education on minds of peculiar structure, reason and experience both forbid us to expect that National morality can prevail in exclusion of religious principle.[3]

Further on in the same address Washington asks rhetorically, "Can it be, that Providence has not connected the permanent felicity of a Nation with its virtue?"[4]

The nation's second president, John Adams, stated during his term of office that "we have no government armed in power capable of contending in human passions unbridled by morality and religion. Our constitution was made only for a moral and religious people. It is wholly inadequate for the government of any other."[5] Reflecting back on the American Revolution in 1818, Adams wrote: "The Revolution was effected before the war commenced. The Revolution was in the minds and hearts of the people; a change in their religious sentiments of their duties and obligations."[6]

WHAT ABOUT THE FIRST AMENDMENT?

It should be noted that these statements by Washington and Adams, the nation's first two presidents, were made *after* the First Amendment to the Constitution, which guaranteed religious freedom, was ratified in 1791. Obviously, they did not see the First Amendment as qualifying or mitigating religion's role in society. Baptists, long-time champions of religious freedom, figured prominently in the First Amendment's successful ratification. The Baptists of Virginia, having suffered persecution at the hands of state and local authorities, were led by their famous evangelist, John Leland, in opposing the Constitution's ratification. However, after conferring with Virginia's Baptists, James Madison "agreed to introduce amendments to the Constitution to safeguard religious liberty."[7]

With the resulting Baptist support, Virginia ratified the Constitution and Madison was elected to the U.S. House of Representatives.[8] This enabled him to bring forward the amendments that resulted in the Bill of Rights, the first of which begins with "Congress shall make no law respecting an establishment of religion, or prohibiting the free exercise thereof."

WHAT ABOUT THOMAS JEFFERSON?

Thomas Jefferson, the nation's third president, was in Europe at the time of the First Amendment's proposal and adoption. He did express his opinion about it, however, in a letter to the Baptist ministers of Danbury, Connecticut, who had castigated him severely during his campaign for the presidency in 1800. Jefferson wrote:

> Believing that religion is a matter which lies solely between man and his God, and that he owes account to none other for his faith or his worship, that the legislative powers of government reach actions only, and not opinions, I contemplate with sovereign reverence that act of the whole American people which declared that their legislature should "make no law respecting an establishment of religion, or prohibiting the free exercise thereof," thus building a wall of separation between church and state.[9]

This is the origin of the now famous phrase "a wall of separation between church and state," which has been used by modern day Supreme Court justices, notably Felix Frankfurter and Hugo Black, to determine that even accommodation of religion in general violates the Constitution. Jefferson, a man far more liberal in his religious views than most of his contemporaries, no doubt envisioned his "wall" as protecting the government from religion rather than mandating a wholly secular society in which government must rigorously exclude religious observance from the public life of the nation. Jefferson's own record was mixed, as he allowed the University of Virginia to have a chapel and to teach religion and he supported frontier schools teaching moral values.[10] For the modern-day Supreme Court to elevate a figure of speech from a letter by a President who had nothing to do with either the framing or the adoption of the First Amendment to the status of *the* interpretive standard for establishment clause doctrine says more about the philosophies and views of twentieth century Supreme Court justices than those of the First Amendment's original eighteenth-century framers.

WHAT ABOUT ROGER WILLIAMS?

Roger Williams, long a popular folk-hero of church-state separation, certainly appears to have never intended church-state separation to mean that people of faith should not bring their faith convictions into the public arena of decision making. In fact, when Williams was banished from the Massachusetts Bay Colony in 1635 the charges against him were enumerated by Governor Winthrop:

> Mr. Williams held these four particulars:
>
> First, that we have not our land by patent from the King, but that the natives are the true owners of it, and that we ought to repent of such a receiving it by patent.
>
> Secondly, that it is not lawful to call a wicked person to swear, to pray, as being actions of God's worship.
>
> Thirdly, that it is not lawful to hear any of the ministers of the (Anglican) parish assemblies in England.
>
> Fourthly, that the civil magistrate's power extends only to the bodies and goods and outward state of men, etc.[11]

Roger Williams, justifiably viewed as a champion of church-state separation, was deeply embroiled in the moral and intensely political question of the colonists' treatment of the Indians; and it was listed first in the bill of particulars against him. Williams, soon to found Providence Plantations (Rhode Island) as a state with no establishment of religion and total religious freedom, saw no contradiction in bringing his religious convictions into the highly volatile political question of land ownership and the colonists' right to receive title to it from the king rather than from its original native American owners.

Williams also believed that while government must never coerce religious belief, general religious sentiments such as belief in God, in eternity, and in divine judgment were essential for what he termed "government and order in families, towns, etc."[12] Given the vital role of religion in the fabric of American society from the early colonial period onward, it should not be surprising that Daniel Webster would conclude in 1820 that

> Our ancestors established their system of government on morality and religious sentiment. Moral habits, they believed, cannot safely be trusted on any other foundation than religious principle, nor any government be secure which is not supported by moral habits.[13]

THE NINETEENTH CENTURY—DE TOCQUEVILLE

In the 1830s an outside observer came to America to investigate American society. This investigator, the Frenchman Alexis de Tocqueville, was fascinated by this new country, America, and this new person, "the American." He wanted to understand what made the country and her citizens so different from their counterparts in the Old World of Europe. The result was his classic *Democracy in America*, which is filled with always interesting, often insightful, and sometimes prescient observations about America.

De Tocqueville made numerous important observations about the role of religion in American life. He related:

> On my arrival in the United States the religious aspect of the country was the first thing that struck my attention; and the longer I stayed there, the more I perceived the great political conse uences resulting from this new state of things. In France I had almost always seen the spirit of religion and the spirit of freedom marching in opposite directions. But in America I found they were intimately united and that they reigned in common over the same country.[14]

Acknowledging the Puritan origins of and influence on America's religious views, de Tocqueville noted that

> The greatest part of British America was peopled by men who . . . brought with them into the New World a form of Christianity which I cannot better describe than by styling it a democratic and republican religion. This contributed powerfully to the establishment of a republic and a democracy in public affairs, and from the beginning, politics and religion contracted an alliance which has never been dissolved.[15]

De Tocqueville concluded that "religion is therefore mingled with all the habits of the nation."[16]

He observed that Americans "show by their practice that they feel the high necessity of imparting morality to democratic communities by means of religion."[17] De Tocqueville concluded that

> in the United States the sovereign authority is religious . . . there is no country in the world where the Christian religion retains a greater influence over the souls of men than in America; and there can be no greater proof of its utility and of its conformity to human

nature than that its influence is powerfully felt over the most enlightened and free nation of the earth.[18]

To say that the institutional separation of church and state mandated by, and the religious freedom guaranteed by, the First Amendment were intended to restrict the political participation of people of faith or to disqualify their religious convictions and beliefs from consideration in the public arena of ideas is to twist and to distort the First Amendment's intent, and America's subsequent historical experience, beyond all recognition.

Religious conviction has profoundly influenced American thought in both its colonial period and its nationhood. As has been demonstrated, the American Revolution would have taken a markedly different course if it were not for people of religious conviction. There would have been no abolitionist and anti-slavery movement without the conviction, the leadership, and the support of people of faith. In the present century, there would have been no child labor reform movement without the impetus of religious conviction. There would have been no civil rights movement without the leadership and moral imperative provided by people of religious conviction, black and white. These spiritual ancestors believed their faith convictions were moral imperatives that left them no choice but to be involved.

RELIGION'S ROLE IN SOCIETY—THE TWENTIETH CENTURY

The deeply religious traditions of America's culture have continued in the present century, but they have encountered the most serious secular challenges ever. In spite of the increasingly militant secularist forces in American life, the American people have remained "determinedly, some would say incorrigibly, religious."[19]

America has become more ethnically pluralistic as a result of successive waves of immigration since the mid-nineteenth century. Consequently, the nation's religious beliefs have broadened from the interdenominational, Protestant evangelical consensus of the antebellum period to a kaleidoscope of beliefs. Roman Catholics now make up the largest group. These developments have not lessened, but only diversified, religious conviction.

Religious permeation in American society has remained broad and deep. Indeed, as late as this century's midpoint, two Americans of strikingly dissimilar political persuasion, President Dwight D.

Eisenhower and Supreme Court Justice William O. Douglas, both bore testimony in their own way to the importance and strength of religion in American life. President Eisenhower, echoing his predecessors, said, "Our government makes no sense unless it is founded in a deeply felt religious faith—and I don't care what it is."[20] Eisenhower remarks reflected his belief in the importance of faith and its diversity in our society.

In 1952 Justice Douglas, in the *Zorach v. Clauson* decision, wrote, "We are a religious people whose institutions presuppose a Supreme Being."[21] He concluded that the state

> respects the religious nature of our people and accommodates the public service to their spiritual needs. To hold that it may not would be to find in the Constitution a requirement that the government show a callous indifference to religious groups. That would be preferring those who believe in no religion over those who do believe.[22]

CONFLICTS AND REACTION

However, the judicial and cultural tides were shifting. By 1963 when the *Abingdon School District v. Schempp* decision struck down officially sponsored Bible reading and recitation of the Lord's Prayer (a decision many Baptists agreed with since it involved the sponsoring of religion rather than its accommodation) Justice Arthur Goldberg worried that

> untutored devotion to the concept of neutrality can lead to results which partake not simply of that noninterference and noninvolvement with the religious which the Constitution commands, but of a brooding and pervasive devotion to the secular and a passive, or even active, hostility to the religious. Such results are not only not compelled by the Constitution, but it seems to me, are prohibited by it.[23]

Perhaps Justice Goldberg had a premonition of things to come. He certainly was a prophet. The "hostility to the religious" on the part of the judiciary in relation to public schools and other public arenas soon reached a fever pitch. The past quarter of a century has produced an aggressive, secularizing neutrality which has been hostile to, and has discriminated against, the religious free-exercise rights of people of faith in the public schools and other sectors of public life.

Increasingly, significant segments of the society, such as the media, have had a difficult time comprehending the motives of those whose convictions come from their faith and understanding how inextricably these beliefs are woven into American life. Richard John Neuhaus in his book *The Naked Public Square* related a classic example of this secular blindness. Quite soon after Martin Luther King's assassination in April, 1968, an ecumenical memorial service was held in Harlem. Neuhaus told of how television covered the event:

> The announcer . . . spoke in solemn tones: "And so today there was a memorial service for the slain civil rights leader, Dr. Martin Luther King, Jr. It was a religious service, and it is fitting that it should be, for, after all, Dr. King was the son of a minister."
>
> How explain this astonishing blindness to the religious motive and meaning of Dr. King's ministry? The announcer was speaking out of a habit of mind that was no doubt quite unconscious. The habit of mind is that religion must be kept at one remove from the public square, that matters of *public* significance must be sanitized of all religious particularity. It regularly occurred that the klieg lights for the television cameras would be turned off during Dr. King's speeches when he dwelt on the religious and moral-philosophical basis of the movement for racial justice. They would be turned on again when the subject touched upon confrontational politics. In a luncheon conversation Dr. King once remarked, "They aren't interested in the *why* of what we're doing, only in the *what* of what we're doing, and because they don't understand the why, they cannot really understand the what."[24]

Newscasters and social analysts like these are not part of a conscious conspiracy against the religious, "but victims of a secularizing mythology of which they are hardly aware."[25]

Increasingly, people of "faith conviction" launched counterattacks through such activities as support for "Equal Access" legislation for public schools and universities, which would guarantee equal access to the public school facilities for voluntary, student-initiated religious clubs that similar nonreligious clubs enjoyed. Equal Access was passed by Congress in 1984 and was declared constitutional by the U.S. Supreme Court in 1990.

However, the public schools are just one significant arena in a pervasive cultural war being waged between the secularizers of our public precincts and the defenders of the free exercise of religion.

What it is that Protestants such as evangelical Baptists want and what they do not want should be distinguished. Most of them *do not* want state government sponsorship of religion. They perceive such activities as a violation of the First Amendment's establishment clause. Most of them *do* want *accommodation* of the free exercise of religion rights of people of "faith conviction" in the public square. This distinction between the establishment and the free exercise clauses of the First Amendment is a helpful one to make and is not used often enough in discussions on this topic.

With increasing vigor, evangelical Baptists and others are rejecting the strictly secular understanding of church-state separation. They are demanding the right to bring their religious convictions to bear on the public policy issues of the day, and they are demanding a recognition of the crucial, pivotal role religion has played in the life and history of America. They understand that if God's name used in a profanity is protected speech, even if offensive to believers, then God's name invoked in a prayer is protected speech, even if offensive to nonbelievers. They understand their right to be involved in the public and legislative arena, and they understand their obligation and responsibility to be involved citizens in their community, their state, and their nation.

They do not want to coerce others' religious convictions. They do want the government to keep perpetrators from coercing their victims. They understand that you cannot legislate attitudes but that you must legislate behaviors. They will not allow their values and convictions to be dismissed simply because they are based on religious convictions. They increasingly see attempts to do so as the bigoted censorious behavior that it is.

People of faith are called upon not just to enjoy but to exercise, not just to preach but to practice their liberties. Surely there could be no better thing for America than citizens of "faith conviction" to awaken to the exercise of their rights and to the fulfillment of their responsibilities.

Religion and Politics

Henry J. Hyde

"Religion and politics" is a hardy perennial in the garden of American controversy. From the days of the Puritans, Roger Williams, and the Maryland colonial experiment in religious toleration, on through to the Constitutional Convention of 1787; during the great debate over slavery and the Civil War; during the nation's westward expansion, the efforts to assimilate millions of immigrants, and the industrial revolution; in the aftermath of World War I and during the 1928 presidential campaign; in the Kennedy-Nixon campaign of 1960 and the civil rights movement; during the war in Vietnam and the presidential campaigns of Jimmy Carter and Ronald Reagan—at these defining moments of our national history and at virtually all the way-stations in between—Americans have vigorously debated how religious convictions relate to the working of government. In that sense, then, there is nothing new about the "religion and politics" controversies of the late 1980s and early 1990s. The fact that Americans continue to argue these questions—and continue to settle them through legal and political means, rather than through violence and bloodshed—is testimony to both the vigor of our democratic culture and the effectiveness of our democratic institutions.

But a new element has entered that perennial debate in recent years. It is the claim—defended by much of American academie, absorbed by much of the prestige press, and publicly asserted in the legal system by organizations such as the American Civil Liberties Union and Planned Parenthood—that democracy itself rests on the conviction that there are no ultimate convictions: no objective moral order, or, as the more nuanced would put it, none about which we can know and on which we can form a public consensus to guide public policy. Democracy is an exercise in the maintenance of "the process." And for so long as religious people play by these rules, and by this conception of "democracy," they can be tolerated, much like the vegetarians, the flat-earthers, and the transvestites.

But skeptical relativists reach the boundaries of their toleration when those Americans who take their understandings of public morality from religiously-derived moral norms attempt to make these norms a matter of public debate about the ordering of our public life. This is, according to the relativists, a basic violation of the rules of the game. This is substituting substance for process. Some even take this further and suggest that there can be no "democracy" if people insist that democratic governance is bound by the norms of a moral order that transcends it. Assert publicly, and as a matter bearing on public policy, the objectivity and knowability of moral norms, the relativists say, and it is but a short step to the thumbscrew, the bastinado, and the stake. In Richard Neuhaus's now-famous image, the only safe democratic arena is the naked public square.

THE CULTURE WAR

Thus what appears on the surface to be a continuation of the ongoing American deliberation about "religion and politics" turns out, on closer examination, to be instead a dimension of what Neuhaus, George Weigel, James Davison Hunter, and others have called the new American *Kulturkampf:* the "culture war" that lurks just beneath the surface of our public life, and that occasionally erupts into public view when particularly divisive issues (of race, education, abortion, or the relationships between men and women) are engaged. The "culture war" is important in its own right; its resolution will have much to do with how, or whether, Americans transmit their values to the next generation. But the "culture war" is also crucial for the future of American democracy.

The claim that democracy is, at bottom, merely a matter of procedures—the claim that democracy has no substantive moral or ethical foundation—is, to my knowledge, a *novum,* a new thing, in our generation. The Greeks didn't believe this. Neither did the scions of the Roman Republic, or the leaders of the Glorious Revolution of 1688 in England. More to the point for our purposes, neither did our Founders and Framers. Perhaps one could make the case that there was one effort to build a modern democracy on something other than morally substantive grounds, but the experience of the Weimar Republic in Germany and the terrible scourge of Nazism that followed its implosion ought to be as profound an historical caution as we can find against the claim that democracy is just a matter of procedures. Weimar teaches us that, absent a substantive basis for democratic procedures, the devil will surely be roaring about the public square, seeking whom it may devour. And succeeding.

As we enter the third century of American public life under the Constitution of 1787, there is no dearth of serious issues on the public agenda. Our schools are in crisis. Race relations are worse than they were thirty years ago, thanks in large part to the continuing efforts of some to Balkanize American society. We are seeing examples of something without parallel in our national experience: the emergence of what seems to be a relatively permanent underclass, locked into a cycle of poverty. The drug crisis feeds the growth of violent crime, particularly in our cities. There is too much litigation, and the litigious temptation feeds the crisis of rising costs in health care. The infrastructure of our national transportation system needs massive overhaul. Four thousand innocents are killed every day by abortion.

Yet there will be no satisfactory resolution of many of these issues until we get the main issues in the *Kulturkampf* settled far more satisfactorily: that is, a broad-based agreement in America that democracy is not a matter of procedures alone; that a republic requires a virtuous citizenry; that there are moral norms that transcend the American democratic experiment and that stand in judgment on us; and that we can know these norms with some surety and bring them into the public discourse as we conduct our public business.

And that will require getting the religion-and-politics debate onto firmer ground. Others in this volume will have much to say about that project, in its many dimensions, but, as a public official, I clearly see the danger of the skeptical relativist position and its claim that the relationship between "democracy" and "truth" is a kind of zero-sum game in which widespread and publicly actionable agreement on "truth" necessarily entails a diminishment of "democracy."

RECLAIMING OUR HISTORY

The relativists claim that theirs is the position most congruent with the intentions of the Founders of the American republic and the Framers of its Constitution. The relativists suddenly transforming themselves into apostles of "original intention" is, of course, ironical, but the problem here is not merely hypocrisy. For the relativists' claim is nothing less than an attempt to rewrite American history in order to advance a partisan agenda in present controversies.

It is an historical absurdity to suggest that the Founders and Framers were skeptical relativists whose vision of the American democratic experiment required the creation of a naked public square. The fact of the matter is that they were far more subtle thinkers than many of today's contemporary relativists and held two convictions simultaneously. First, based on their study of ancient republics, they were convinced that democracy was a substantive experiment in self-governance and that a republic could not long survive without a virtuous citizenry. Second, based on their understanding of American pluralism (as Madison, for example, experienced in his own election campaigns in Orange County, Virginia), they were convinced that a state-sponsored religious establishment would impede the development of a successful democratic republic.

William Lee Miller of the University of Virginia reminds us of the first of these convictions in his reflections on the Founders and Framers. These great men, according to Miller, wanted an American republic "whose hallmarks were . . . public virtue, public liberty, [the] public happiness of republicanism, the humane sociability of the Scottish Enlightenment." For them, in other words, "the concept of public virtue stood at or near the center of republicanism."[1] No naked public square here. The free exercise of religious and moral conviction was essential to the life of the republic, as our Founders and Framers saw things.

As for the question of the relationship between the government and religious institutions, the Founders and Framers were not historians and politicians for nothing. As students of history (whose comprehension of the ancient world, for example, was far superior to what we find in graduates of our most prestigious liberal arts colleges today), they knew all about the problems the Roman Empire experienced when civic virtue broke down, particularly among its ruling elites. As Protestants (primarily) and from a dissenter heritage, the Founders and Framers had sharp memories of the European wars of religion and even clearer views of the dangers of absolutist altar-and-throne arrangements. As politicians, they had to deal as a matter of course with the religious plurality of the American people. For example, Madison, an Episcopalian, to insure his election to the Virginia legislature, had to assure the good Baptists of Orange County that he would take a firm stand against any preferential treatment being given to the Episcopal Church.

And thus the Founders and Framers came up with their distinctive answer to the age-old problem of religion and politics: free exercise of religion, with a constitutional proscription on governmental favors being bestowed on any one church. We usually speak, in our ordinary discussions of the First Amendment (in which the Framers' answer was embodied), of "the religion clauses" of the Constitution, meaning "free exercise" and "no establishment." But the deeper truth of the matter is that there is but *one* "religion clause," in which "no establishment" serves the purpose of "free exercise." I sometimes wonder if this debate wouldn't have been clearer if the First Amendment had just one more word in it so that it read, "Congress shall make no law concerning an establishment of religion, or *otherwise* prohibiting the free exercise thereof." The point is moot, of course, but the addition of that one adverb *otherwise* clarifies what the best historical scholarship now acknowledges: that the purpose of disestablishment was to enhance the free exercise of religion, which the Founders and Framers believed was essential to their republican project. What else would disestablishment be *for*? What other purpose could it possibly serve? Disestablishment in the service of free exercise was *not*, in other words, an accommodation to the adherents of a medieval mythology. It was, in the Founders' and Framers' view, an essential component of the creation of that virtuous citizenry on whose shoulders the future of the democratic experiment lay. Thus those who contend for the naked public square cannot claim to be "on the side of history."

THE REAL DEMOCRATS

In addition to its implausibility as history, there is also something unpleasantly undemocratic about the naked public square proposal, for it ignores one of the most distinctive facts about the

American people: namely, that we are an incorrigibly religious people (in Neuhaus's wonderful phrase) among whom religiously grounded warrants are essential to our commitment to democracy.

The demographic data on American religiosity should be beyond reasonable dispute. Whether the survey team in question is Gallup, Roper, or Yankelovich, the results are the same: the American people are overwhelmingly theistic. Moreover, the American people, in a manner far beyond any comparable advanced industrial society, practice their religion: they pray; they attend religious services; they belong to church organizations; they give money to religious institutions. No doubt American religion could be even deeper; but, however one parses the data, modernization has not inevitably led to secularization and a radical decline in religious belief and practice in the United States.

The persistent religious nature of Americans may explain why democracy continues to work in the United States. Democracy is, after all, an historically abnormal way to organize a society. Why is it that the American people are, in the main, tolerant of others' religious convictions, others' deepest convictions? Why is pluralism perceived as a virtue in America? Why do Americans believe that discrimination is wrong? Why do people believe that elections and courts, rather than guns and mobs, are the right way to settle arguments over public policy? Why is the ballot box, not the cartridge box, the American way of doing public business? Why do Americans accept, with usually graceful chagrin, the defeat of their preferred candidates for public office? Why do the winners feel an obligation to create space in the public square for those who have lost? What sustains our politics of consent when so much of human history has been dominated by the politics of coercion?

Although the religious commitment of the American people may not explain everything, survey research suggests that, for the overwhelming majority of Americans, commitment to the values and attitudes that sustain our democratic politics is an expression of *religious* conviction. We are tolerant of others' deepest convictions, even others' deepest religious convictions, because we believe it is the will of God that we not kill each other over what constitutes the will of God. We accept the give-and-take of democratic politics—including the occasional loss of power for our side—because we think this is a sensible way to do things, but even more fundamentally because we believe this is the *right* way to do things, the way God intended human beings to treat each other. We believe in the rule of law because we believe that God has ordained the rule of law as the way in which human societies are to be organized.

To be sure, there is pragmatism in the continuing American commitment to democracy, just as there is a measure of routine in our democratic politics. But if we ask ourselves how this country called the United States of America, ethnically, religiously, and racially plural and big, rich, continental, raucous, and cantankerous ever holds itself together and, more than that, prospers, then I think we have to reach for a deeper answer than pragmatism or routine. America works because the overwhelming majority of the American people believe that the values and attitudes that make America work are divinely ordained.

To argue for the naked public square, therefore, is to disenfranchise the overwhelming majority of the American people, to declare them *personae non gratae* in their own country, to declare them public dangers.

To argue for the naked public square is to declare oneself undemocratic.

THE LANGUAGE OF THE DEBATE

The Founders and Framers expected that religiously derived moral norms would be a part of the American public conversation, and they welcomed that prospect as a crucial means toward the sustaining of a virtuous citizenry. The great majority of our fellow citizens, even today, in this last decade of the supposed century of secularization, are religiously motivated in their understanding of, and commitment to, the values and attitudes that make democracy possible. These may come as startling (or startlingly obtuse) propositions at the Harvard Law School or in the editorial chambers of the *New York Times*, but they seem to me rather close to what Mr. Jefferson would have called "self-evident truths."

But the assertion of those truths, and the confidence that my understanding of them *as* truths is shared by tens of millions of Americans, doesn't solve the problem. For there are many forms and styles of religious conviction in America. And there is the secularist minority, which has a legitimate place in the debate over the right-ordering of this society. How can we argue amidst the plurality of convictions in American public life? What is the language in which Catholics, evangelical Protestants, liberal Protes-

97

tants, Orthodox and Conservative Jews, Reform Jews, Muslims, Buddhists, and secularists can communicate with each other about hotly contested issues of public policy?

I believe such a "grammar" for the public debate exists, and that it can be found in what has been called the "natural law" approach to moral reasoning.[2] That is another essay, but there are a few rules of the road by which religiously serious people can work in the public square.

The debate, if it is going to be fruitful, has to be a genuinely *public* debate. That means that everyone who wants to be a part of it—including skeptical relativists—ought to be a part of it. The problem today, of course, is getting space in the public square for those functionally disenfranchised because of religious conviction. But I assume I am talking here to believers. And the answer to our problem is not to repeat the errors of our adversaries.

A genuinely *public* debate requires that all of us—religious people and secularists—be able to make our case in ways that can be heard by those who don't share our denominational frame of reference. Catholics have to be able to make their case in ways that Protestants can hear and engage. Similarly for Protestants vis-à-vis Catholics, and for Christians and Jews in public conversation with each other. This doesn't mean that Catholics can't talk about church teaching, or Protestants about the letters of St. Paul, or Jews about the Torah and the Talmud. It does mean that Catholics ought to have the skill to "translate" their understanding of church teaching so that it appeals to the moral warrants that Protestants and Jews honor. It does mean that Protestants ought to be able to "translate" biblical injunctions into publicly accessible moral categories so that Scripture doesn't get reduced to the status of a divine trump card slyly slid into the Protestant rhetorical deck. It does mean that Jews have to relate the moral wisdom of the Torah and the Talmud to a controverted public question in categories and language that Christians can intelligently engage. And it means that religious people have to be able to make their arguments in ways that can be engaged by the secularist minority.

This kind of democratic "translation" process need not result in a kind of moral gruel, a least-common-denominator moralism, an ethical culture society writ large. There is no reason why a Catholic can't say, publicly, and to Protestants, Jews, and secularists, "Here is what my church teaches about the morality of abortion. That teaching, though, is not for Catholics only, because it is based, not on moral insights that are peculiar to Catholics, but on a moral analysis of the nature of the human person. Let me make the case to you on those grounds." So also for Protestants, Jews, and secularists vis-à-vis Catholics. Were that kind of conversation to happen in America, the public square would not simply be reclothed: it would be immeasurably enriched by the moral wisdom of the centuries.

The skeptical relativist attempt to mandate a naked public square is undemocratic. It is also a danger to democracy. As a man of faith and as a public official, I insist on participating in the conversation. I also accept the responsibility to make moral arguments in ways that can be heard by those who do not fully share my religious convictions. In doing so, I believe I am doing my duty as both a Christian and an American.

Chapter 4

HUMAN LIFE

William E. May

William E. May is the Michael J. McGivney professor of moral theology at the Pope John Paul II Institute for Studies on Marriage and the Family in Washington, D.C. He recently completed twenty years of teaching moral theology at the Catholic University of America. A native of St. Louis, he received his B.A. and M.A. from the Catholic University of America and his Ph.D. in philosophy from Marquette University. Prior to entering academic life, he was an editor. He is the author or co-author of more than a dozen books, the latest being *An Introduction to Moral Theology*. Pope John Paul II appointed him a member of the International Theological Commission in 1986, and a *peritus* to the 1987 Synod of Bishops. In 1991 he received the *Pro Ecclesia et Pontifice* medal.

Norman L. Geisler

Norman L. Geisler is a former professor of Trinity Evangelical Divinity School and Dallas Theological Seminary. For the past three years he has been dean of the Liberty Center for Research in Lynchburg, Virginia. He received his B.A. and M.A. from Wheaton College and his Ph.D. in philosophy from Loyola University in Chicago. He has written more than thirty books, most recently *Thomas Aquinas: An Evangelical Appraisal*. For forty years he has lectured extensively around the world on philosophy, ethics, and related topics.

The Sanctity
of Human Life

William E. May

In an unforgettable homily on the Capitol Mall in Washington, D.C., on October 7, 1979, Pope John Paul II eloquently proclaimed:

> ... all human life—from the moment of conception and through all subsequent stages—is sacred, because human life is created in the image and likeness of God. Nothing surpasses the greatness or dignity of a human person. Human life is not just an idea or an abstraction. Human life is the concrete reality of a being that lives, that acts, that grows and develops.... Human life is precious because it is the gift of a God whose love is infinite; and when God gives life, it is forever.[1]

Pope John Paul's affirmation of the sanctity of human life in this homily was by no means a surprise, for the Catholic Church has, from its very inception and throughout its entire history, proclaimed this sublime truth. After presenting the reasons why the Church teaches that human life is sacred, I intend to focus on the

- the *bodily* character of human life,
- the critical importance of this bodily character,
- the moral norm, proposed by the Church as absolute or exceptionless, that one ought never intentionally kill an innocent human person,
- and the sanctity of human life and the issue of contraception.

WHY THE CHURCH TEACHES
THAT HUMAN LIFE IS SACRED

The Church teaches that human life is sacred because it holds that God has himself revealed this truth, and God can neither deceive nor be deceived. This truth is at the heart of biblical revelation, for, as we are told in the first chapter of Genesis, "God said, 'Let us make man in our image, after our likeness. . . .' So God created man in his own image, in the image of God he created him: male and female he created them" (Gen. 1:26–27 RSV), and to his creature man God gave dominion over all the earth and every earthly living thing. Of all his material creatures, man and man alone is made in the image and likeness of God. Man, in short, "is the only creature on earth which God willed for himself."[2]

Every living human being, the living body that comes to be when new human life is conceived, is a living image of the all holy God and is therefore a being of incalculable dignity and sanctity. Every human being, of whatever age or sex or condition, is a being of moral worth, an irreplaceable and nonsubstitutable person. Because of this inherent dignity and sanctity, a human being, as Karol Wojtyla has said, "is the kind of good that does not admit of use and cannot be treated as an object of use and as such a means to an end." Because of this dignity and sanctity, a human being "is a good toward which the only adequate response is love."[3]

When we come into existence we *are* already, by reason of this inherent dignity, persons. We do not *become* persons after a period of development or achievement. As persons in God's image, we are endowed by God with the capacity to discover the truth and the capacity to determine our own lives by freely choosing to conform our lives and actions to the truth. A baby (born or preborn) does not, of course, have the *developed* capacity for deliberating and choosing freely, but it has the *natural* capacity to do so because it is human and personal in nature.[4]

This is the kind of being human persons are by virtue of their being made in the "image and likeness" of God. But there is an even deeper and more profound reason for their dignity and sanctity. God made human beings to be the *kind* of beings they are (their nature) precisely because he wanted there to be a creature to whom he could communicate his very own divine life through grace. Such a creature had to be, therefore, inwardly open (open by nature) to receive this sublime gift, and to be inwardly receptive of divine life, such a being had to be gifted with the capacity to know the truth and to make free choices, for God can *give* himself only to a being capable of freely *receiving* him. Just as a man can not give himself to a woman in marriage unless she is free to receive him, and, in freely receiving him, to give herself to him, so God can not give himself to a being incapable of receiving him. He can give himself only to a creature, a human being, whom he has made inwardly capable of receiving him.

God cannot become incarnate in a pig or cow or ape because these creatures of his are not capable of reflecting the divine image. But, as we know from divine revelation, God can become incarnate in his human creature, and in fact he has freely chosen to become truly one of us, for his eternal and uncreated Word, true God of true God, became and is a human being, a man. Thus every human being can rightly be called a "created word" of God, the created word that his uncreated Word became to show us precisely how deeply we are loved by the God who formed us in our mother's wombs (cf. Ps. 139:11–19). Nature, in short, is for grace; creation is for covenant. Human persons enjoy a dignity not enjoyed by other material creatures because they are the *kind* of beings they are: persons made in God's image and likeness. In addition, they are sacred, for they are the kind of beings they are precisely because they are the beings to whom God wills to give a share of his own divine life. He wills to share with them his divinity just as they shared with his only begotten Son their humanity. They are called to be his children, to be members of the divine family. This is the ultimate reason why human life, the life of the human person, is sacred.

THE BODILY CHARACTER OF HUMAN LIFE

When God created humans, he did not create a disembodied spirit to whom he then added a body as an afterthought. Rather, in creating humans, he made them living flesh (cf. Gen. 2:7). In fact, in creating humans, "male and female he created them" (Gen. 1:27 RSV), i.e., he created a sexually reproducing species. Bodiliness, therefore, is integral to the human person, so much so that when God's eternal and uncreated Word became "man," he became "flesh" (*sarx egeneto*) (John 1:14).

The Catholic understanding of human life, therefore, is opposed to the radical dualism so characteristic of Platonic and much modern and contemporary thought. In the Nicene-Constantinople

Creed, affirmed every Sunday in the Mass, the Church professes its belief in the "resurrection of the dead," the resurrection of the body. While not denying—indeed affirming—the immortality of the soul,[5] the Catholic faith insists on the truth that human persons are composed of body and soul and that the body is integral to the human person.[6]

The human person is a unity of soul and body. The human soul, which is the person's intellectual principle, is united to the body; the soul is *not* an agent of which the body is an instrument. To the contrary, the soul is an intrinsic principle of the human person and makes the person *to be* the *body* he or she is. Nor is there any other component that makes the body be body than the soul by which the person has the capacities of knowing the truth (intellect) and choosing freely. Each person has his or her own soul. But since soul and body are not distinct beings, no link is needed to unite them. The human soul, integral to the form called body, makes it *to be* a person, and the entire soul is present in every part of the body.[7]

But, inasmuch as the *person* is the unity of soul and body, the separated soul as such is *not* the person.[8] For the person is the living body. This truth of faith has very important implications. We are not selves having and using bodies. *We are bodies*. As one of the leading Catholic theologians of our day has put the matter, "the human person is a certain, special kind of body. Moreover, in the light of the teaching of faith that the human person becomes by adoption a member of the divine family (cf. Rom. 8:14–17) and a participant in divinity (cf. 2 Pet. 1:4), we also can conclude that the organic life and the biological processes of the human body belong to divine life. . . . And, as the dogma of the Assumption makes clear, the person as body is destined for heavenly glory."[9]

We can, in truth, say that a *living human body is a person*. Thus, at conception, we have in our midst a living human person, a being of unsurpassed dignity and sanctity. And we have such a person in our midst so long as we have a living human body, no matter how debilitated, weak, and suffering it might be. The life of that person, "even if weak and suffering, is always a splendid gift of God's goodness."[10]

Today many, infected with the dualism that has permeated Western thought since Descartes, separate the person from his body. The person is the "conscious subject," aware of itself as a self and capable of relating to other selves, and the body is the instrument of the person. But if the person really is not his body, then the body is subpersonal and subhuman, and the destruction of the life of the body is not an attack on the person. On this view the lives of the unborn and of those not fully in possession of themselves—the severely retarded and the "vegetating" senile—along with the lives of those no longer able to engage in "meaningful" activities are of no inherent value. Such lives can thus be set aside, destroyed, killed without doing violence to any "personal subjects." For those who share this dualistic view of the human person, "membership in a species," including the human species, "is of no moral significance."[11]

According to this dualistic view of the human person—and today its influence on public policy is enormous—only certain members of the human species have moral worth, those, namely, who are "meaningfully" alive, those with *developed* capacity for reasoning, willing, desiring, and relating to others, and the ability to exercise this developed capacity.[12]

In this view bodily human life is a good *for* the person, an instrumental good. When it no longer serves as the condition for experiencing allegedly personal values, i.e., values dependent upon consciousness for their being, then bodily life is no longer a good.

But the human person, as we have seen, is a *body* person. The life of the human body, therefore, is personal in nature, not subpersonal. Human bodily life, precisely because it is personal, is a good *of* the person, participating in the dignity and sanctity of the person. Hence, to violate bodily life is to violate the person.

THE INTENTIONAL OR "DIRECT" KILLING OF THE INNOCENT IS ALWAYS GRAVELY IMMORAL

The sacred writers present "You shall not kill" (Ex. 20:13; Deut. 5:17 RSV) as a divine command and "Do not slay the innocent and righteous" (Ex. 23:7 RSV) as a norm for judicial procedures[13] God is the absolute Lord of life; he gives it and takes it away (cf. Deut. 32:39). But God does not make death (Wisd. Sol. 1:13); this results from the devil's envy (Wisd. Sol. 2:23–24). Satan, a murderer from the beginning (John 8:44) seduced Eve by telling her that sin would not lead to death (Gen. 3:1–4).

The Catholic tradition, in its interpretation of Holy Writ, has always maintained that the intentional, deliberate killing of innocent human beings is gravely evil. This tradition is ably summarized in the section devoted to killing in the *Catechism of the Council of Trent*.[14]

According to this source of Catholic teaching, the commandment forbidding killing "was the very first law given by God to man" after the deluge (Gen. 9:5). "Our Lord began his authoritative commentary on the Decalogue . . . by pointing to this commandment" (Matt. 5:21). In explaining what this commandment forbids, the *Catechism* excludes certain kinds of killing: the killing of animals, the execution of criminals, killing an enemy in a just war, killing by accident (although such killing can also be wrong), and killing in self-defense. Setting aside these kinds of killings, "all other killing is absolutely forbidden by the law of God—whatever might be the circumstances of the person killing, or the person killed, or the manner of the killing." In addition, the *Catechism* instructed pastors to communicate to their people "a true horror for this sin of willful murder," whose enormity is manifest in Scripture (Gen. 4:10; 9:5; Ex. 21:12; Lev. 24:17).

The teaching that the intentional killing of the innocent is absolutely immoral, traditional in the Church long before the Council of Trent, is the teaching of the Church today. Pope Pius XII properly formulated this teaching when he said: "As long as a man is not guilty, his life is untouchable, and therefore any act directly tending to destroy it is illicit, whether such a destruction is intended as an end in itself or only as a means to an end, whether it is a question of life in the embryonic stage or in a stage of full development or already in its final stages."[15]

Pope Pius's statement helps clarify the meaning of "innocent." The term *innocent* has a very precise meaning: it refers to persons *not* within one of the two classes of killing recognized as justifiable in the tradition: those guilty of capital crimes and those engaged in the forcible violation of society's just social order.[16] His statement also helps to clarify the meaning of "direct killing," a term frequently used by popes in setting forth Catholic teaching. A killing is "direct" when one intends the death, either as the end or *as the means* that one adopts (whether gladly, indifferently, or reluctantly) by one's own free *choice*.

Such "direct" or "intentional" killing is, within the Catholic tradition, understood to be quite different morally from "indirect" killing or killing that is outside the scope of one's intention. In indirect killing, although one's own freely chosen action brings death about, and one foresees that it will, one does not intend it either as means or end; one does not freely adopt by choice the proposal to kill an innocent human person. Thus the same Pope Pius XII wrote:

> We have on purpose always used the expression "*direct* attack on the life of the innocent," "*direct* killing." For if, for instance, the safety of the life of the mother-to-be, independently of her pregnant condition, should urgently require a surgical operation or other therapeutic treatment, which would have as a side effect, in no way willed or intended, yet inevitable, the death of the fetus, then such an act could not any longer be called a *direct* attack on innocent life.[17]

The distinction between the "direct" or intentional killing of the innocent and the "indirect" or unintended killing of them is grounded in a truth central to the Catholic faith, namely, that God himself is absolutely innocent of evil. God never intends that evil *be*, although he does permit evil to occur. God intends only the goodness that he communicates to his creature; the evil to which such goodness is prey falls outside his intention, caused indirectly, insofar as he causes corruptible things, but not intended by him. "And thus God, by causing in things the good of the order of the universe, as a consequence, and as it were *per accidens*,[18] causes the corruption of things; according to 1 Kings 2:6: 'The Lord kills and gives life.' When it is said in Wisdom of Solomon 1:13 that 'God has not made death,' it means *per se* intended,"[19] but human persons, created in God's image and likeness, are like God in that they do not *intend that evil be*, although at times they may permit or allow evil to occur.

Precisely because human persons are not to do evil for the sake of good to come (cf. Rom. 3:8), precisely because they are not to *intend* the death of the innocent, i.e., to embrace by choice their death either as end or as means, the norm forbidding such killing is absolute or exceptionless. John Finnis has summed up concisely and perceptively the reasons why the Church holds that this is an absolute norm. He wrote:

> Christian morality is more in the heart than in the results; one's intention is morally more basic and important than any performance or behavior by which that intention is carried out. Any performance—i.e., any outward action, considered as the execution of a choice—has its primary moral significance from the act

109

of the will (the choice of intention of means or end) which it embodies or carries out. . . . Directly killing the innocent—i.e., carrying out a choice (intention) to kill the innocent—is excluded from Christian life precisely because it is straightforwardly a choice against human life. Given the Christian understanding of the significance of choice and action, the traditional norm thus follows from the first principle of Christian ethics: love of neighbor. For human life is intrinsic, not extrinsic, to the human person. A choice against human life is thus a choice against the person: anti-life, therefore, anti-person. It is thus incompatible with love of the person, *i.e.*, with that first principle of Christian and rational ethics.[20]

It is, then, no wonder that at Vatican Council II the assembled fathers did not hesitate to say: "*All* offenses against life itself, such as murder, genocide, abortion, euthanasia and willful self-destruction . . . are criminal; they poison civilization; and *they debase their perpetrators more than their victims* and militate against the honor of the Creator"[21] (Council's italics). Freely to choose to kill an innocent human being is to give to oneself the identity of a *killer* and *murderer.* It is to close one's heart, one's person, to the good of human life.

CONTRACEPTION AND THE SANCTITY OF HUMAN LIFE

Today the majority of people in the Western world apparently think that contraception is not only morally right and just but even morally mandatory. According to them, it does not seem to harm anyone and it helps married people (and the unmarried as well) cope with a serious problem, the problem of an "unwanted" pregnancy. I grant that many people accept contraception in good faith; after all, the culture in which they live accepts it and indeed advocates and promotes it, so they grow up with the notion that it is morally acceptable.

Yet, I submit, the choice to contracept is not a good moral choice and that it is, indeed, an anti-life choice serving as the gateway to abortion. Although in this essay, I cannot discuss the subject as fully as it merits,[22] I hope that I will be able to show briefly why husbands and wives who seek to be responsible in their parenthood and in their married lives ought not to contracept.

To show this it is necessary, first of all, to be clear about what contraception is. Contraception itself is not a sexual act, although it is inescapably related to a sexual act. That it is not a sexual act can be seen by the following example. Suppose that a tyrant who is himself celibate and never engages in intercourse wishes to limit the population of his subjects and, in order to do so, puts a sterilizing agent into the water supply. This tyrant is practicing contraception both by his intention and subsequent action. Thus contraception is best understood as the choice to impede the beginning of a new human life prior to, during, or subsequent to an act of sexual union. Thus a couple that contracepts makes a twofold choice and engages in two distinct acts. They choose to have sexual union, and they choose—and this is the contraceptive act—to "close" this freely chosen act of sexual union to the transmission of human life. They realize, quite reasonably, that the act of sexual union is the sort of act through which human life can be given. Precisely because they do not want that life to be given, they contracept. Their contraceptive act is the adoption by choice of a proposal to impede the beginning of a new human life. Should human life be given, despite their efforts to impede its beginning, the life thus given would be "unwanted," at least initially, and to "want" it they would have to change their minds and wills.

But it is not morally good to set one's will and heart against the goodness of human life. It is not morally good to "unwant" a new human person. The moral evil of contraception consists precisely in this anti-life will. While contraception is not the same as abortion, and while many who practice contraception would never consider abortion, contraception itself is the gateway to abortion, for it is, as such, contra- or anti-life.

"No unwanted child ought ever to be born" is the slogan of those who advocate contraception and abortion. "No human person, including a child, ought to be unwanted" is the truth proclaimed by the Church in the name of Jesus Christ. This is a basic truth of Christian faith, a truth rooted in the sanctity of human life. Christian spouses can, of course, rightly regulate conception by choosing to abstain from the marital act if there is a serious reason why they ought not to pursue the good of handing on human life here and now. But they ought also "let the little children come to them" and not set their wills against their conception. To do so is to make a contra-life choice, one not compatible with a respect for the dignity and sanctity of human life.

The Natural Right

Norman L. Geisler

All governments presuppose some moral basis. Otherwise there is no standard for measuring justice or preserving the life of the community. So it is not a question of *whether* but of *which* moral laws should be used as the basis of civil government. Basically there are three answers to this question: human law, natural law, and divine law.

THE SEARCH FOR A COMMON BASIS
FOR THE SANCTITY OF HUMAN LIFE

Standing on One's Own Shadow

Humans have an incurable ego. We stand on our own shadow and then congratulate ourselves for finding a firm foundation for our lives. The attempt to ground human rights in the human will inevitably generates human wrongs. Earlier this century, John Dewey and other influential Americans signed the *Humanist Manifesto* (1933) that proclaimed that "the nature of the universe depicted by modern science makes unacceptable any supernatural or cosmic guarantees of human value."[1]

Reassuringly, they later added, "Values derive their source from human experience. Ethics is autonomous and situational, needing no theological or ideological sanctions."[2]

One of the signatories, whose imprint is on the *Humanist Manifesto II* (1973), Joseph Fletcher, argued that "only the end justifies the means: nothing else,"[3] and all "decisions are made situationally, not prescriptively."[4] He rejected all contentful ethical norms and insisted that we should avoid absolutes like the plague.[5] In the name of this moral relativism, *Humanist Manifesto II* went on to approve of abortion, euthanasia, and suicide.[6] So much for the sanctity of human life based on purely human law—at least so-called "humanistic" law. Other forms of strictly man-based governments—whether of the Nazis' right or of the Marxists' left—have scarcely fared better, accounting as they do for the slaughter of multimillions of innocent human lives. It does not seem to occur to humanistic ideologues that their espousal of solely human law (also called positive law) is contrary to their own human inclinations. Which of the signatories of their *Manifesto* that favors abortion was naturally inclined to believe that his mother should have killed him in her womb? Yet this is what the present humanistically based law allows to happen to over four thousand babies every day—1.6 million a year. Obviously, such "human" law does not provide an adequate basis for the sanctity of *human* life—at least not unborn human life. Nor is it much more assuring for those who have reached the other end of the life continuum, commending as it does suicide and euthanasia as a means of human extermination.[7]

Furthermore, the antinomian denial of an objective moral law is self-defeating. Joseph Fletcher, for example, seemed blissfully oblivious to the self-defeating nature of his insistence that we should never use the word "never."[8] Humanists are content to stand on the pinnacle of their own absolutes while they are relativizing everything else. They are apparently unaware that as they wield their sword to behead the monster of absolutism they decapitate their own relativism on the back swing. The sober truth of the matter is that one cannot move the world unless one has some place to put a fulcrum. Relativism self-destructs in its vain attempt to destroy all absolutes.

There must be some common moral law or else objective moral judgments cannot be possible. C. S. Lewis insightfully made this point in *The Abolition of Man* when he wrote:

> This thing which I have called for convenience the Tao, and which others may call Natural Law . . . is not one among a series of possible systems of value. It is the sole source of all value judgment. If it is rejected, all value is rejected. If any value is retained, it is retained. The effort to refute it and raise a new system of value in its place is self-contradictory. [9]

Professor Allan Bloom made a similar case for an absolute moral law in his academic bombshell, *The Closing of the American Mind*. He chided the prevailing academic view that "there were no absolutes; freedom is absolute." As to the oft-repeated claim that the study of different cultures proves that all values are relative, Professor Bloom responded: "All to the contrary, that is a philosophical premise that we now bring to our study of them." He added: "This premise is unproven and dogmatically asserted for what are largely political reasons." The fact of different opinions on values does not prove value is relative. "To say it does so prove is as absurd as to say that the diversity of points of view expressed in a college bull session proves there is no truth."[10]

So is there an absolute in which to ground the sanctity of human life? Absolutely?

From the Secular Frying Pan into the Religious Fire

A purely human law basis for government provides no ultimate guarantee of human rights. Each government can do that which is right in its own eyes. Might makes right. Where man is under no moral law, he becomes his own law.

The religious right is at least as dangerous as the secular left. Religious theonomy (divine law) as the basis for human dignity can be as frightening as secular anarchy. The latter extreme destroys the integrity of law, while the former the liberty of those under the law. Theonomists, or reconstructionists, as they are called, mistakenly superimpose divine law on unbelievers rather than on believers.

Theonomy is an unworkable ethical basis for government in a religiously pluralistic society, whether it be Muslim or Christian in form. Of course, a given government could choose "divine revelation" as its basis for civil law, but herein lies the evil of theonomy. For what is voluntary for believers is involuntary for unbelievers. Perhaps the easiest way for a Christian to understand this is to imagine himself living in the late Ayatollah's Iran. If this is unacceptable, then on what grounds can we choose to impose the Christian's divine law on non-Christians? Sooner or later the question arises: whose religious book will be the basis for the civil laws? It is sheer religious bigotry to answer: "Mine."

Indeed, it is not necessary to envision a Muslim theonomy to make us recoil in horror. The Christian theonomy some are offering is enough to give pause to fellow believers. After all, Roger Williams was not fleeing from a Catholic emperor named Constantine. We are fooling ourselves if we really think that the solution to secular antinomianism is puritan legalism. Some Christian theonomists are urging that America base its government in the Old Testament Law of Moses, which mandates that we execute all kidnappers, adulterers, homosexuals, and even rebellious children![11] Thoughtful reflection reveals that this "cure" of reconstructionism is worse than the disease of secularism. Its harsh reality is hidden beneath its deceptively appealing plea to return to "the good old days" of America's Christian roots. However, by superimposing its religious book on others, it violates their First Amendment religious rights. And in depriving others of their First Amendment rights, it undermines its own.

The Law behind the Law: Natural Law

Recent Supreme Court appointee Clarence Thomas made headlines for his belief in natural law. It was interesting to see how the secular media responded to this allegedly dinosauric belief. Some, of course, dismissed it as an outmoded archaeological curiosity of the Dark Ages. Others begrudgingly acknowledged that it could be found in our venerable national birth certificate under the rubric of "Nature's laws" and "unalienable rights" such as "the right to life, liberty, and the pursuit of happiness."[12] Even these, however, hastened to say that while natural law *existed*, it was *unusable* in determining the viability of civil laws. They never seemed to ask themselves how our Founding Fathers could have made it the very basis of our government, even to the point of specifying "the right to life" by it, unless it was thought to be of very practical value in determining just laws.

Although natural law is mentioned in the Bible,[13] belief in natural law did not begin with Christians. Even though it is embraced by both Catholics and Protestants, it is unique to neither. In point of fact, it is found in ancient Hindu, Chinese, and Greek writings. Even before Socrates, the Greek philosopher Heraclitus believed in an unchanging Logos (Reason) behind the changing flux of human experience.[14] Plato held to moral absolutes.[15] The Stoics developed natural law theories well before the time of Christ.[16]

The concept of natural law has a venerable history among great Christian thinkers on both sides of the major theological fence. Like others before him, Saint Augustine believed that God gave the Gentiles "the law of nature."[17] He referred to it as "the system of nature."[18] This law is "implanted by nature" in all men.[19] While believing in human depravity, he insisted that "the image of God is not wholly blotted out in these unbelievers."[20] Thus he held that God was just in punishing unbelievers for not living in accordance with this "law written on their hearts."[21]

Following Augustine, Thomas Aquinas declared that "natural law is nothing else than the rational creature's participation in eternal law."[22] Law is "an ordinance of reason made for the common good. . . ."[23] "It is the rule and measure of acts. . . ."[24] Eternal Law is the divine reason by which God governs the universe.[25] Natural law is simply the human participation in this eternal law. It is the first principle governing human action, as the laws of logic are the first principles governing human thought.[26]

Aquinas distinguished natural law, which is common to all rational creatures, from divine law, which is imposed only on believers. Natural law is directed toward man's temporal good; divine law is aimed at his eternal good.[27] Divine law is for the church; natural law is for society as a whole. In short, the basis for human law is natural law.

However, natural law is not unique to Catholic thinkers. Just like Augustine and Aquinas before him, John Calvin believed it to be beyond dispute that since "the Gentiles have the righteousness of the law naturally engraved on their minds, [so] we certainly cannot say that they are altogether blind as to the rule of life."[28] He called this moral awareness "natural law" that is "sufficient for their righteous condemnation"[29] but not for their salvation. By means of this natural law "the judgment of conscience" is able to distinguish between "the just and the unjust."[30] God's righteous nature "is engraved in characters so bright, so distinct, and so illustrious, that none, however dull and illiterate, can plead ignorance as their excuse."[31]

For Calvin, not only is the natural law clear but it is also specific. It includes a sense of justice "implanted by nature in the hearts of men."[32] There "is imprinted on their hearts a discrimination and judgment, by which they distinguish between justice and injustice, honesty and dishonesty." It is what makes them "ashamed of adultery and theft."[33] Even the heathen "prove their knowledge . . . that adultery, theft, and murder are evils, and honesty is to be esteemed."[34] Calvin summarized man's "natural knowledge of the law [as] that which states that one action is good and worthy of being followed, while another is to be shunned with horror."[35]

The roots of early American natural law view derived from John Locke,[36] who in turn was influenced by Richard Hooker.[37] Locke believed that the "laws of Nature" teach us that "being all equal and independent, no one ought to harm another in his life, health, liberty, or possessions; for men being all the workmanship of one omnipotent and infinitely wise Maker. . . ."[38] This same view was expressed by Thomas Jefferson in the Declaration of Independence (1776) when he wrote: "We hold these truths to be self-evident, that all men are created equal, that they are endowed by their Creator with certain unalienable Rights, that among these are Life, Liberty and the pursuit of Happiness."

Jefferson believed that these unalienable rights are rooted in "Nature's Laws" which derive from "Nature's God." On the Jefferson Memorial in Washington, D.C. are inscribed his own words: "God who gave us life gave us liberty. Can the liberties of a nation be secured when we have removed a conviction that these liberties are the gift of God?" Here again it is clear that Jefferson's America was not a uniquely Christian America. Rather, it is based on the concept of unalienable rights grounded in "Nature's Laws."

In their zeal to advertise their commitment to God's infallible revelation in Scripture, some evangelical Protestants overstate their case. In so doing they diminish or negate the need for the natural law and thereby undermine a socially viable basis for protecting the sanctity of human life in a religiously plural society.

Apart from any religious justification,[39] there are strong reasons for grounding the sanctity of human life in natural law. This is true both socially and internationally.

A society cannot function without some kind of common moral code that binds people together in a social unit— a kind of moral cohesive. Without this ethical cohesive, there would be no unity in a society. But it is obvious that not every society accepts a divine law, such as the Bible or the Koran. This being the case there is evident need for some kind of naturally available moral code to bind people together.

Most of the great cultures of the past and present embraced a common moral law. C. S. Lewis collected quotations reflecting a common natural law from the great civilizations of the past.[40]

These are ample testimony to the universal social need for some natural moral principles by which human conduct can be governed. To argue that there is no adequate moral basis for society apart from special revelation runs contrary to the moral writings of the great cultures of the past. It is tantamount to saying that these great civilizations have not expressed moral character. This is not only blatantly false, it is also contrary to the Christian teaching on common grace and general revelation (cf. Rom. 2:12–15).

The very concept of fundamental rights transcending all government demands a moral law that is above and beyond all particular governments and religions. The desire for a transnational moral code is a will-o'-the-wisp unless there is a natural law that transcends all governments.

Natural law is manifested in at least two ways in addition to writings. There is both an inner and outer side to natural law. It is impressed inwardly on the human heart and outwardly in human actions. The natural law is written in the most readily available place for people—in their own heart. It is also written in a way everyone can read—intuitively. No lessons in language are necessary, and no books are needed. Natural law can be seen "instinctively."[41] It is known by inclination even before it is known by cognition. We know what is right and wrong by our own natural intuitions. Our very nature predisposes us in that direction.

To be sure, being selfish creatures, we do not always desire to do to others what is right, but we do nonetheless desire that it be done to us. This is why Jesus summarized the moral law by declaring: "In everything, do to others what you would have them do to you" (Matt. 7:12 NIV). Confucius recognized the same truth by general revelation when he said: "Never do to others what you would not like them to do to you."[42] The natural law is not difficult to understand; it is hard to practice. The truth is that we know what we want others to do to us, even if we do not always want to do the same to them.

Since we do not always do what we know we ought to do, natural law is more manifest in human reactions than in human actions. That is, people's real moral beliefs are revealed not so much in what they do but in what they want done to them. Some may kill others, but they do not believe others should kill them. Even though Seneca's stoic culture taught his mother that abortion was justifiable, nonetheless, he thanked his mother for not aborting him.[43] So it is that we "do by nature" the things that "show" the moral law "written on our hearts."[44]

COMMON VALUES AND THE SANCTITY OF HUMAN LIFE

Whatever dispute there may be over which moral actions are prohibited by natural moral law, there is no dispute about one—the common value of protecting human life. All agree that we should never intentionally take the life of an innocent human being. If this is so, then there is only one relevant question when it comes to abortion—are unborn babies human beings? If they are human, then abortion is morally wrong. Not simply because the church or the Bible says it is wrong but because a moral law written on the heart of every human beings says so.

Let's spell out the natural law argument for the sanctity of unborn human life and then take a look at the evidence for the humanity of the unborn.

- It is morally wrong to intentionally take the life of an innocent human being.
- Unborn babies are human beings.
- Therefore, it is morally wrong to intentionally take the lives of unborn babies (i.e., abort them).

The first premise is not in dispute, being part of our common values as human beings. And totally apart from the biblical evidence, which is considerable,[45] the purely moral case against abortion stands or falls on the factual evidence that can be provided in support of the humanity of unborn babies as human beings.

The Scientific Evidence

Modern science has provided a window on the womb. As a result, the evidence is now clearer than ever that individual human life begins at the very moment of conception (fertilization).

GENETIC FACTS

It is a genetic fact that a fertilized human ovum is 100 percent human. First of all, from that very moment all genetic information is present. No new information is added from the point of conception till death. Second, all physical characteristics for life are contained in that genetic code present at conception. Third, the sex of the individual child is determined at the moment of conception. Fourth, a female ovum has only 23 chromosomes. A male sperm has 23 chromosomes. A normal adult human being has 46 chromosomes. But at the very moment of conception, when the male sperm and female ovum unite, a new tiny 46-chromosome human being emerges. Fifth, from the moment of conception till death nothing is added except food, air, and water.

EXPERT TESTIMONY

On April 23, 1981, scientific experts from around the world testified as to the beginning of an individual life. Here is a summary of what was said:

- In biology and in medicine, it is an accepted fact that the life of any individual organism resulting from sexual reproduction begins at conception, or fertilization. (Dr. Micheline M. Matthew-Ruth of Harvard University, supported this from over 20 embryology and other scientific texts.)
- To accept the fact that after fertilization has taken place a new human has come into being is no longer a matter of taste of opinion. The human nature of the human being from conception to old age is not a metaphysical contention, it is plain experimental evidence (world famous French geneticist Jerome LeJeune).
- But now we can say, unequivocally, that the question of when life begins is no longer a question for theological or philosophical dispute. It is an established scientific fact. Theologians and philosophers may go on to debate the meaning of life or the purpose of life, but it is an established fact that all life, including human life, begins at the moment of conception (Dr. Hymie Gordon).

EMBRYONIC DEVELOPMENT

Modern fetology has brought to light some amazing things about the growth of this tiny person in his/her mother's womb which fetologists call their second "patient." The following summary of fact is vivid testimony to the full humanness of the prenatal child (say, a girl):

First Month—Actualization

Conception—All her human characteristics are present.

She implants or "nests" in her mother's uterus (1 week).

Her heart muscle pulsates (3 weeks).

Her head, arms, and legs begin to appear.

Second Month—Development

Her brain wave can be detected (40–42 days).

Her nose, eyes, ears, and toes appear.

Her heart beats and blood flows (her own type).

Her skeleton develops.

She has her own unique fingerprints.

She is sensitive to touch on her lips and has reflexes.

All her bodily systems are present and functioning.

Third Month—Movement

She swallows, squints, and swims.

She grasps with her hands, moves her tongue.

She can even suck her thumb.

She can feel organic pain (8–13 weeks).

Fourth Month—Growth

Her weight increases six times (to 1/2 birth weight).

She grows up to 8–10 inches long.

She can hear her mother's voice.

Fifth Month—Viability

Her skin, hair, and nails develop.

She dreams (i.e., has rapid eye movement, REM).

She can cry (if air is present).

She can live outside the womb.

She is only half way to her scheduled birth date.

These make the identity of human embryos unmistakable. They are not mineral, vegetable, or animal; they are human. Since the factual evidence is overwhelmingly in favor of a new individual human life beginning at conception (fertilization),[46] and since intentionally taking an innocent human life is morally wrong, it follows rationally and necessarily that abortion is morally wrong. And since abortion has taken over 25 million human lives, it is the Number One moral problem in America—with no close second.

It should be stressed again that it is irrelevant as to whether or not any religious document is against killing tiny babies. It is morally wrong, and their lives must be protected by law. We do not tolerate, for example, child sacrifice or even parents refusing to allow life-saving procedures (like blood transfusions) for their children. Religious *belief* may be absolute, but religious *practice* is not. The law must protect the lives of the unborn and the born, from abortion and from infanticide. Abortion is not a religious issue; it is a *human* issue. It takes human lives.

The Constitutional Right to Life

In addition to the strong scientific evidence that unborn babies are tiny human beings, there are also good legal grounds for the right to life of unborn children. This is evident from several official sources.

In the English Common Law tradition the unborn, since the thirteenth century, have been protected by laws prohibiting abortion. They were protected against battery since the seventeenth century. In the twentieth century laws were added to protect the unborn against maternal neglect, against death by execution of the mother, and against loss of inheritance.

The Declaration of Independence declares the "unalienable" "right to life" for all. From this it is clear that our Founding Fathers believed that the right to life was an inalienable right. That is, it is something to which "Nature's God entitle[s] them." In short, the right of life is a God-given right that governments cannot give and governments cannot take away.

But did the Founding Fathers envision this right to life for the unborn or only for those who were born? That an affirmative answer is called for is evident from several facts: First, the English Common Law tradition, from which our laws come, embraced laws against abortion. Second, the moral law (natural law) tradition from which Thomas Jefferson came, and to which he referred in the phrase "Nature's Laws," also opposed abortion. Third, during the time the Founders lived, the unborn were described in dictionaries as a "child in the womb" and a child was defined as a "very young person." Finally, as early as 1716, sixty years before the American independence, the Common Council of New York passed a law forbidding midwives to perform abortions.

Our Bill of Rights embraces the Fifth Amendment (1791), which reads (in part) as follows: "Nor shall [any person] be deprived of life, liberty, or property, without due process of law." In other words, everyone has not only the right to life, liberty, and property, but also the right to due process of law in regard to being deprived of these rights. Now abortion is a violation of the Fifth Amendment both because it deprives the unborn of life and because it does so arbitrarily. The unborn are accused, pronounced guilty, and given capital punishment for no crime, with no lawyer, before no jury. No greater injustice could occur to any person under our Constitution. The Fourteenth Amendment to the Constitution likewise protects against the deprivation of human life without due process of law.

In brief, it is unconstitutional to take anyone's life without due process of the law. But does the word "person" in the Fourteenth Amendment include an unborn child? There are many reasons for a yes answer. First, there were legal references to the unborn as a "child" during the time when the Fourteenth Amendment was written. Second, the dictionaries of the day defined a fetus as a "child in the womb." Third, the killing of the unborn was called "manslaughter." Fourth, at that time all abortions were prohibited, except for saving the life of the mother. Fifth, at that time they exacted the same range of punishments for killing the baby as for killing the mother. Sixth, the punishment was greater when it was proven that it was the abortion, not something else, that killed the baby. Seventh, some of the congressmen who voted for and helped draft the Fourteenth Amendment also approved of strong anti-abortion laws in United States territories. Hence, if the Fourteenth Amendment was meant to include the right to abortion and exclude the unborn from legal protection, it was completely unknown to those who were chiefly responsible for the Amendment's existence. And finally, "the most direct piece of federal legislation relating to abortion in this period was enacted by Congress in 1873, five years after the Fourteenth Amendment was proposed." This legislation prohibited the selling, lending, or giving away of "any article . . . for causing unlawful abortion" as defined by the criminal law of the state in which the federal enclave was located. Six years before the Supreme Court legalized abortion in 1973 there were laws in all fifty states prohibiting abortion except to save the life of the mother. Then, some states began to make exceptions for "hard cases," such as when a pregnancy is the result of either rape or incest. New York, for example, legalized abortion for difficult cases in 1967. But prior to *Roe v. Wade* (1973) all states forbade abortion on demand. Hence the *Roe* decision reversed centuries of anti-abortion legislation and common law tradition in one fell swoop.

The Testimony of History

Most cultures since ancient times have opposed abortion. The ancient Canaanite Code of Hammurabi (1728–27 B.C.) exacted a

123

penalty for even unintentionally causing a miscarriage. The Jewish law gave the same penalty for causing the death of an unborn as for any other person.[47] The Assyrian king Tiglath-Pileser I (twelfth century B.C.) punished a woman who caused herself to miscarry. The famous Greek physician Hippocrates (fourth century B.C.) opposed abortion, insisting that doctors pledge: "neither will I give a woman an abortive remedy."

In spite of the fact that the Stoics generally favored abortion, their Roman philosopher Seneca (first century A.D.) praised his mother for not aborting him. In the same century, the poet Ovid pronounced that those who abort are worthy of death. In the second century, Rufus insisted that abortion was a "danger to the commonwealth." During the same period the Roman thinker, Soranus, opposed abortion, claiming that physicians should save lives, not kill them.

In the early Middle Ages (fourth century A.D.), Saint Augustine opposed all abortions as a violation of the moral law of God. Likewise, at the end of the middle ages, Saint Thomas Aquinas strongly opposed the abortion of all human fetuses. The Reformer, John Calvin (sixteenth century), called abortion abominable. English Common Law punished abortion when it could be shown that a life was taken. And an early American law (1716) forbade midwives to perform an abortion. In brief, there has been a nearly unanimous prohibition against abortion on demand from the great cultures and moral codes down through the centuries. Present U.S. policy stands in stark contrast to this long and widespread moral tradition.

ABORTIONS OF TRUTH AND LOGIC

In spite of the strong factual, legal, and moral cases against abortion, there are many who think that there are good arguments in its favor. All of them, however, have two fatal flaws: they make sense only if the unborn are not human beings, and these same arguments can be used to justify infanticide and euthanasia as well. Let's briefly consider some of these "good" arguments for abortion.

First, there is a woman's right over her own body. Second, there are situations in which the baby will be born hopelessly deformed. Third, there is the need to alleviate the insufferable indignity forced upon a woman by a pregnancy resulting from rape. Fourth, there are those unwanted pregnancies that make the child vulnerable to neglect and abuse. Fifth, why should a woman be forced against her will to bring into this world a baby she does not want? Finally, there is need for compassion for the many women whose lives would be threatened by illegal abortion in back alleys with rusty coat hangers.

There is merit in all these arguments. Indeed, they are persuasive—granting one major assumption that the Supreme Court made when it legalized abortion on demand—namely, that the unborn being is not a human person protected by the Constitution but only a "potential [human] life." If the unborn is not an individual human being, then not only are these arguments good, they are even convincing.

On the other hand, if the unborn being is not an individual human being, but merely a "potential life," then all these arguments are at best little more than emotional appeals with no moral justification whatsoever. For example, who would argue—on similar grounds to those used by abortionists—that Hitler had the right to kill Jews because they were unwanted? Or what abortionists would insist that because Jews would otherwise have been killed by a more painful death, that this justified passing laws to insure them a safe and less painful death in a gas chamber? And surely no reasonable abortionist would insist that the mother of Ethel Waters would have the right to kill her daughter years after her birth because her mother was still haunted by the memories of the rape by which Ethel was conceived. And what abortionists of Jewish descent (or any other) can justify the moral rightness of snuffing out the lives of millions of Jews simply because it was made legal to do so? And who would accept the argument, implicit in *Roe v. Wade*, that the decision to kill two-year-old children was "essentially a matter between the woman and her attending physician." Insisting, as the *Roe* Court did, that is primarily a medical decision, is like arguing that capital punishment by the electric chair is primarily a problem in electrical engineering! If these cases seem absurd, it is for one reason—they all involve the intentional taking of an innocent human life. But since the factual evidence overwhelmingly supports the full humanity of the unborn from the moment of conception, then it is equally absurd to abort them.

Then there are always the more evasive intellects—often trained in philosophy—who insist on making distinctions not grounded in reality. For example, some argue that an unborn baby may be human but it is not a *person*. In response, several things

125

should be noted. First, the argument is *philosophically arbitrary*. It has no essential grounds by which it makes this distinction, only accidental ones (such as size, shape, and location). Second, this distinction is *morally irrelevant*. The moral duty is to protect human life, not just persons. Third, it is *legally misdirected*. Corporations and even baby eagles are protected by our laws—how much more should unborn humans be protected! Fourth it is *socially disastrous* since by the same reasoning one could declare all small children and adults who lack certain functions to be "nonpersons." Fifth, it makes the question of when life begins *objectively indeterminable* since there is no other observable point at which to place the inception of life. Sixth, it leads to a *moral absurdity*, such as declaring that personhood begins at self-consciousness. But this would justify infanticide up to nearly two years after birth, the point at which self-consciousness is attained. One can already hear Rachel weeping for these her children.

There is a second fallacy in all the "good" arguments for abortion. As the late Princeton ethicist Professor Paul Ramsey warned, the same "good" reasons put forward in defense of abortion are equally "good" arguments for infanticide and euthanasia. In short, if we can kill babies before they are born because they are deformed, socially inconvenient, undesired, etc., then there is no ethical reason we cannot kill two-year-olds—or eighty-two-year-olds—on the same grounds.

Unfortunately, infanticide and euthanasia are not merely *logical consequences* of the pro-abortionists' arguments; they are *actual occurrences*. Consider just a few of the fatalities in recent years.[48]

In 1981 the Indiana Supreme Court rules that the parents of a "Baby Doe" could starve her to death. She had Down Syndrome and a correctable deformity. The parents' attorney was quoted as praising them for their courage and compassion for the child in taking the action!

In 1983 a New York federal judge gave permission to allow the death of a "Baby Jane" without treatment of her infection.

In 1990 Dr. Jack Kevorkian of Michigan constructed a "suicide machine," complete with a button to release deadly chemicals into the blood, so that his patient could kill herself. More recently (1991) he helped two more persons commit suicide.

In addition there are voluntary euthanasia groups, such as Exit, which produce "how to" books on committing suicide. Derek Humphrey, the founder of Exit, helped his first wife commit suicide. He

boasts, "We have made it respectable to debate and discuss euthanasia. We've also helped a lot of people die well." Euthanasia is
already common in some European countries, like the Netherlands,
and is growing in the United States.

The disastrous consequences of not following the factual evidence and the sound reasons of the natural law perspective is that
now that abortion is accepted we find that we no longer have any
basis for stopping infanticide and euthanasia. We have killed "Baby
Doe" and now do not know how to save "Granny Doe." We have
bifurcated our public ethic from our private ethic and are left
without any operative ethic. We have rejected natural law and are
engaged in the unnatural and unlawful slaughter of innocent lives,
young and old.

One of the more irrational responses to the arguments in favor
of legally protecting the sanctity of human life has been known to
slip from the lips of prominent politicians from time to time: "I
personally do not believe abortion is right, but I don't oppose the
rights of others to have abortions." Or, "Abortion is against my
personal religious beliefs, but I do not want to impose my beliefs
on others." In response, it should be noted that this bifurcation of
private and public ethic is both morally absurd and constitutionally
mistaken.

First, everyone would consider it absurd for a politician to argue
"I don't personally think murder is right, but I don't object to
someone else's doing it." Or, "Rape and murder are against my
beliefs, but I don't think it is right to impose my religious views on
others." What they forget is that if the unborn is a human being,
then there is absolutely no difference between these statements
and their stand in favor of legal abortion.

Second, the idea that abortion is a religious point of view is both
legally and philosophically mistaken. Most laws reflect morality
and that fact does not invalidate them under the First Amendment.
If it did, there could be no laws against rape, child abuse, spouse
abuse, infanticide, or murder since the belief that these are wrong
are deeply held religious convictions as well. Further, the Constitution does not forbid the establishment of morality; it only forbids
the establishment of religion. If it prohibited establishing morality,
then it would be unconstitutional to enforce moral behavior, which
is obviously absurd.

Mark Twain was not a Christian, but he saw what was wrong
with the public/private ethic disfunction some Christians use to

justify legal abortion. In words well worth pondering by both Catholic and Protestant politicians, he wrote:

> This is an honest nation in private life. The American Christian is a straight and clean and honest man, and in his private commerce with his fellows can be trusted to stand faithfully by the principles of honor and honesty imposed on him by his religion. But the moment he comes forward to exercise a public trust he can be confidently counted upon to betray that trust in nine cases out of ten, if 'party loyalty' shall require it. . . . His Christianity is of no use to him and has no influence upon him when he is acting in a public capacity.[49]

Once we have recovered from these sobering words, we should contemplate carefully Twain's conclusion, which is amazingly relevant to the contemporary debate over legalized abortion:

> He has sound and sturdy private morals, but he has not public ones. . . . There are Christian Private Morals, but there are no Christian Public Morals, at the polls, or in Congress or anywhere else—except here and there and scattered around like lost comets in the solar system.[50]

Chapter 5

FAMILY

Randall J. Hekman

Randall J. Hekman is the executive director of the Michigan Family Forum, a family-policy council associated with Focus on the Family. Prior to this he served fifteen years as a probate judge for Kent County, Michigan, in the juvenile court division. He has written numerous articles on juvenile crime, child abuse, and neglect, as well as a book, *Justice for the Unborn*. He is a graduate of MIT and George Washington University Law School.

Carl A. Anderson

Carl A. Anderson is vice president for public policy of the Knights of Columbus, an international Catholic fraternal society. He came to this post in 1987 after eleven years of government service, most recently as special assistant to President Ronald Reagan. He is dean and professor of family law at the Pontifical John Paul II Institute for Studies on Marriage and Family in Washington, D.C. In 1990 he was appointed to the United States Commission on Civil Rights.

The Attack on the Family: A Response

Randall J. Hekman

Family is incredibly important not merely to conservative evangelicals and Catholics but to all Americans. A recent Barna study showed that most Americans believe family is more important than health, close friends, religion, the Bible, career, or even money.[1] Fully 94 percent of all Americans rate family as "very important." In contrast, only 59 percent of Americans rate religion as "very important," 55 percent place the Bible in the same light, and only 33 percent view money as "very important" to them.

Not surprisingly, evangelicals and Catholics responding to the Barna survey were even more enthusiastic than the average American about the importance of family to them: 98 percent of those calling themselves evangelicals and 95 percent of those calling themselves Catholics felt family was "very important."

Whether these responses by Americans are an accurate reflection of what they truly believe will be challenged by some of the data in this chapter. But there can be no denying that the vast majority of Americans know beyond any doubt that family *needs* to be a priority for all of us, that life for individuals, groups, communities and our nation itself has little meaning apart from irreplaceable family relationships.

We Christians understand that God also believes family is extremely important. In the early biblical account of Adam and Eve in Genesis, God, the creator of family, provided this commentary: "For this reason a man will leave his father and mother and be united to his wife, and they will become one flesh." (Gen. 2:24 NIV).

Both Old and New Testaments contain much instruction—both direct and by example—about the value of family life and the principles to follow to ensure that families prosper.

Unfortunately, even though nearly all Americans believe that family is "very important," families in the 1990s are under incredible attack in our culture. Innumerable books, articles, and studies have been published documenting the many struggles our families confront.

SPIRITUAL WARFARE

Alert Christians know that behind much of the conflict in the world is a cosmic struggle between God and Satan. Throughout history Satan has utilized different strategies in an attempt to thwart God's plans for man. One tactic that has been particularly effective from Bible times until the present has been an attack on family integrity. Intermarriage of God's people with pagan nations was strongly condemned as corrupting family, and ultimately national integrity. Even the otherwise brilliant King Solomon lost his spiritual vitality by relationships with wives who did not share his love for the one true God of the Hebrews. As he aged "his wives turned his heart after other gods, and his heart was not fully devoted to the LORD his God, as the heart of David his father had been." (1 Kings 11:4 NIV).

Proper family relationships are absolutely critical to our spiritual health. Since Satan knows this better than we do, he will attack at this level. His attacks are both direct and indirect. Many of the indirect attacks come through ungodly cultural trends and values.

SOCIETAL STRESSES

Probably the single biggest problem hurting families in America today is divorce. Approximately 50 percent of the marriages currently being consummated in America will end in divorce. Despite calling the process "no fault," the impact on the parties—especially the children—is by no means "no harm." More and more studies are showing the short-term and long-term emotional and economic consequences to children when their parents divorce.

Coupled with divorce is the growing number of children born out of wedlock. In 1950, one in 25 American children was born out of wedlock. By 1980, this number had grown to one in four, where it remains today. More than 60 percent of black children born in the United States are born to unmarried women. In fact, the probability of a black child being raised to age 17 by both parents is only 6 percent. Children of all races stand about a 50 percent chance of spending at least some of their childhood with only one parent. While single parenting can work, there is growing unanimity among researchers that two-parent families are significantly more likely to produce emotionally and physically healthy children than single-parent families.[2]

The teenage years are fraught with pitfalls in our modern culture, as the following facts indicate:

- The teen pregnancy rate has increased 621 percent since 1940, obviously related to a greatly increased rate of teen sexual activity.
- The number of teens being murdered has increased 222 percent since 1950, and murder is now the leading cause of death among minority youth aged 15 to 19.
- Teen suicide has increased 300 percent since 1940 and is now the second leading cause of death among adolescents.
- Teens continue to use alcohol and other drugs at an alarming rate; 13 is the average age for the first use of drugs, and one-third of all high school seniors claim to become drunk once per week.

In addition to these troubling statistics, the modern media through music, videos, and associated paraphernalia have helped to spawn a new youth culture. Catering to a teen's desire to be part of the "in crowd" and to wield power among peers, these media industries have preached a nihilistic message of anarchy, death, drugs, and violent sexuality.

Crime greatly affects the quality of life for families, particularly in urban settings and for children at school. Since 1950, crime rates in America have increased nearly 1000 percent, with juvenile arrests up fifteenfold. One in four of black youth is under some form of court supervision.

Certain educational programs are negatively influencing families by having teachers devote inordinate amounts of classroom time to "safe" sex practices, "responsible" use of drugs and alcohol, and "values clarification." Most are taught without a solid moral foundation. Academic essentials, safety basics, and school discipline have been sacrificed.

With the quality of human life having become more important than its sanctity, the value of life for handicapped, elderly, and infirm family members has been demeaned. Inevitably, this has cheapened the value of life for all of us. We now view people biologically and economically without regard for their status as creations of an infinite God. If children or "burdensome" adults are not wanted we throw them away: one in three conceived children is aborted, and an openness to infanticide and euthanasia has increased.

Pornography and obscenity are legally sold in many of our cities. Some of this material gets in the hands of children, robbing them of childhood innocence and purity. Sexual deviants use hard-core pornography to break down the resistance of victims or to heighten their own perverse drives, and these deviants are perpetrating such acts in families.

Economic problems also strike home with families. In fact, when adjusted for inflation a worker's weekly pay has been reduced from $295 in 1970 to $257 in 1990. This is caused not only by sluggish economies but also by increased federal income taxes. The tax rate for a family of four has grown from 2 percent of gross income in 1950 to 24 percent in 1990. State and local taxes have typically mushroomed as well. These economic numbers have forced more women to leave their children for employment and more fathers to take second and third jobs. Little wonder parents today spend about 40 percent less time with their children than parents did 25 years ago.

Two other cultural trends now working on the family are the gay rights and "green" movements. The first claims that a homosexual relationship is a valid life-style choice and the second pits humans against other life forms in a struggle for control. Unless these trends are biblically addressed, they will overtake the family as others have.

PERSONAL STRESSES

Some people feel that the combination of satanic spiritual warfare and a culture that opposes Christian values leaves Christians with no choice but to cave in to the pressure and be defeated in their lives and families; however, Scripture indicates otherwise. Such phrases as "we are more than conquerors," "we can do all things through him who strengthens us," and "greater is he that is in us than he that is in the world" should give us courage. We also have the marvelous biblical examples of Moses being raised in secular Egypt but keeping his faith; of Joseph flourishing as a leader in a pagan land; of Daniel rising to greatness in Babylon after being taken away from his parents and forced into captivity. In New Testament times, many of the new Gentile churches were established in cultural settings where the gospel was totally out of step with the existing pagan culture. Nowhere do New Testament authors suggest other than for God's people to be "blameless and pure, children of God without fault in a crooked and depraved generation, in which you shine like stars in the universe" (Phil. 2:15 NIV). In a world where immorality, unfaithfulness, disloyalty, dishonesty, and confused priorities exist, Christians are to find in the power of God the strength to live righteous lives for Him.

And this is no pipe dream. God is eager to give us his Spirit to indwell and empower us to be the husbands, wives, fathers, mothers, and children he wants us to be. I have seen this truth played out many times in my own life and family as well as that of friends.

The problem is not whether God is powerful enough to help me; the real problem is whether or not I want to obey God in my family. The crisis of moral authority that exists in the culture at large has seeped into the church.

George Barna's group asked a sampling of Americans whether or not they agreed with the statement, "There is no such thing as absolute truth; different people can define truth in conflicting ways and still be correct." Sixty-seven percent of all Americans agreed with this statement either "strongly" or "somewhat"; 53 percent of those calling themselves evangelical agreed, as did 74 percent of mainline Protestants, and 68 percent of Catholics. Even 52 percent of those calling themselves born again felt absolute truth does not exist![3]

If absolute truth does not exist, I can simply decide for myself whatever I feel is right or wrong. If I want to commit adultery, get divorced, ignore my children, use pornography, fail to tithe my income to my church, abuse my children, get an abortion, it is my decision and mine alone. Needless to say, this is antithetical to orthodox Christian faith.

When I was being raised, I was told that the primary difference between Protestants and Catholics was that the former believed in salvation by faith alone and the latter in salvation by works. To the extent this is true, Catholics should be more in tune with the need to obey God's precepts, while Protestants would find it very easy to join in our culture's infatuation with relativism: believe in Christ for salvation and do anything you please. Unfortunately, the mental fog of relativism has clouded the brains of both groups significantly.

True believers know that God demands obedience of his followers—not to earn God's love but to show their love for him. Jesus made this point:

> If anyone loves me, he will obey my teaching. My father will love him, and we will come to him and make our home with him. He who does not love me will not obey my teaching (John 14:23–24 NIV).

Some believers, in trying to make these clear words of our Lord jibe with the modern precepts of relativism, suggest that all Jesus really meant was that we love our neighbor, which gets translated into an amorphous, gooey, universal niceness. However, God *does* expect us to live different lives from the culture around us as the New Testament demonstrates over and over again. Indeed, even we evangelical, salvation-by-faith-alone Protestants will answer to God for our activities after salvation. Paul reminds the Corinthian Christians, reminds them that "we make it our goal to please [the Lord]. . . . For we must all appear before the judgment seat of Christ, that each one may receive what is due him for the things done while in the body, whether good or bad." (2 Cor. 5:9–10 NIV).

And what could be a more important area to obey God in than the love we show to our closest neighbors, those in our immediate family?

The family is important to ourselves and our nation, but family life in America is under heavy attack from spiritual forces and cultural trends that oppose strong families. Even more deadly to the family than external attacks are the rebellious minds and wills of Christians that will not bow to God's non-negotiable, absolute will.

In fact, it is *because* those calling themselves Christians, those whom Christ called the salt of the world to preserve culture, have capitulated to the mores of the world that families languish around us. When we, the conscience of our nation, do not lead with distinctively righteous lives, it is no wonder people watching us do no better. It is time we provided the moral leadership God expects of us and our nation needs from us. And this moral leadership must begin at the level of belief and practice in our own lives. When we fail to provide the example we should, let us freely acknowledge our wrong choices and ask forgiveness so as not to give our wonderful Lord a bad name.

A fascinating thing occurs when we begin to encourage each other to live for God. The entire culture eventually becomes touched by the quality of our lives. While there will always be some opposition to God's people living distinctively Christian lives, there have been times in the history of America that massive religious revivals have swept our nation, bringing incredible social change. We will never achieve heaven on earth, but the closest we can come to it is when a large percentage of the population is God-fearing such as we see happened in the years subsequent to a time of religious revival. Soon thereafter comes modification of laws and other reforms. Such occurs naturally in a democratic republic since public policy always rests on private policy, the beliefs of individual people.

We have abortion, pornography, national debt, and easy divorce as public policies because the private policies of our people—including many, if not most, Christians—currently support these perspectives. We have abortion not because people love to kill babies but because we virtually worship sex as a culture and demean the value of bearing and raising a child. We have pornography because we tolerate absolute garbage on *our* TV's, in *our* books and magazines, and in *our* thoughts. We have national debt because our longing for material things has left us in personal debt. Easy divorce exists because too many feel their own choices are more important than their solemn word.

If change is to come about, Christians must address public policies on family from two fronts: individual and public. We need to change the hearts of Americans, starting with our own, to create a climate of change; and we need to pursue public policy changes with our local, state, and national leadership. But merely to do the latter is hypocritical, shallow, and unlikely to be successful in the long run.

BASIC PRINCIPLES OF FAMILY LIFE

What are the principles essential to orthodox evangelicals and Catholics in the area of family life?

Marriage[4]

We believe that the institution of marriage is a permanent, life-long relationship between a man and a woman, regardless of trials, sickness, financial reversals, or emotional stresses that may ensue. Marriage should not be entered into lightly; we must truly see it as a high and holy relationship, the best analogy of which is that of Christ and his bride, the church.

Since God ordained the institution of marriage, he knows how to maintain it. Churches can do much more than to prepare couples for married life. The concept of Community Marriage Policies, advocated by columnist Michael McManus, wherein all the pastors and priests in a given community agree not to perform a wedding for a couple until they have undergone four or more months of premarital counseling and mentoring by a mature married couple, is an excellent one with great results.

Divorce laws can and should be modified to make it more difficult to sever what God has joined together. We should advocate a return to "fault" divorce standards. Other ideas to consider include procedures to ensure that child support ordered by the judge is, in fact, paid. Perhaps when divorce occurs to a couple that has been married a long time or who have children, significant alimony in addition to child support should be ordered by trial court judges, particularly where the "fault" lies more with the husband. One other possibility would be to consider returning to the common-law principle that places primary responsibility for custody of minor children on the father in cases of divorce.[5] This policy had the effect of making a wayward man think twice or even three times about running off with some young woman: he was unable in those days to shirk his God-given responsibilities of fatherhood. With our current laws, however, husband and fathers can be much more cavalier about familial duties.

Proper Priorities for Fathers and Mothers

We believe the responsibility of raising children is one of the highest callings for Christian parents. We oppose the notion that women can only find their satisfaction by mirroring career paths pursued by men. We also oppose the notion that men should pursue their careers with little regard for the spiritual, emotional, and physical needs of their children. Scripture teaches that *fathers* are to bring up their children in the "training and instruction of the Lord" (Eph. 6:4 NIV) and that fathers are involved in the loving discipline of their children (Heb. 12:7, 9, 10). Raising children is not women's work alone but the responsibility of both parents. Having said this, however, we believe the primary responsibility for daily child care should fall to the mother in most situations (Titus 2:4–5). Farming children out to surrogate caretakers merely for economic or career advantage is contrary to wisdom and a proper view of what is truly important in life. While self-denial and meekness are qualities spurned by our macho-man, self-sufficient woman culture, they are still revered by God and will be ultimately rewarded by him.

We should support efforts to pay breadwinners—typically fathers—in proportion to the number of children and other dependents they have. We should also support all efforts to cut taxes so that parents can spend more time with their children rather than working excessive amounts merely to meet the basics of life. In no way should we financially reward the couple who chooses to have both parents working while neglecting financially the mother who chooses to stay at home to raise her children. We also should support voluntary efforts to create "family days" in communities, asking local groups to avoid scheduling meetings a certain day each week.

The Value of Children

We believe that children are a gift of God, a heritage from the Lord. We are therefore accountable to God for molding, shaping, and preparing them for a life of service to God and to their fellow men.

The Bible teaches that God creates children in the womb by working through the sexual relations between a man and a woman. God in his sovereignty decides whether the child will be a boy or girl, what personality and physical features the child will have, and other factors, down to the fingerprints. For God there is no such thing as chance. As God's creation, all children belong to him; parents merely have the children "on loan" for a few years with the responsibility of raising them for the glory of God.

Since children are a blessing of God and created by him, healthy Christian parents should be open to God for the children he wishes to create through the parents. The decision of family size is an issue that needs to be under the lordship of Christ.

Hence, we oppose any effort to provide governmental restrictions on childbearing for environmental, overpopulation, or eugenic reasons. In reality, according to Census Bureau projections, since 1973 American women have not been bearing enough children even to have our population break even in the long run. There is growing concern in all Western nations about the likelihood of economic crises from the burgeoning numbers of elderly and the paucity of working people to pay for social security and medical costs associated with these demographic shifts. While the governments of Germany and France are now paying citizens to have additional children, American thinking is seemingly locked in the time warp of the 60s with visions of a catastrophic population bomb ticking away. Children are inaccurately viewed as being economic and environmental burdens: the average person gives back to his or her economy about ten times what he or she consumes during their lifetime. Besides, advanced nations are better able to contain pollution than are developing nations. We need to advocate tax credits or increased tax exemption rates per child to reward the parents who are willing to make an investment in the future of our nation by bearing and raising children.

The Value of All People

We believe that human life is of inestimable worth and significance in all its dimensions, including the aged, the widowed, the mentally retarded, the unattractive, the physically handicapped, and every other condition in which humanness is expressed from conception to the grave, including the unborn.

As a result, we oppose all attempts to create a quality of life ethic in place of the sanctity of human life ethic taught by the Judeo-Christian tradition. We therefore oppose abortion, except to save the life of the mother, and infanticide and euthanasia. God is the author of life and in him we live and move and have our being.

Human Sexuality

We believe that the human sexual relationship is intended to find its full expression within the bonds of marriage between a man and a woman. We are, therefore, opposed to premarital and extramarital sexual activity, as well as any attempts at recognizing homosexual activity as a normal life-style.

Educational programs of sex education must avoid the "safe sex" approach, which may mention abstinence as an option but fails to authoritatively teach extramarital abstinence as the only right way to live. In place of these programs that have had no impact on reducing teen sexuality and pregnancy rates but explicitly teach sexual information and promote decision making and self-esteem without a moral basis, we support programs that are truly abstinence based, family centered, and age appropriate in their approach. These latter programs have been incredibly successful with youth from all socio-economic classes and have actually reduced sexual activity and pregnancies.

We oppose the expansion of special legal rights for individuals engaging in homosexual activities, including the enacting of "domestic partnership" laws to permit adoptions by homosexual couples and to obligate businesses, educational institutions, and private organizations to hire otherwise qualified homosexuals. AIDS and other deadly sexually transmitted diseases should not be politically protected diseases. Those with these diseases—regardless of how they contracted them—need to be treated in such a way as to reasonably guarantee safety for those not infected. At the same time, we support a vigorous effort to minister to the physical and spiritual needs of all people who suffer with AIDS and other such diseases—especially those who wish to escape the sexually perverse life-style inherent in homosexuality and other unbiblical sexual relationships.

Pornography

We oppose the sale and distribution of pornographic material. We believe that pornography degrades women and can lead to sexual exploitation of children and even harm to those who use it. Pornography offends the dignity of human sexuality and fosters a callous and permissive attitude toward sexual violence.

We support strong and effective laws restricting the sale and distribution of obscene material (as defined by the U.S. Supreme Court) and the vigorous enforcement of such laws.

We oppose the continuing increase of sex and violence in the media and would encourage television and radio management to move toward more responsible and wholesome programming. We also oppose the increasing incidence of sexual and violent messages contained in the lyrics of certain contemporary music.

We are appalled that our federal tax dollars continue to be used to support "art" projects that are wholly obscene and antithetical to the religious and moral principles upon which our nation was founded.

Alcohol and Drugs

We support the vigorous and impartial enforcement of all state liquor laws. We support effective policies and programs designed for the treatment and rehabilitation of the alcoholic and his family. We support strong and effective laws against drunk driving and the diligent enforcement of such laws.

We also support the enactment of strong and effective laws against all illegal drugs and their strict and impartial enforcement. We also support effective programs designed to provide treatment and rehabilitation for the drug addict and his family. We support effective drug and alcohol education in all schools.

We affirm the public's right to live and work in a smoke-free environment and support reasonable and effective laws to protect the personal rights of nonsmokers.

Crime and Punishment

We believe the primary responsibility of the criminal justice system is to punish wrongdoers and reward those who do right and to create a climate in which wrongdoing is discouraged and justice is promoted (Rom. 13:3–4). "Rehabilitation" is more the province of the church than the government.

As such, we oppose programs that tend to treat many adult offenders as "sick" or as otherwise being in need of treatment. Those programs underpunish some offenders and overpunish others—all in the name of treatment. We support the use of multiple restitution for theft offenses and other creative methods of punishment for offenders that will be just yet humane.

Discipline of Children

We believe parents need to courageously train their children to obey reasonable authority. In this effort, parents need to understand the strengths and weaknesses of their children so they can do their part to encourage the growth of positive qualities and discourage qualities that are harmful. We believe the appropriate spanking of a child is one method parents should use to help their younger children avoid self-centered and harmful behaviors.

We oppose any efforts to criminalize "corporal punishment," including efforts by the child welfare system (child protective services) to equate spanking with a form of child abuse.

If orthodox evangelicals and orthodox Catholics can work together to support the sort of approaches to family life contained in this chapter, we can expect, with the blessing of God, significant changes in our lives, then in our families, in our churches and parishes, and in our communities, our states, and our nation.

Symbol of the
Eternal Covenant

Carl A. Anderson

The communion between God and His people finds its definitive fulfillment in Jesus Christ. . . . This revelation reaches its definitive fullness in the gift of love which the Word of God makes to humanity in assuming a human nature, and in the sacrifice which Jesus Christ makes of Himself on the Cross for His bride, the Church. In this sacrifice there is entirely revealed that plan which God has imprinted on the humanity of man and woman since their creation; the marriage of baptized persons thus becomes a real symbol of that new and eternal covenant sanctioned in the blood of Christ.[1]

With this meditation on chapter five of Paul's letter to the church at Ephesus, Pope John Paul II concisely summed up the place of marriage, its central importance within the Christian tradition, and why it is that the church has sought to protect the institution of marriage and the family founded upon it. Within the tradition, marriage and family are understood as "willed by God in the very act of creation."[2] "Accordingly," wrote Pope John Paul, "the family must go back to the 'beginning' of God's creative act, if it is to attain self-knowledge and self-realization in accordance with the inner truth not only of what it is but also of what it does in history."[3] Because this "inner truth" has been "imprinted on the humanity of man and woman," the Christian tradition has realized that the natural realities of marriage and family are present not only to believers. As the apostle Paul wrote, pagans who never heard of the

Law "still through their own innate sense behave as the Law commands. . . . They demonstrate the effect of the Law engraved on their hearts" (Rom 2:14 NJB).

Yet, from the very beginning of Christian communities, it was apparent that while the "substance" of the laws of marriage and family might be "engraved" on the hearts of the pagans, their family culture failed to reflect such realities. From the fourth through the sixth centuries, the struggle between Christianity and classical pagan culture increasingly focused upon the family. The views of marriage by both Saint Jerome and Saint Augustine would ultimately form the basis for a new conceptual ordering of family life embodied in the laws enacted by Christian emperors such as Justinian. This increasingly Christian culture recognized the responsibility of the lawgiver to protect the family. The roots of this tradition ran deep: three of the Ten Commandments sought to preserve the family. Moreover, the Gospel accounts of statements made by Jesus on the subject of marriage made clear two profound obligations of the lawgiver. First, the law of marriage arose not from the whim of the lawgiver but from within the very nature of the human person and the natural order. "Have you not read that the Creator from the beginning made them male and female and . . . This is why . . . the two become one flesh?" (Matt 19:5 NJB). But, secondly, the lawgiver was not only under an obligation to respect marriage and family as a requirement of the natural order; a decision of the lawgiver that contradicted natural justice could not itself do justice to the family. "Now I say this to you: anyone who divorces his wife . . . and marries another, is guilty of adultery" (Matt. 19:9 NJB). The insistence of the tradition on the stability of marriage and the family and its view that the permanence of marriage as an institution be protected and upheld by the law was, in the words of the English historian Paul Johnson, "one of the most fundamentally creative inventions of Judeo-Christian civilization."[4] By the twelfth century, churchmen such as Thomas Aquinas would ground the tradition's view of marriage firmly in nature and nature's law.

While this medieval synthesis unraveled with the denial of the sacramentality of marriage during the Reformation, it was not until the Enlightenment that the Christian view of marriage, whether in its Catholic or Protestant understanding, was rejected. For the *philosophes* of eighteenth-century France, Christian marriage was simply a reflection of the "irrationality, cruelty, and unnaturalness of Catholic society."[5] Rousseau argued that "the state ought to emancipate itself from the notion of marriage as a sacrament and treat it exclusively as a civil and, of course, dissoluble, contract."[6] The Protestant reformers had earlier held marriage as a civil contract and, in returning to the Mosaic tradition, permitted divorce in cases of adultery. But here the similarity between evangelical Christianity and the Enlightenment ended. The *philosophes'* view of marriage was based on a radically different view of nature and of the ultimate end of the human person. For Diderot, whose *Encyclopaedia* was perhaps the single most important book of his time, the Christian era was at an end and it was time for a new order. He wrote:

> The presence of Man it is that gives interest and meaning to the existence of living things, and how better could we record the history thereof than by taking this consideration for our guide? Why not give to man in this work the place which is allotted him in the universal scheme of things? Why not make him the centre round which everything revolves?[7]

Elsewhere Diderot posed the question: "What, in your opinion, are the duties of man?" To which he answered: "To make himself happy."[8] Similarly, Saint-Lambert would reflect the moral code of the new age in his *Universal Catechism:*

- Q: What is man?
- A: A being possessed of feelings and understanding.
- Q: That being so, what should he do?
- A: Pursue pleasure and eschew pain.[9]

Perhaps the highest recognition of the new view came in America when Thomas Jefferson wrote that among the fundamental rights of the person was the right to "the pursuit of happiness." According to Max Rheinstein, "the philosophy of the Enlightenment conceived of marriage as one of the avenues open to man in his pursuit of happiness, and man's right to pursue happiness was one of those inalienable rights which no government ought to be able to block."[10] Moreover, the *philosophes'* understanding of nature itself mandated a radical change in their understanding of marriage. John Locke's *Essay Concerning Human Understanding* advanced a fundamental tenet of the new moral order:

> . . . if nature be the work of God, and man the product of nature, then all that man does and thinks, all that he has ever done or thought, must be natural, too, and in accord with the laws of nature and of nature's God.[11]

Thus, Rousseau, Voltaire, and Diderot discovered in the "unspoiled innocence" of native societies and the "noble savage" an alternative to the Christian tradition of marriage. Especially for Rousseau, the individual can only be free when liberated from the "corrupting" social institutions around him. The ties of marriage and family, far from protecting and promoting human freedom, are for Rousseau chains that bind the person in oppression. To be free, man must first be liberated from the family. As Robert Nisbet has written,

> Rousseau sees the State as the most exalted of all forms of moral community. For Rousseau there is no morality, no freedom, no community outside the structure of the State. Apart from his life in the State, man's actions are wanting in even the minimal conditions of morality and freedom.[12]

During the French Revolution, this Enlightenment ideology became official policy. Title II of the revolutionary Constitution of 1791 proclaimed marriage as a civil contract. The revolutionary divorce law of 1792 proclaimed marriage "a secular institution designed to serve individual human beings in their pursuit of happiness" and enumerated broad grounds for its termination.[13] The law reflected the idea that "any indissoluble tie is an infringement of individual liberty and that therefore the principle of individual liberty presupposes a natural right to divorce."[14]

With the Bourbon Restoration, the mantle of the Revolution was cast here and there for some time before falling to the early Marxist revolutionaries. While their claim as its inheritors was perhaps nowhere better justified than in the Great Terror, it was also clearly evident in early Soviet policies regarding marriage and family. Marxist theory of the family rests on Frederick Engels' *Origin of the Family, Private Property and the State.*[15] Engels described his work as "the fulfillment of a bequest" to Karl Marx and in it he sought to place the family at the center of Marx's theory. He argued that the evolution of the family was directly related to the evolution of the means of production. According to Engels,

> monogamy does not by any means make its appearance in history as the reconciliation of man and woman, still less as the highest form of such a reconciliation. On the contrary, it appears as the subjection of one sex by the other, as the proclamation of a conflict between the sexes.[16]

Quoting from his earlier work with Marx, *The German Ideology,* Engels insisted that "the first class antagonism which appears in history coincides with the development of the antagonism between man and woman in monogamous marriage, and the first class oppression with that of the female sex by the male."[17]

Because he maintained that "the modern individual family is based on the open or disguised domestic enslavement of the woman" in which the husband represents the bourgeois and "the wife represents the proletariat . . . the first premise for the emancipation of women is the reintroduction of the entire female sex into public industry."[18] Men and women could be fully liberated only when they were both fully incorporated into the public economy. Early Marxists were eager to point out that the fundamental premise of Marxism "demands that the quality possessed by the individual family of being the economic unit of society be abolished."[19] One precondition for the "reintroduction" of women "into public industry" and the destruction of the family as a unit of society was the absolute control of women's fertility. Thus, the inevitable consequence of the socialist view of the liberation of women was ready access to abortion. Following the October Revolution, the Soviet regime would initiate a pattern, now familiar among subsequent socialist governments, of the legalization of abortion as a method of family planning.[20]

Marxist family theory was given political expression within weeks of the Russian Revolution. The first general decree of the Soviet regime concerned the dissolution of marriage. The more comprehensive Soviet Family Code of 1918 rejected the recognition of any religious character of marriage: only a civil ceremony conducted in a registry office would establish binding rights and obligations. The 1926 Soviet Family Code removed even the requirements of a civil ceremony and for the first time recognized *de facto* cohabitation as equal to marriage and enjoying many of the same legal rights and social benefits. By 1930, the withdrawal of the Soviet state from the regulation of marriage reached the point where "marriages could be terminated by informal mutual consent, unilateral declaration, or mere desertion without any announcement or agreement whatsoever."[21] The objective of such laws was stated by the Soviet sociologist Volfson in 1929. In his *Sociology of Marriage and the Family*, he argued that the family under Marxism would lose its productive function, its joint household function, its child-rearing function, and its function in regard to the care of the aged. Since, therefore, "the family will be purged of its social content, it will wither away."[22]

Earlier, the Soviet theorist Liadov had framed the underlying issue bluntly: "Is it possible to bring up collective man in an individual family?" His answer seemed clear as a matter of Marxist ideology: "A collectively thinking child may be brought up only in a social environment. . . . The sooner the child is taken from his mother and given over to a nursery, the greater is the guarantee that he will be healthy."[23] But to understand the new, healthy, collectively thinking child who was to emerge from the new Marxist social environment liberated from traditional family structures, one must first understand the socialist view of equality. Socialist equality is not an equality in the sense of *external* factors, such as equality of rights, opportunities, or benefits. Instead, it is an equalization of *internal* factors, of "the abolition of differences . . . in the inner world of the individuals constituting society. . . . The equality proclaimed in socialist ideology means identity of individualities."[24]

Marxist socialism presents a philosophy of the human person in which the individual identity of each human being dissolves into the communal "being" of the state. In this view, the person no longer finds legal expression as an individual with the right to a personal self-determination and unique destiny. Instead, the individual must find his destiny exclusively in terms of the communal good, in what Marxist legal philosophy describes as a "species being."[25] Each person no longer possesses inherent and inalienable rights. Each individual, whatever the dictates of his or her conscience, may only make the morally correct choice when choosing what the majority has willed. Because "equality" is understood in the plurality of individualities, the individual is held to be nothing more than a fungible component of the larger society—as one of the "masses." And just as a baker may form a mass of dough or a steelworker a mass of molten metal, each individual, as part of the "masses," is subject to such social manipulation by the state. This denial of the uniqueness of human identity and of human experience makes possible a social environment in which abortion, nonmarital cohabitation, and easy divorce are promoted as routine.

Here we find most starkly presented the contrast with the Judeo-Christian tradition that has unwaveringly asserted the uniqueness of creation: no two snowflakes are identical; no two human cells are identical; no two children are identical; no two married couples are identical; no two human families are identical.

Indeed, within the Christian tradition, it is the family that stands as the focus of the unique and unrepeatable act of creation; as John Paul II has stated, "it is the family that takes each man and woman out of anonymity, and makes them conscious of the personal dignity, enriching them with deep human experiences and actively placing them in their uniqueness within the fabric of society."[26] Equally important is the Christian development of our understanding of the integrity of the human *conscience*—a word that appears nowhere in the Old Testament, but approximately thirty times in the New Testament.[27]

Unlike Marxist societies, where the state asserts itself as the embodiment of morality, Western democracies have tended toward a different extreme of Enlightenment philosophy—the morally neutral state. This view of the state is also rooted in the Enlightenment's view of the human person, its rejection of the Christian recognition of "the createdness of nature," and its replacement of the moral natural law with the abstract state of nature.[28] Having lost a sense of the moral natural law and thus of a highest good to which the human person is directed by his nature, the morally neutral state deals with questions of justice in terms of social contract. George Parkin Grant observed that the influence of Immanuel Kant upon legal philosophy was to lead to "a sharp division between morals and politics."[29] As he explained,

> Properly understood, morality is autonomous action, the making of our own moral laws. Indeed any action is not moral unless it is freely legislated by an individual. Therefore the state is transgressing its proper limits when it attempts to impose on us our moral duties. . . . The state is concerned with the preservation of the external freedom of all, and must leave moral freedom to the individual.[30]

From this perspective, it is easy to see how in *Roe v. Wade* the Supreme Court judged the interest of personal choice to be paramount.[31] While the Court discussed abortion in terms of privacy, in reality the Court established a zone of autonomous decision making. The Court based its ruling in *Roe* that the child before birth was not a person and therefore not entitled to the protection of the law upon the assertion that government could not resolve the difficult question of when the life of a human being begins. However, in choosing to hear the appeal in *Roe* rather than the appeal of a case with a more developed trial record on the question of the biological humanity of the unborn child, the Supreme Court itself did much to foreshadow the outcome in *Roe*.

For example, on appeal before the Supreme Court there was also a case in which a New York State court upheld that state's newly enacted permissive abortion statute against a challenge that it denied unborn children their right to life. The New York court found "that upon conception a fetus has an independent genetic 'package. . . .' It is human . . . and it is unquestionably alive."[32] In spite of that factual record, the court nonetheless held that this "human entity" need not be recognized as a person or protected under the law. The court concluded that "[i]t is a policy determination whether legal personality should attach and not a question of biological or natural correspondence."[33] In *Roe v. Wade*, the Supreme Court held that this "policy determination" would pass from the legislature to the individual woman. Both court decisions portray different facets of a legal philosophy committed to a moral neutrality in matters of life and death, which, having rejected the natural law tradition, is now inadequate to protect fundamental human rights.

The Supreme Court's abortion jurisprudence has its roots in a case regarding the constitutional status of marriage decided only eight years earlier. In the 1965 case of *Griswold v. Connecticut*, the Supreme Court ruled that the State of Connecticut's ban on the use of contraceptives by married couples was unconstitutional.[34] Connecticut had defended its statute by asserting that the use of contraceptives, even in marriage, was immoral. The Supreme Court disagreed. In its opinion, defending the "sacred precincts of marital bedrooms" through a new right of privacy, the Court stated:

> We deal with a right of privacy older than the Bill of Rights—older than our political parties, older than our school system. Marriage is a coming together for better or for worse, hopefully enduring, and intimate to the degree of being sacred. . . . It is an association for as noble a purpose as any involved in our prior decisions.[35]

By placing marital activity within a newly defined constitutional zone of autonomous decision making, the Supreme Court sharply limited the authority of society to regulate marriage and nonmarital cohabitation.

Seven years after *Griswold*, the Supreme Court found in *Eisenstadt v. Baird*[36] that the "sacred precincts" of the marital bedroom recognized in *Griswold* were really no more sacred than any other bedroom. "Whatever the rights of the individual to access to contraceptives may be," wrote the Court, "the rights must be the same for the married and the unmarried alike."[37] If under *Griswold* the distribution of contraceptives to married persons cannot be prohibited, a ban on distribution to unmarried persons is equally impermissible. The Court reasoned:

> It is true that in *Griswold* the right of privacy in question inhered in the marital relationship. Yet the marital couple is not an independent entity with a mind and heart of its own, but an association of two individuals each with a separate intellectual and emotional make-up. If the right of privacy means anything, it is the right of the individual, married or single, to be free from unwarranted governmental intrusion into matters so fundamentally affecting a person as the decision to bear or beget a child.[38]

In *Griswold*, marriage was "a coming together . . . intimate to the degree of being sacred." It was the "sacredness" of the intimate relationship within marriage that required protection according to the Supreme Court, not the institution of marriage itself. As the Court later stated in *Eisenstadt*, such intimacy may occur outside the bonds of marriage. With the *Eisenstadt* decision, the Court began to "blur the distinction" between the legal institution of marriage and informal, non-marital cohabitation.[39] The fearful symmetry between life and death in the Court's abortion jurisprudence surfaced with equal force in its imposed neutrality between marriage and cohabitation in its marriage jurisprudence.

These changes in the law have not occurred without profound consequences for family life in the United States. First, the newly established constitutional right of privacy when combined with previously enacted "no-fault" divorce legislation radically changed many couples' expectations regarding marriage. A legal system that permits divorce at the will of either spouse does more than simply effect an easier exit from marriage. It changes the social "rules" for entry into marriage. A system of "no-fault" divorce rewards a spouse's commitment to individuality and the individual's good; it does not promote a commitment to the common good of the two spouses. Because a commitment to marriage is not protected by the "no-fault" legal environment, such a commitment is made solely at the spouse's own risk. Thus, the new legal framework actually enhances those tendencies that foster individuality and separation of the marital couple rather than tendencies that support unity and mutuality. Since the "no-fault" legal structure tells the marital couple to invest less in the marital community, it is not surprising that they increasingly expect—and get—less from it. With fewer legal, economic, and social returns from marriage, it is not surprising that more couples find less reason to stay married.[40]

While the Supreme Court's decisions in *Griswold* and *Eisenstadt* have been roundly criticized, supporters of the Court's decision in these cases continue to defend the "right of privacy." They even succeeded in denying confirmation of a critic of these decisions who was nominated to be an Associate Justice of the Supreme Court, in part because of his opposition to the Court's reasoning.[41] But in considering the institutions of marriage and family in light of the Constitution, it is not sufficient to speak simply of the "sacred precincts of the marital bedroom" or to praise marriage as an institution that is "intimate to the degree of being sacred." To view sexual intimacy or one's expectation of privacy associated with it as the defining characteristic of marriage is to misunderstand the precise point on which the unique position of marriage has been based within Western culture. This tradition has viewed matrimony as a natural institution that arises out of the concrete reality of the human person. It is an institution that has as one of its principal ends the good of the offspring. Procreation concerns more than simply the decision to bear or beget a child. It is also a commitment to the upbringing, education, and development of the child—a commitment in which the larger community has a vital interest. To reduce the procreative good of marriage to merely sexual activity is to fundamentally redefine the meaning of marriage. The institution of marriage has been legally protected by society not because of any "privacy" interest that the couple may have but because of a decision by the larger community that a stable, monogamous relationship is the preferred community to promote the good of children and of the spouses themselves. That is why once individuals have entered into this relationship, the tradition protected their expectation that the state must respect the intimacy of their married life.

The unique position of marriage in Western culture arose not only as a result of a more complete understanding of procreation but also as a consequence of the Judeo-Christian insight that the commitment of the spouses to one another was faithful and exclusive until death. This gift of one person to another within marriage, irrevocable in the canon law of the Roman Catholic Church and nearly irrevocable in civil law, distinguishes the married state from all other relationships. It is this commitment of the spouses to treat each other as irreplaceable and nonsubstitutable that is precisely denied by cohabitation outside of marriage. Sexual activity outside of marriage by its very nature communicates to the other that he or she is replaceable and that a substitute may be found. Outside the marriage bond or within a bond that may be easily dissolved, sexual activity ceases to be the unique gift of one person to another person.[42] The Western tradition, in holding that one of the principal ends of marriage includes the good of the offspring, developed through time a comprehensive legal structure around the institution of marriage and family life to protect not only the spouses themselves but also their children. That structure was based on the realization that there existed a profound connection between the begetting, nurturing, and educating of children. It was a legal structure founded upon a respect for the integral reality of the human person and upon the recognition that the marital community is not extrinsic to that reality but arises from it. That recognition has provided the best opportunity to protect the integrity of the human person while at the same time providing for genuine human fulfillment within the larger society. All too evident today is the fact that society rejects this insight at its own peril and at the peril of future generations. The task confronting the Christian today is the same as it was in Saint Paul's time: to communicate to those who "may not actually 'possess' the Law" how it is that the "the Law engraved on their hearts" may bear fruit in their lives.

Chapter **6**

EDUCATION

Robert A. Destro

Robert A. Destro is associate professor of law at the Columbus School of Law, Catholic University of America, where he also directs the Law and Religion Program. From 1983 to 1989 he sat on the United States Commission on Civil Rights, leading its discussions of discrimination on the basis of disability, national origin, and religion. He also serves on the executive committee of the board of directors of the Catholic League for Religious and Civil Rights. He has been an adjunct associate professor of law at Marquette University, before which he was engaged in the private practice of law in Cleveland, Ohio. He graduated from Miami University in Ohio and earned his law degree from the University of California at Berkeley.

James W. Skillen

James W. Skillen is executive director of the Association for Public Justice headquartered in Washington, D.C. He has written numerous articles and books, most recently *The Scattered Voice: Christians at Odds in the Public Square*. He coedited *Political Order and the Plural Structure of Society* and both translated and edited a new edition of Abraham Kuypers's *The Problem of Poverty*. He earned his Ph.D. at Duke University and has taught political science at Messiah, Gordon, and Dordt colleges.

Parental Choice and Educational Equity

Robert A. Destro

A BRIEF INTRODUCTION

Some fifteen to twenty years ago, a friend who was at that time an activist in the field of parental choice in a Midwestern state hosted a private dinner in her home for a former United States senator and his wife.

"Now tell me," said the senator's wife, "why is it that you Catholics want our tax money to educate your children?" The Senator nodded; for he too wanted to know the answer. My friend was a bit nonplused by the frankness of the question but was pleased nevertheless: it was the direct question for which she had been waiting for a long time.

"That's an easy one," she replied. "We don't want your money. We want some of *our* tax money to be used for the education of *all* the children in this state, including our own."

Her guests smiled politely—and dropped the subject. It was never raised again.

Such experiences, I believe, give Catholics a uniquely personal vantage point from which to view the issue of educational choice. I use the term *uniquely personal* for several historical and cultural reasons that will appear below; however, the Catholic perspective is neither distinctively different from that of other advocates of choice nor self-interested.

The point here is the political one made in 1963 by William Gorman, then a staff member of the Center for the Study of Democratic Institutions. Expressing "a vague discontent with [his] Conference billing, "A Catholic View," he reminded his audience that "though a Catholic viewer, what I am looking at, or for, is the structure and content of our constitutional consensus signable, so to speak, by all members of our body politic."[1] That point cannot be over-emphasized: educational choice is an issue of justice and equity for all Americans. The "religious" issue is a weapon employed by the opponents of choice in education

WHAT IS CHOICE IN EDUCATION?

From the perspective of the consumers (all parents, children, and taxpayers), education in the United States is not a matter of "choice": it is compulsory. Every state requires children to attend school and will prosecute parents who refuse or neglect to educate them.[2] Most States prescribe minimum standards for educational content, facilities, and teachers and will enforce them vigorously, though only selectively. There is growing political and professional support for early childhood education, and minimum educational and facility standards for day-care centers are a part of the same trend. The inevitable next step will be to debate whether to make both mandatory. Education programs concerning human sexuality, drug and alcohol abuse, AIDS prevention, the use and distribution of contraceptives, and a whole host of programs on other sensitive topics (most recently, "multi-culturalism"[3]) inevitably metamorphose from "experimental, pilot programs" to required courses.[4]

On a more tangible level, titanic political and judicial battles are fought regularly over mandatory student assignment plans. It matters little whether the issue is busing for school desegregation, a redrawing of district lines to reflect demographic change and diversity, or the availability (or lack thereof) of education for children with special needs: choice in education, or, more appropriately, lack of choice, is a perennial and sensitive issue. It has been for a long time.[5]

And last, but certainly not least, is the question of money. The cost of public education is borne by all the taxpayers, who have no more "choice" in the matter of making timely tax payments than the "choice" they will have in the face of death. Public education is big business but with one important difference: it has no competition. Neither taxpayers nor consumers can vote with their wallets; they pay anyway. Choice is "extra." Federal, state, and local government support for public education totalled $148.6 billion in 1986, an average of $3733.67 for each child enrolled in the public schools.[6] Private sector spending on non-public education during the same period amounted to $13.2 billion, an average of $2421.13 per child.[7]

Because education funding is the largest single item in the budget of most local governments and because the school system may often be one of the largest employers in a community, issues that affect either education funding or policy become political issues of the first order as their effect ripples through affected sectors of the community.[8] And as political issues they are subject to all of the factional cross-pressures, log-rolling, and legal disputes that affect other aspects of the political process.[9] From the perspective of those who provide and control public education, the range of permissible choice among legitimate alternatives is usually limited only by the amount of money available and what the political "traffic" will bear. Control within budgetary limits is virtually absolute.

Toss the concept of educational choice into this roiling cauldron of "hot" political and social issues, and the mixture becomes volatile indeed. *Fund* the choice, as the state of Wisconsin did for poor children in inner city neighborhoods, and it explodes.[10] The reason is as simple as it is straightforward. The debate is not really about "choice" at all; it is about *control*. Loss of students to the private sector means loss of the government's control over them and, more importantly, over the money the state allocates for their education. In 1988, the most recent year for which statistics were available, only 11.5 percent of school-age children attended non-public schools, and the National Center for Education Statistics projects about the same percentage through 1992.[11] Funded choice would inevitably cause that percentage to rise, but no one knows to what degree. At this point at least it is not the potential *size* of a competition fueled by pent-up parental demand[12] that bothers the educational establishment; it is the *concept* that there might be parental control and competition at all.[13]

This is why listening to and reading the debates over educational choice will leave the discerning reader with the impression that there is as much "choice" in selecting the appropriate meaning of the term "choice" as there is promise in the concept itself. It is only when an appropriate descriptive adjective defines the nature of the "choice" to be permitted that the contours of the debate—and its critical importance—becomes clear.

REAL VS. IMAGINED CHOICES:
THE POLITICS OF EDUCATIONAL FINANCE

What Are the Choices?

The right to a free public education is expressly provided in state constitutions,[14] and the right *not* to attend state schools has been held by the United States Supreme Court to be a component of the "liberty" protected by the Fourteenth Amendment to the Constitution of the United States.[15] As a result, the first choice is not *whether* to educate the children (that is already required) but how.

There are only two choices widely available: attend a school run by the government and funded by tax dollars or attend a school (including a home one) that is run and funded, either in whole or in part, by the private sector.[16]

Other forms of "educational choice"—neighborhood choice, inter-district choice, statewide choice, enrollment lotteries, and pairs, clusters, and magnet schools (to name only a few of the options)—are choices *within* a government-run, -managed, and -funded educational system. The debates over these choices also raise profound questions concerning the efficiency, equity, and effectiveness of state schools, but those questions are beyond the scope of this essay.[17] More pertinent is why from a Catholic perspective children have the right to utilize their fair share[18] of tax monies allocated for education in the manner best suited to their respective futures and why this should be a valid option for children in any community that is committed to education, freedom, pluralism, and democracy.[19]

The Nature of Parental Choice

Parents are obligated by law to assure, among other things, that their children attend school. Their obligation as parents, however, is far broader: they are bound, both morally and legally, to ensure that the best interests of their children are served by the educational choices which they, as parents, are empowered to make.[20] This is so because "[t]he child is not the mere creature of the State; those who nurture him and direct his destiny have the right, coupled with the high duty, to recognize and prepare him for additional obligations."[21] Any concerned parent will consider the range of legally available educational choices with a view toward what is best for the child and the family under the circumstances.[22]

Because parents who have no choice rarely feel any need to elaborate on the choices made for them, it may appear to some observers that, to the extent choice becomes an option, important choices will be made reflexively by parents who are not well-informed (or worse, do not care) about either the nature or the consequences over the short and long terms. The implicit paternalism of such predictions aside, the fact that there will be some parents who will not choose well underscores the nature of the dilemma facing those who advocate choice in education.

To the extent that options are limited, most parents will make rational choices within the range of permissible options.[23] If there are incentives or disincentives attached to choices within a permissible range, such factors will inevitably influence the choice made.[24] The passive appearance of a choice to an "objective" observer (a rare bird indeed), however, does not mean that it is either irrational or ill-informed; more information is needed. The Supreme Court of the United States recognized the sensitivity of such inquiries in *Wisconsin v. Yoder:*

> The unique role in our society of the family, the institution by which 'we inculcate and pass down many of our most cherished values, moral and cultural,' requires . . . sensitivity and flexibility [with respect] to the special needs of parents and children.[25]

Factors Influencing Parental Choice

THE FINANCIAL INCENTIVE TO CHOOSE PUBLIC EDUCATION

Since the factors involved in the choice between public and private education are so complex and vary from family to family, it may be useful to list some of the most important: location, safety, convenience, cost, overall quality, program content, culture, language, demographics, religion, family, history, teachers, and physical facilities. To the extent that there is a choice, families will engage in a fairly sophisticated trade-off, selecting among the available options in a manner that suits their respective needs, financial abilities, and aspirations.

But all things are not equal. There is a powerful incentive to choose education in the public sector: money. Children are entitled by state constitutions to a free and "uniform" education at public expense. (Whether they receive it or not is, of course, another question entirely.[26]) But there is a catch: in order to receive the benefit, one must make the "right" choice (i.e. a public school).

Such a dilemma raises a number of questions from the perspective of civil rights and constitutional law; for the question is no longer whether the state will provide free education but *to whom* that education will be afforded. The reason for the dilemma is generally ascribed simply to "public choice."[27]

But choices are not made in a vacuum. "Public choices," like their private counterparts, reflect the attitudes and, sometimes, the prejudices, of those who make them. In the context of educational choice, public choice is influenced by attitudes and prejudices concerning not only the relative importance of education, its goals, and content but also about the nature of the community at large, who shall be considered a member, and on what (and whose) terms.

NON-FINANCIAL INCENTIVES TO CHOOSE PUBLIC EDUCATION

Another fact rarely articulated but central to the debate over choice is that private education is not value-neutral. Neither is public schooling, nor should it be. Parents know this instinctively, and so do the school authorities.

By definition, education is not (nor can it be) simply the transmission of information. The courts have long recognized that education is a moral and cultural endeavor of the highest order, designed to mold the minds, bodies, and spirits of children and young adults. As a result, "every educational system has a moral goal that it tries to attain and that informs its curriculum. It wants to produce a certain kind of human being. This intention is more or less explicit, more or less a result of reflection; but even the neutral subjects, like reading and writing and arithmetic, take their place in a vision of the educated person."[28]

If a community elects to fund only education that is acquired in schools run by the government, it is making an implicit judgment concerning the moral environment necessary to a well-rounded education. At the same time, it limits the range of meaningful options available to parents who, for whatever reasons, may not share that vision. No longer may they choose on the basis of what environment is best for their children; they must make the initial decision in light of the powerful financial incentive to attend state schools. Unless resources or other benefits available in the private sector counterbalance this financial incentive, those for whom cost is a significant factor (i.e. most Americans) will receive great *community* pressure to choose a state school, and most families will make the only rational choice they can afford: a public school.

Once that step is taken, everything—books, teachers, curricula, facilities, and all other important components of education (including the school to which the child is assigned)—become matters of "public" rather than parental or private choice.[29] Even the possibility of choice within the public setting is limited by the politics of educational choice itself. The only real alternatives are to move to another city or town (i.e. public school "choice" funded by the parents), or to leave the system entirely by selecting a school that is not run by the government. For most parents, such a "choice" is no choice at all.

So why does the public choose only "public" education? Although they might choose a more "open" mix of public and private options if left to their own devices, the complicated and troublesome answer is that fear and misunderstanding often get in the way of the central task Americans have set out for themselves: building a vibrant, pluralistic society from the rich diversity of our people. (*E pluribus unum.*)

Factors Influencing Public Choice: The Common School and the Politics of Religion

The debate over parental choice in education is not a new one. Because of the role it plays in shaping the lives and beliefs of their children, parents have always been concerned about the nature and content of education; and from the time of the Pilgrims through the early 1800s, Americans looked, in part, to their churches to provide it. The first schools in what is now the United States were founded by Spanish Catholic missionaries in Florida and New Mexico between 1594 and 1630. The school of the Dutch Reformed Church and the Boston Latin School followed shortly thereafter in 1633 and 1635 respectively.[30] In the Colonies, which were overwhelmingly Protestant, education was officially Protestant as well, and remained unofficially so well into the twentieth century—one of the last vestiges of what Mark DeWolfe Howe has described as America's *de facto* establishment of religion.[31]

In those early years, both the churches and their educational efforts were funded by the community. James Madison's "Memorial and Remonstrance Against Religious Assessments"[32] was directed

163

against the collection of tax money "for teachers of the Christian religion," who would, of course, teach it from the perspective of the established Anglican church. That, in fact, was the problem and the essence of the push for the religious liberty guarantees of the First Amendment.

"Official" religion was often neither free nor tolerant of dissenters, and when the last established church in the United States lost its status in 1833, the equality of religious ideas before the law had taken a great step forward. Schools were open, and parents could choose freely among them. In New York, for example, a law passed in 1813 provided that the Free School Society (later the Public School Society) should allocate the educational funds at its disposal to, among others, "such incorporated religious societies in said city, as now support or hereafter shall establish charity schools within the said city, who may apply for the same."[33] But funded educational choice was not to last.

The development that eventually changed everything, including attitudes concerning the relationship of churches to schools, was immigration—specifically, immigration of Catholics. In 1790, Catholics numbered only about 35,000 out of a total population of over four million, and together, Catholics and Jews amounted to only about 0.1 percent of the population.[34] "The great Atlantic migration," first of the Irish, later of Germans and Scandinavians, and finally of Eastern and Southern Europeans, brought in over 40 million immigrants, including large numbers of Catholics with "foreign" ways, languages, and loyalties. For many, this was not a welcome development. Americans expressed their fears over immigration as early as the eighteenth century. In his notes on the state of Virginia, Thomas Jefferson referred to immigrants as a "a heterogeneous, incoherent, distracted mass" who would need to rid themselves of their old world ways if America was to prosper. Such views only grew in intensity in the nineteenth century.

The Rev. Lyman Beecher of Boston saw immigration as containing the seeds of "the conflict which is to decide the destiny of the West" and that it "will be a conflict of institutions for the education of her sons, for the purposes of superstition, or evangelical light; of despotism or liberty."[35] Catholics, because of their faith commitments, were not fit to be called "Americans" because they were "considered lower in the scale of mental cultivation and refinement than the Protestant . . . due to their being deprived of the Bible by their priesthood."[36]

To men like Beecher, it was clear that *something*, obviously, had to be done promptly. The logical answer was to "educate" them:

> If we do not provide the schools which are requisite for the cheap and effectual education of the children of the nation, it is perfectly certain that the Catholic powers of Europe intend to make up the deficiency, and there is no reason to doubt that they will do it, until, by immigration and Catholic education, we become to such an extent a Catholic nation, that with their peculiar power of acting as one body, they will become the dominant power of the nation.[37]

But there was, already, "cheap and effectual education" being provided at public expense by church-related schools and the newly established public schools. The problem, from the Catholic perspective, was that the newly established public schools "tended to be close copies of the Protestant schools they replaced." When they were unsuccessful in their attempts "to remove Protestant sectarianism from the public schools,"[38] Catholics began to request their fair share of the tax monies allocated to the schools of other religious organizations under the 1813 statute. The result was a change in the law of New York; under this new law funds were denied to any school that taught "sectarian doctrine" (i.e. Catholicism).[39]

One of the striking things about the politics of school choice is how it has changed since the ascendancy of the common school education reformers and how it has consistently feared that democracy and community will not survive if parents may freely choose among educational alternatives. Even though it was an article of faith in the early years of the republic that "schools and the means of education shall be forever encouraged" because "religion, morality and knowledge" were thought "necessary to good government and the happiness of mankind,"[40] *certain* religious beliefs were viewed as inimical to the common good and inconsistent with the mission of the schools.

To some in positions of political power, including Blaine and Grant, Catholicism, and to a lesser extent other minority religions, fit that description. Other "sectarian" practices, such as Bible reading and organized prayer, however, continued until well into the twentieth century.[41]

When the laws designed, in the words of the anti-Catholic propagandist Paul Blanshard, to prevent "[t]he capture of a public educational system" by the "Catholic hierarchy" for their sundry nefarious purposes[42] came to be used by Catholics and Jews to protect their own children enrolled in the public schools from being proselytized and trained in Protestant traditions, the fact that public schools "tended to be close copies of the Protestant schools they replaced" was forgotten. Such attempts proved, as it were, the un-American nature of those who objected; their valid religious concerns were cast aside as attacks on both Christianity itself[43] and "America's most treasured institution,"[44] the public school.

Anti-Catholicism, the official policy of all colonies but Pennsylvania (which nevertheless required religious oaths for public office, which were abhorrent to Catholics) and Rhode Island (where no Catholics were known to have lived),[45] was thus yoked together with nativism and fed fears that the immigrants would wreak havoc upon the economic and political life of those already here.[46] Educational choice simply had to be curtailed—or eliminated[47]—to guarantee that alien cultures and ideas would not survive the assimilation process. The Official Ballot Summary printed by the state of Oregon in preparation for the 1922 initiative that sought to eliminate all private schooling makes the point quite clearly:

> What is the purpose of our public schools . . . ? Because they are the creators of true citizens by common education which teaches the ideals and standards upon which our government rests. . . . Mix those with prejudices for a few years while their minds are plastic, and finally bring out the finished product—a true American. . . . Our children must not under any pretext, be it based upon money, creed or social status, be divided into antagonistic groups, there to absorb the narrow views of life, as they are taught.[48]

It is a story which those of us who the writers of that pamphlet would believe have "absorb[ed] the narrow views of life, as . . . taught" by our parents and clergy, are tired of hearing. Yet we hear the same old arguments today, dressed up to look a bit more inclusive, compassionate, and less xenophobic. Americans who desire to maintain a distinctive cultural or religious identity are just as much "true Americans" as those who do not or cannot.[49] Most immigrants, including my own grandparents, who make the effort to reach these shores (or cross the Southern border) are choosing to join the American experiment *because* it is *different* from what they left behind. There is no threat to pluralism because they bring cultural, religious, and linguistic baggage to their new home. The real threat arises because well-intentioned xenophobes and, more recently, hard-line advocates of cultural diversity do not know how to deal with them. A pluralistic democracy is a rich amalgam of different peoples, each with a unique cultural and religious heritage, contributing to the constant renewal of culture and freedom. Without them, the "American" culture we know today would not have been possible.

Penalizing the "Wrong" Choice:
Making Parental Choice a Lose-Lose Proposition

That the public schools have been an essential component in the building of the United States as it exists today is a given. No one really questions that fact or wishes it were not so. A position in favor of parental choice says nothing about either the intrinsic value of public schooling (which I wholeheartedly support) or the current value of the public schools as a force for positive change in society. The *only* thing to be said about public schooling in light of the controversy over parental choice is that public schools are not necessarily the best choice for everyone.

What is intriguing about the debates over school choice is how little attention is given to the issue of discrimination. After *Pierce v. Society of Sisters*,[50] parents had a constitutional right to make the choice not to send their children to a public school—if they were willing to pay for the alternative education. But as the law developed over the years, the implicit (and, sometimes, explicit) message handed down by the courts was that to exercise one's constitutional right to choose an education influenced by religion (any religion) was the wrong choice, both for the student and for society. Legislation that sought to lighten the burden of the choice was routinely struck down as an unconstitutional "establishment of religion." Opponents selectively cited the historical antipathy of the Virginia Founding Fathers to the support of religious education, even though the programs at issue bore little resemblance to the establishment problems the Virginians sought to remedy.

From the beginning, however, the controversy has been over public money, control and, most importantly, over whose children (and values) would be nurtured by its use. It is the same today.

The church-state cases decided by the Supreme Court of the United States to date make it clear that virtually all manner of educational benefits available to public school students, from maps to diagnostic services for children with special needs, can be denied to parents and school children who exercise their constitutional right to choose a non-public education.[51] One need not even show that educational funds were improperly used;[52] for the risk that someone might perceive a "symbolic" relationship of church and state is, for a majority of the Justices, too great.[53] Some simply prefer the public schools (Justice Powell, now retired, once led the Richmond, Virginia, school board); while others solemnly intone the words of Professor Paul Freund to the effect that it is better [for whom?] to deny equal treatment than to argue divisively in public over the allocation of tax funds.[54]

What the "danger" is, why it violates anyone's individual rights to pay their fair share of the educational tax burden,[55] and why the perception of the parents whose children are denied tax benefits—that the Congress and State Legislatures designed for all school children[56]—does not "count" in the constitutional calculus is never discussed. Like the senator's wife, sophisticated opponents of parental choice simply drop the subject. In October 1991, the less sophisticated among them forgot themselves and bought full-sized advertisements in the Washington, D.C. subway system, featuring pictures of Catholic Justices on the United States Supreme Court and a text that proclaims unless "Americans" are vigilant, Catholics (note the contrast) will take over.

Only in recent years, as religiously devout citizens of other Christian and non-Christian traditions have sought to make the public schools less antagonistic to their beliefs,[57] or to set up their own schools,[58] or to leave the educational system entirely,[59] have the historical complaints of observant Catholics and Jews been seen in a fresh light. As the public schools attempt, in their traditionally bureaucratic way, to comply with court orders designed to extirpate the last vestiges of Protestant Christianity from school buildings and curriculum,[60] the essential truth of Professor Allan Bloom's observation that "every educational system has a moral goal that it tries to attain and that informs its curriculum" is emphasized.

The public school system in the United States does "want to produce a certain kind of human being." Its "intention is more or less explicit, more or less a result of reflection" and clearly reflects "a vision of the educated person."[61] She is well-versed in multiculturalism; bilingual; well- informed and open-minded about sex

168

and sexuality; practices "safer sex"; does not use drugs, alcohol, or tobacco; and has been exposed to a modicum of science (especially evolutionary theory), history (except the parts about religion, though this is changing), social studies (including values clarification), and a bit of literature and math to round things out. The *only* things that person does not carry are two: *any* recognizably religious tradition or even an appreciation for the richness fostered by the myriad religious traditions that flourish in America. In a world where sex education is placed on a par with mathematics and given equal time in the schedule,[62] it is not surprising that the "educated person" might perceive religion as irrelevant at best and "divisive" and troublesome at worst.

Such a vision of the educated person is, in a heterogeneous society, an understandable one, though I do not share it. It is not, however, the only one or, more to the point, the only legitimate one.

And that, of course, is the point: if the Establishment Clause forbids anything, it is the anointing of any tradition, religious or secular, as the "official" dogma of the Republic. Parents, in short, must be free under the First and Fourteenth Amendments to choose for themselves and their children among the available and legitimate educational alternatives, without a financial inducement to make what the government perceives to be the politically or theologically "correct" choice at the moment. None other than Professor Laurence Tribe—no friend of funded parental choice in education[63]—describes the problem in the following terms:

> Whenever both religion clauses are potentially relevant,—the dominance of the free exercise clause follows from the principles underlying both clauses. For both clauses embody a broad concept of the relationship between religion and the state, which must be modified to adapt to changing conceptions both of religion and of government. If individuals and groups are to enjoy meaningful religious freedom, the protection afforded by the free exercise clause must vary with the extent of governmental regulation and subsidy in society generally. The opinions of the Framers offer general guidance, expressed in such core values as voluntarism and separatism. In the context of these general values, we must consider whether a nation committed to religious pluralism must, in the age of the affirmative state, make active provision for maximum diversity; we must ask whether, in the present age, religious tolerance must cease to be simply a negative

principle and must become a positive commitment that encourages the flourishing of conscience. Whenever tension is perceived between free exercise and non-establishment, " . . . a value judgment [is required] as to which is to become dominant . . . the one premised on a vital civil right, or the one premised on . . . eighteenth century political theory. The resolution [is] preordained— to pose the conflict is to resolve it." Even if one takes a more charitable view of the political theory underlying the opposed position, it seems doubtful that sacrificing religious freedom on the altar of anti-establishment would do justice to the hopes of the Framers—or to a coherent vision of religious autonomy in the affirmative state.[64]

While I do not agree with Professor Tribe's implicit view that all religious liberty interests can be subsumed under the rubric of individual "religious autonomy,"[65] I do agree that the type of autonomy involved here—that of parents to choose the value systems in which their children shall be raised—is consistent not only with a "coherent vision of religious autonomy in the affirmative state," but also it is consistent with the autonomy of all parents, who are charged in law and morality to protect and further the best interests of their children.

CONCLUSION

The argument made above is twofold, for it speaks of rights and duties. First, parents, as voters and taxpayers, are entitled as a matter of justice and equity to demand from their elected representatives the funds they need to educate their children to be good, productive citizens in a pluralistic democracy. That the public fisc cannot possibly meet the entire need is a given, and that painful choices must be made and priorities set in the process simply underscores the communitarian nature of the task. The books cannot be forever balanced on the backs of those who choose to exercise their constitutional right to select legitimate alternatives.

The duty component rests on the assertion that the community and its leaders must take responsibility for the public choices it has made, both present and past, which have inhibited the ability of parents and families who are members of identifiably religious, ethnic, and racial groups to make the same choices about educational values and environments that the community has made for the public schools. Recent studies by James Coleman show that, while the packaging and moral content of the education may be different in private schools, the commitment to diversity and democratic values is the same, if not stronger, than that found in their public counterparts.[66]

Knowledge of these facts—through academic study and personal experience as a Catholic child educated in Catholic schools through graduation from high school—is what, in the end, led me to agree to pen this essay "from a Catholic perspective." I can do so because, to borrow again the words of William Gorman, my argument rests squarely on "the structure and content of our constitutional consensus." And when the day comes that that consensus is "signable, so to speak, by all members of our body politic" parents will, after many years of waiting and discrimination, be free to choose what is best educationally for the children they love so much.

Parental Freedom
of Education Choice

James W. Skillen

Glowing pride and tearful dismay, liberating joy and devastating sorrow—these emotional extremes pull at the hearts of American parents today as they try to raise and educate their children. Good grades in school bring pride to all; a child's early distaste for learning produces sorrow. A developing talent that allows a child to go on to college or to successful employment gives a sense of liberating fulfillment; academic or social failure in school that may threaten a child's maturation can break a parent's heart.

Today, perhaps more than ever before, schooling appears to be both increasingly urgent and deeply troubled, both obviously essential and clearly problematic. Citizens and public policy makers look for ways to promote the schooling of young people in order to secure America's future. But how should they promote it, and what, precisely, should they promote? Who should do what kind of promoting? Who is best equipped to educate children? How should schools and teachers best complement and supplement the learning patterns and moral training children receive at home and in their neighborhoods? How can government's education policies do justice to all of America's parents, students, and teachers? How can schooling best assist the development of moral, economic, and civic life for each citizen?

These and thousands of other questions come to the fore if one looks seriously at the educational challenge that faces American society and its families. Yet there is no simple answer to the questions just posed. We live today in a social and political context

172

shaped by centuries of experimentation, policy making, and institutional development. Much of what exists is good and should be conserved; much is bad and needs to be reformed. But how do we sort out the good from the bad? How may we hold on to what is positive while genuinely overcoming what is negative?

To address even a few of these important questions one ought to present an argument that shows sensitivity to historical reality. One must help to dispel some of the perplexities and confusions we face and not simply spin out a yarn of wishful thinking or utopian expectations. Moreover, anyone who is concerned with the moral revitalization of American society must gain a clear understanding of the specific and differing responsibilities of families, governments, churches, voluntary agencies, schools, and other institutions. Realizing the need for this kind of serious reflection and argument, I want to make a case for the crucial importance of doing greater justice to America's parents and guardians who remain chiefly responsible for raising and overseeing the education of their children.

A BRIEF GLANCE BACKWARD

Schooling was not defined by constitutional mandate at America's founding. Two or three hundred years ago, education was not conceived strictly as either governmental or non-governmental, as either religious or non-religious, as either belonging to the family or belonging to the state. Common law and tradition, which reflected diverse educational patterns in families, schools, churches, and other agencies, ruled the day. Not until the ideas of Thomas Jefferson, Horace Mann, and others began to take hold in the 1840s did a system of government-run common schools start to dominate the American landscape.[1]

When European Catholic immigrants began to pour into Boston and New York in the 1840s, local and state governments decided it was time to organize schooling in a way that would help to solidify and promote a common culture. Over the next century and a half, a system of uniform, democratically mandated, bureaucratically governed schools came to be established. Cultural, religious, educational, and family differences were variously ignored, rejected, or celebrated depending on governmental decisions that reflected majority will and then, eventually, the Supreme Court's interpretations of the U.S. Constitution.[2]

In the nineteenth century, a white, Anglo-Saxon, Protestant (WASP) majority held an idea of society that led them to exclude Catholic schools from public recognition. The majority believed not only in the political principle of majority rule but also that some degree of cultural homogeneity is essential to the maintenance of a stable society. Therefore, as the majority turned over more and more responsibility for schooling to city and state governments, those governments moved to define Catholic schools as private, "sectarian" enterprises undeserving of public support because of their threat to the cultural homogeneity of a WASP society.

Catholic schools were not outlawed completely but were denied access to public funding and recognition. The consequence was that government gradually monopolized public funding and legal privilege for the benefit of a single system of schools, namely, the system run directly by the government itself. That system took as its purpose to train all children in a common way of life.[3]

The government-organized schools were called "public" because they were governed directly by public law as departments of either cities or states and were supported by public tax dollars. Catholic and other non-government schools, which the authorities defined as private or "sectarian," were allowed, for the most part, to govern themselves. Despite the fact that the non-government schools performed the same public service as did the government schools, they were permitted to exist only on the periphery of the public square so as not to interfere with the homogeneous common life of the majority culture. Catholics were, in essence, told that they could be citizens as long as their schools, like their churches, confined their activities to a private sphere and paid their own way. Consequently, Catholics were forced to separate their private, non-conforming lives from their civic lives.

At the time, the Protestant majority did not experience the same tension between their public and private lives because the Protestantism of the majority (including its King James Bible, moral codes, etc.) remained the dominant ethos of the so-called "nonsectarian" schools. Not until the 1960s did a growing number of Protestants begin to experience the exclusion that Catholics felt in the 1840s. The system of majoritarian school governance established by a WASP majority during the preceding century had become firmly entrenched. The dominant tendency was to define all traditional religious views as "sectarian." In the name of neutrality and "non-sectarianism" those older views had to be dismissed from the government's increasingly "secularized" school system.[4]

A major point to stress here is that the governance of American education from the 1840s on has manifested a highly restricted sense of justice controlled by the idea that government should act uniformly in accord with majority will to advance a culturally homogeneous *public* program for society. Anything not approved by public governance or that appeared to exhibit diversifying cultural or religious tendencies has had to be pushed into private space. The full reality of education—as it has actually taken place in diverse families, ethnic groups, churches, schools, and other distinctive circles of citizens—has consequently suffered maltreatment at the hands of public educational bureaucracies.

Anything not able to fit the majoritarian, homogenizing mold has had to be discounted or privatized and therefore either squeezed out of government-run schooling or redefined within those schools in ways that would accord with the governing will.[5]

Most Americans take the existing educational governance patterns for granted whether they like them or not. Those patterns are rooted in the conviction that the civic community is a simple republic whose members ought to govern themselves entirely through their representatives by majority will even while they agree not to tyrannize individuals and minorities in the legitimate enclaves of their private lives. Institutions such as families, non-government schools, voluntary associations, and churches are often, or usually, not recognized as having both a non-government character *and* a legitimate function in the public realm. The assumption underlying current patterns is that the public law may legitimately try to advance a general purpose of benefit without regard to the diversity of non-governmental institutions that might also be closely involved in that same public purpose. The civic community is conceived as a simple, homogeneous, single-willed (through majority) community, rather than as a pluriform, complex society in which government's actions should promote the *public* freedoms of diverse institutions and cultural traditions.

With respect to education these patterns have meant that the majority has often felt free to ignore or to overrule the desires for diverse schooling expressed by many families, churches, and non-government schools. When "the people" decide, through due process of law, to offer a public service, they simply assume that their actions are, by definition, good and legitimate since they reflect majority will. Whatever does not conform to the uniformly defined public educational purpose may then, with equal legitimacy, be eliminated or relegated to a private sphere. The central concept here is homogeneity of public life under government with an allowance for diversity and peculiarity outside the public domain.

Few in the 1840s imagined (and perhaps fewer today imagine) that the general public purpose of advancing education might be realized with much greater justice if the government's mandates and funding were to recognize the primacy of parental choice from among a diversity of school systems. Justice has been conceived too narrowly as the product of majority will that merely respects minority rights in private. Insofar as non-government institutions (such as families, churches, schools, and so forth) have exhibited diversity and/or dissented from the majority's decisions about schooling, they have suffered real injustice and discrimination in public life despite their supposed freedom in private. Protecting private freedom is not sufficient for the achievement of public justice. Not only have religious, philosophical, or cultural convictions of many citizens been thwarted; many citizens have also been put in the position of feeling alienated (to some degree) from the very democratic polity to which they belong. The simple majoritarian process, operating in a political system that aims for the homogeneity of the political community, leads to all-or-nothing decisions. The majority wins control of the public terrain; the minority loses and has to retreat into privacy.

A pluriform or pluralist conception of a democratic polity requires the adoption of quite a different posture when it comes to the governing of a complex society.[6] It is both more sensitive to the common law tradition and more alert to the fact that justice requires fair *public* treatment of the diverse, nonpolitical institutions in society and not simply the privatizing of everything that does not conform to the programs inaugurated by a governing majority will. Freedom for parents to relate the morality of their homes to the full process of educating their children requires, I believe, the public justice of a pluralistic framework of school governance.

DOING JUSTICE TO EDUCATION IN A COMPLEX SOCIETY

It is not hard to see that a society founded upon democratic governance should be concerned with the literacy and intelligence of its citizens. Enlightened self-rule is surely superior to self-rule that remains mired in ignorance. Moreover, if a democratic society is highly diverse and is being shaped by immigrants from many different cultural and linguistic backgrounds, one can see the wisdom of civic education that tries to give all citizens some knowledge of the republic they share in common.

However, when "the people" begin to legislate on matters of education, the complexity of society and of the educational process must be sorted out clearly if justice is to be done to all concerned. There is nothing inherent in literacy training and civic education, for example, that requires government itself to establish or control the agencies of schooling or to do all the educating of citizens. The fact is that schooling occurred for hundreds of years before government-run common schools were established. Moreover, basic literacy training and civic education are only part of what most schools and families want to provide for young students.

When government acts, its responsibility should be to do justice to its citizens. It must be able to answer questions such as: How should education be justly funded? For how many years of schooling should government subsidies (if any) be provided, and from where should those funds be derived? What is a just system for raising and distributing funds for schooling? Is it ever just for a government mandate or service to exclude anyone? Should schooling be required of every citizen by force of law or simply offered for those who want it? Should newer immigrants be given extra educational service if they start below the literacy level of natural-born citizens, or should a standard amount of schooling be offered to every person, regardless of the level at which he or she begins? What about the other institutions and agencies also concerned with education, such as families, non-government schools, churches, and voluntary associations? How can justice be done to all of them?

A utilitarian answer to these questions can never adequately address the demands of justice. To say, for example, that it is better to provide schooling for some citizens (instead of offering nothing) even if everyone cannot benefit, is to leave open entirely the question of whether it is just to educate some but not all citizens. To argue that government should do something to provide a greater good for a greater number says nothing about the justice of leaving some people at a disadvantage if education is not provided for them or if the means of providing the education is inequitable in one way or another. If an educational effort is to be initiated by government, its *just* character is of preeminent importance. And the demands of justice must be met by the *manner* in which government deals with all citizens and institutions of society, not simply by the fact that it is able to muster a majority vote.

One of the convictions underlying this essay is that justice has not yet been done to the citizens of the United States in regard to education, and one of the chief reasons is that parental responsibility has not yet been given its proper due.

TOWARD A SYSTEM OF FREEDOM
WITH JUSTICE IN EDUCATION

Taking into account the various elements discussed above, I am driven to the conclusion that a fundamental, pluriform transformation of the structure of American schooling is urgently needed.[7] Such a change is fully compatible with our constitutional system of government, including the U.S. Constitution's First Amendment, though such change will challenge the way the First Amendment has been interpreted by some members of the Supreme Court since the 1940s.[8] The changes required to do justice to all parents and children can be achieved by means of simple legislation at state and federal levels that will, however, in all probability, require changes in many state constitutions. The legislative and state constitutional changes will also have to be backed up by revised Supreme Court rulings. If the Supreme Court continues to stand opposed to the reasoning offered here, then a federal constitutional amendment may be necessary.

What will comprise a just system of education in which parental responsibility is finally given its due?

First, the obligations presently resting on parents or guardians (the principal parties accountable for minors) should henceforth be upheld in a non-discriminatory fashion. For example, to the extent that states, for legitimate civic reasons, mandate education for all children, they ought to allow, without any legal or financial discrimination, parental choice of the *means* of schooling, since parents, not the state, hold the principal responsibility for raising children and overseeing their education. Among other things, such non-discrimination entails a proportionately fair investment of public educational dollars in every child. Even among government-controlled schools today there is a highly inequitable distribution of educational tax dollars because of the residential, district basis of taxation and school funding. But in addition, the highly inequitable distribution of tax dollars that favors government-run schools only aggravates the injustice. The way to redress these financial inequities is to set up a new system of statewide (or even nationwide) distribution of education dollars to each school-age child (whether directly or indirectly) regardless of the school he or she attends. Whether the tax monies are raised through a property tax or some other means, the distribution should *not* be made on the basis of the residential neighborhood of the child as is now done. And since religious and other conscientious convictions of parents and their children ought to be respected under the First Amendment, governments have no right to mandate the education of all children and then to discriminate financially against those tax-paying citizens who choose religiously qualified schools for their children's education.[9]

Fairness and equity certainly may justify discrimination in some cases of funding. For example, handicapped or learning-disabled children may require a proportionately larger expenditure if they are to receive the same level of schooling. High school education costs more than elementary education, so a greater proportionate investment can be justified there. But beyond these and many similar reasons for proportional discrimination, there can be no justification for discrimination simply because of skin color, religious conviction, or differing pedagogical methods and philosophies of education that parents freely choose.

The First Amendment ought to be interpreted to protect each citizen's freedom to exercise his or her religious convictions without inhibition by government except where government must act to protect the lives, liberties, and properties of all citizens. If, for reasons of conscience, some parents feel compelled to educate their children in Catholic, or Protestant, or Jewish, or Muslim, or other faith-guided schools, then the First Amendment's protection of their religious freedom should also govern the distribution of public education dollars so as not to discriminate against them. Once we recognize that it is not necessary for government to own and run all the agencies of education, then government's support of a variety of different school systems can be recognized as completely compatible with First Amendment requirements. The danger to the First Amendment arises when government puts its financial and legal support behind only one system of schools to the exclusion or disadvantage of others. That is the error that currently predominates.[10] Whether 5 percent or 95 percent of public funding goes to support religiously oriented schools, no infringement of the First Amendment's Establishment Clause exists as long as those schools are freely chosen by citizens without either compulsion or special privileging by government. Articles in many state constitutions that prohibit aid to religious schooling represent an unjust attack on the very meaning of the First Amendment.[11]

The question of racial, cultural, and gender discrimination can also be met by means of the same pluriform openness to parental choice in education. As long as no child is excluded from equal educational opportunity, and as long as equitable funding follows every child to the school of choice, then government need only watch to protect the pluriform openness of the public terrain. If all parents and educators are free to choose and to establish schools of every variety—Montessori schools; schools with classically oriented curricula; Asian, Latin, European, or other culturally unique schools; religiously and philosophically distinct schools; and so forth—then no one suffers discrimination simply because different schools have different degrees of particularity and exclusivity. Government should indeed act to ensure that every child has access to adequate schooling, but its actions should encourage the opening of pluriform opportunities rather than hamper diversity in an attempt to force some kind of homogeneous public conformity.[12]

Certain kinds of public, legal requirements binding on all parents and schools can be perfectly compatible with a pluriform system of school choice. For the sake of civic well-being and fairness toward every citizen, there is no reason why governments may not require a certain level of competence in English from children at different age levels, or a certain level of competence in basic civic knowledge. But these public mandates laid on all parents alike can be met by any number of means—in schools, at home, or by special tutoring agencies. Government's right to issue mandates for the protection and enhancement of the public welfare needs to be carefully distinguished from its right to own and operate educational agencies. The former does not grant a right to monopoly control of the latter. Basic linguistic and math skills, civic knowledge, and other educational achievements have been nurtured in America by Catholic, Jewish, Protestant, and other nongovernment schools for more than two centuries. Those skills can continue to be nurtured in a wide variety of schools equitably and proportionately supported by public funds.

A pluriform system that does full justice to parental choice can also do greater justice to educators, schools, tutoring programs, and more. There is no constitutional or other argument from justice that says government should be allowed to privilege its own agencies of schooling to the disadvantage of other agencies run by churches, parent associations, and independent educators. Once the distinction between state and society is made and once the distinction between governments and schooling is accepted, then government's ability to treat all parents and schools fairly becomes possible. Governments will always need to make laws to protect the public, and they may need to do many things in order to promote an educated citizenry. But all such actions should be based on prior foundations of justice that recognize the independence of families and schools. Government's consequent actions to promote the public good should build on the recognition of the right of parents to choose schools for their children without any financial or legal discrimination.

Chapter **7**

HIGHER EDUCATION

George C. Fuller

George C. Fuller has recently served as president of Westminster Theological Seminary, where he is now professor of practical theology. (This seminary, located in Philadelphia, affirms the inerrancy of the Bible and is committed to historic Reformed theology.) He previously served as a pastor in Maryland, Minnesota, Alabama, and Massachusetts. He has written articles on South Africa, on a ministry of mercy, on time management, and on other subjects.

Russell A. Kirk

Russell A. Kirk, president of two educational foundations and editor of the quarterly *University Bookman*, is the sole American to hold the highest doctoral degree of the senior Scottish university, St. Andrews. He is the author of thirty books, among them *The Conservative Mind* and *Eliot and His Age*. He was the only man of letters awarded the Presidential Citizens' Medal by President Ronald Reagan.

Evangelical Higher Education

George C. Fuller

Job's prayer (Job 3) falls into a convenient but dismal outline: "Why was I ever conceived, why did I have to be born, and why can't I die now?" You can recall the geometrically cumulative causes of his pain: his children killed, his home destroyed, his business lost, his faith severely challenged.

His smug, theologically precise friends knew he must have committed some grievous secret sin; why else would God bring such suffering? Job knew of no such sin. So his greatest agony was religious, spiritual, theological—"God, I have served you; now for no justifiable reason your archers all aim at me. God, you seem so distant. Don't you care? Is there no one to act as a mediator between us?"

Out of the depths of his pain come the words of Job 28, a prologue for Christian education. Job's topic is wisdom, not information or knowledge or skill. He seeks wisdom for life, for living, wisdom touching pain and suffering, even death, and God.

Job has earned the right to be heard today. He first speaks of the great technological achievements of his time (Job 28:1–11), including vast excavations, extensive mining enterprise, and the building of great dams. Introduce only a few minor changes in Job's words, and his comments look like a summary of modern industrial accomplishments.

All of man's works bring him no answer to the question that Job addresses in 28:12–22: "But where can wisdom be found?" (NIV). The peoples of this earth have found the iron, the silver, the gold. They dig deeper and go higher, but they are no closer to wisdom, not wisdom for life, not the wisdom Job was seeking. They make many discoveries but are no wiser. They gather facts and information, but they wage battles against their brothers and against themselves. They see themselves at the center of a limited universe and exclude God from their formulations. Even if they were inclined to do so, they could search everywhere, offer to pay any price, and never gain wisdom. "It is hidden from the eyes of every living thing, concealed even from the birds of the air" (Job 28:21 NIV).

Wisdom is to be found in God, nowhere else. "God understands the way to it, and he knows its place" (Job 28: 23 RSV).What then are humans to do? They must heed the admonition of God himself: "The fear of the Lord—that is wisdom" (Job 28:28 NIV). However far they may think that they have advanced, they will find wisdom only as they recognize their own weaknesses and sin and then come to worship in gratitude and praise before the God of creative majesty and forgiving grace. "The fear of the LORD is the beginning of wisdom" (Ps. 111:10 NIV).

In the book of Proverbs, wisdom speaks: "The Lord brought me forth as the first of his works, before his deeds of old; I was appointed from eternity, from the beginning, before the world began" (8:22–23 NIV). Wisdom existed with God before creation and was described as virtually having its own personal identity.

The Christian's wisdom is Jesus Christ. Ultimately Job's lament ("If only there were someone to arbitrate between us, to lay his hand upon us both" [Job 9:33 NIV]) and his exaltation of wisdom find their fulfillment in the life and death of the Son of God. "Jews demand miraculous signs and Greeks look for wisdom, but we preach Christ crucified: a stumbling block to Jews and foolishness to Gentiles, but to those whom God has called, both Jews and Greeks, Christ the power of God and the wisdom of God. . . . We speak of God's secret wisdom, a wisdom that had been hidden and that God destined for our glory before time began. None of the rulers of this age understood it, for if they had, they would not have crucified the Lord of glory" (1 Cor. 1:22–24, 2:7–8 NIV).

The Lord Jesus is before all that was created and was indeed the agent of the Father in creation. "He was with God in the beginning. Through him all things were made; without him nothing was made that has been made" (John 1:2–3 NIV). If we understand Jesus to be wisdom for the Christian, specific content follows.

John Henry Cardinal Newman, for example, understood Catholicism to teach "the ruined state of man; his utter inability to gain

Heaven by anything he can do himself; the simple absence of all rights and claims on the part of the creature in the presence of the Creator; the illimitable claims of the Creator on the service of the creature; the imperative and obligatory force of conscience; and the inconceivable evil of sensuality." He saw it as teaching "that no one gains Heaven except by the free grace of God, or without a regeneration of nature; that no one can please Him without faith. . . ."[1]

Given these predispositions, Christians see God as not only alone all-powerful and all-knowing, but as gracious in mercy toward his people, all those who by faith seek to please him. The proper posture then is to understand the universe, every known and undiscovered fact, all of life as under the creation and sustaining providence of God. And for Christians, the position of Jesus is focal; concerning him, Paul wrote, "He is before all things, and in him all things hold together" (Col. 1:17 NIV).

Understanding creation, man bows before the Creator. Acknowledging the law's demands, unbelievers repent in contrition. Recognizing the grace of God in the person of Jesus, they humble themselves before the Cross of Jesus. Wisdom accepts the ultimate autonomy of only one, God, and will not share in the arrogance of any educational process that sees man as the beginning or end of that endeavor. Newman said, "Such, I say, is the theological method, deductive."[2]

For Christians, the role of Scripture is critical. They see it as God's written and authoritative word. Newman again wrote, "What is known in Christianity is just that which is revealed, and nothing more; certain truths, communicated directly from above, are committed to the faithful, and to the very last nothing can really be added to these truths. From the time of the Apostles to the end of the world no strictly new truth can be added to the theological information which the Apostles were inspired to deliver."[3] The evangelical understands Jesus to be the Living Word and the Bible to be God's authoritative word of revelation concerning his Son.

A radical choice must be made, one that may cause discomfort. In the educational process, are humans the servants of their Creator and Redeemer, or are they autonomous, to be measured by their own accomplishments and potential? The universities in Augustine's two cities operated under diametrically opposed presuppositions. He divided the human race "into two parts, the one consisting of those who live according to man, the other of those

187

who live according to God. And these we may also mystically call the two cities, or the two communities of men, of which the one is predestined to reign eternally with God, and the other to suffer eternal punishment with the devil."[4] Can we reasonably imagine a third university established in the empty desert between the two cities, that is staffed by visiting faculty members from each city? Cornelius van Til, professor at Westminster Seminary for more than fifty years, wrote,"The Christian . . . will not obscure the line of demarcation between that culture which is the expression of darkness for all its seeming brilliance and gaudiness, and that culture which is the expression of the kingdom of light, however insignificant it may seem to be. To grasp for culture without Christ, is to lose culture as well as Christ."[5] Christian education takes place under God, the Creator and Redeemer; other education finds an invalid unity for the maze of facts confronting it, or falls into ultimately confusing subjectivism or relativism.

The environment in which Christian higher education takes place is Jesus Christ, the Christian's wisdom. He is not the subject alone of isolated courses or lectures or chapels. He is not apparent only on the crucifix in each room. He is the Creator and Sustainer of every person, every fact, every relationship among facts. For example, "the mathematician should work for the glory of God. He should praise God for the beauty and usefulness that he finds in mathematics, for the incomprehensible nature of God which it displays, for the human mind which God has enabled to understand mathematics."[6] The study of aesthetics and zoology is cause for praise, as beauty and life find their origin and ultimate purpose in God's wisdom. "The real distinctive [of Christian education] is a holistic integration of faith and learning, an active penetration of all the disciplines and all life's callings with the beliefs and values that make up a Christian worldview."[7]

In higher education, Christians may find and prepare for careers. Vocational choice is not made in a vacuum but in Christ Jesus. "To become self-consciously and therefore intelligently Christian requires one to become aware of the nature of Christ's person and work, and then to relate one's own work to that of Christ."[8] Christians will prayerfully evaluate their gifts and abilities in order to offer their best to the church and the world for useful service. Christians know that fulfillment is not found in seeking higher education alone but in serving the Lord. As they delight themselves in the Lord, he will give them the desires of their heart

(Ps. 37:4). In education and career, Christians live and move and breathe in Christ (Acts 17:28). Whatever they do, they should work at it with all their heart, as working for the Lord, not for men, since they know that they "will receive an inheritance from the Lord as a reward" (Col. 3:23–24 NIV).

Christian higher education prepares leaders for the church, both lay and clergy. Their service may be in the church and to the world, in the latter case in the verbal sharing of the gospel or in giving a cup of cold water in the name of Christ. Because Christians serve in varied fields, Christian higher education develops wisdom for professions and trades (Ex. 35:35) and wisdom to administer justice fairly (1 Kings 3:28). True Christian education gives instruction in the moral demands of God, specifically understood in the context of the Christian's relation to Jesus, and then says to its students, "Observe them carefully, for this will show your wisdom" (Deut. 4:6 NIV).

Christians are to be Christ in the world, ministering to those who sin and to those who suffer because of the sin of others. The Bible speaks of "a new creature in Christ Jesus" (2 Cor. 5:17 KJV), and we can assume for Christians a different motivation, a different attitude from those of the non-Christians. The kingdom of God is like yeast that works "all through the dough" (Matt. 13:33), and the subjects of that kingdom, those who worship King Jesus, influence the world they contact, sometimes quietly, slowly, gradually for the cause of Christ. Their "attitude[s] should be the same as that of Christ Jesus: Who, being in very nature God, did not consider equality with God something to be grasped, but made himself nothing, taking the very nature of a servant, being made in human likeness. And being found in appearance as a man, he humbled himself and became obedient to death—even death on a cross" (Phil. 2:5–8). Wisdom for living is to have the mind of Christ. Those who praise and thank God for his gracious mercy in Jesus will humbly seek to do that which benefits others, obey the Father's will, and demonstrate their aliveness in Christ Jesus. Christians may fail, even seriously, and may act in a manner that is contradictory to this high calling, but they continue to respond appropriately to God's love in Christ, which is in no way earned. "God demonstrates his own love for [them] in this: While [they] were still sinners, Christ died for [them]" (Rom. 5:8 NIV).

The Christian mindset has a foundational base of moral values. These are derived from faith in and commitment to God as both

Creator and Redeemer. God's creative act in forming man and woman and their high calling under God set an utmost value on each human being. Therefore the act of murder is wrong: "Whoever sheds the blood of man, by man shall his blood be shed; for in the image of God has God made man" (Gen. 9:6 NIV). In the Sermon on the Mount Jesus spoke of his "fulfilling the law" (Matt. 5:17 NIV), perhaps meaning that he "fills it full with new meaning" for the Christian: "You have heard that it was said to the people long ago, 'Do not murder, and anyone who murders will be subject to judgment.' But I tell you that anyone who is angry with his brother will be subject to judgment" (Matt. 5:21–22 NIV). The mind of Christ, being formed in the Christian, does not permit anger toward others and knows that the setting of moral values and the exhibition of proper moral behavior originate in God's creative act and are implemented through people whose world-view has been radically changed. No longer self-centered, they seek to demonstrate the kind of love with which they have been loved by God, love for the unlovable, the difficult-to-love, the needy, the lost. The apostle John wrote, "This is love: not that we loved God, but that he loved us and sent his Son as an atoning sacrifice for our sins. Dear friends, since God so loved us, we also ought to love one another" (1 John 4:10–11 NIV).

Christian higher education begins with the Creator and His revelation in the written and living Word. Its first task therefore is to distinguish between that which is ultimately "given" (for example, the teaching of Scripture) and what may be our uncertain understanding of a portion of Scripture. But with the foundation of the authority of Scripture in place and affirmed, the Christian can then explore anywhere in the universe of available and potential knowledge. "The aim of Christian education is . . . to assist individuals to discover and develop a sense of competence and to dedicate that competence to the service of God and of men in the name of Christ."[9] In doing so, individuals fear no contradictions because the foundation and all facts (at present whether known and unknown) are part of the truth of God. Cardinal Newman spoke to this point: "I say that we may wait in peace and tranquility till there is some real collision between Scripture authoritatively interpreted, and results of science clearly ascertained, before we consider how we are to deal with a difficulty which we have reasonable grounds for thinking will never really occur."[10] Under God, human beings inquire freely into the universe of created facts. Recognizing Jesus as the gift of God's love and the wisdom of God, they learn the will of God which their new hearts yearn to find and obey.

The emphasis in Christian higher education is on predisposition, disposition, the heart, the will, the inner self. While Christian higher education operates on a firm and given foundation and teaches on that basis, indoctrination is useless. The basic issue is the student's prior commitment to the God of creation and redemption. When that factor is in place, derivatives of that wisdom find their place. Indoctrination is the pointless cacophony of details beating on a deaf heart. While imposed moralistic standards may organize some behavior, the result cannot be called Christian. The Lord said, "These people come near to me with their mouth and honor me with their lips, but their hearts are far from me. Their worship of me is made up only of rules taught by men" (Isa. 29:13 NIV). Evangelism and nurture are therefore proper but clearly separate activities in Christian education. The Christian teacher "frankly begins with the presupposition of the absolute truth of the Christian position. It is this that the teacher tells the pupil."[11] But the wisdom of God must first find root in the heart. Harsh prodding and pushing clearly display error of two kinds: a contradiction of Christian spirit toward others and a denial that the power to effect the required radical change is God's alone.

Christian higher education affirms certain presuppositions about God and man. One of its tasks is to challenge an educational system that is founded on contradictory assumptions. Of course, the confrontation must be done in humility (or the gospel is misunderstood), and it must be done with sensitivity (or our calling in Christ is contradicted). But, given the Christian's posture and, indeed even more importantly, given his love for those who do not comprehend theocentric life and thought, he must speak. So he asks the non-Christian system: "What presuppositions do you make, or do you suppose yourself to begin with a 'clean tablet'? Do you still think you can work in a value-free environment; can such an atmosphere exist, or, like a vacuum, does it soon fill with some material? Is a genuine liberalism possible, one that can even admit the possibility of the Christian theistic position, or are Newman's words too threatening?

> Admit a God, and you introduce among the subjects of your knowledge, a fact encompassing, closing in upon, absorbing, every other fact conceivable. How can we investigate any part of

an order of Knowledge, and stop short of that which enters into every order? You will soon break up into fragments the whole circle of secular knowledge, if you begin the mutilation with divine.[12]

Where does Christian higher education take place? We recognize that not all evangelicals or their institutions, perhaps only very few, will agree with the distinctions drawn above. And it should be further admitted that Christians and their work may only imperfectly achieve goals upon which they place the highest value. But it is still reasonable to ask: Where are we likely to find evangelical higher education?

We might look first to colleges committed to a distinctively evangelical posture. A Carnegie Commission report affirmed in 1972 that since the founding of Harvard "Protestants have established well over 1,000 colleges."[13] But at Dartmouth College, for example, the early motto (*vox clamantis in deserto*, "a voice crying in the wilderness") now better describes a mission *to* the college than the intended mission *of* the college. Today perhaps 800 colleges affirm some degree of church or religious identity,[14] but their levels of commitment to evangelical education very widely.

The Christian College Coalition, founded in 1976, is an association of more than 80 evangelical colleges and universities. Among its shared commitments, these are listed first: "an institutional commitment to the centrality of Jesus Christ to all campus life, integration of biblical faith with academics and student life, hiring practices that require a personal Christian commitment from each full-time faculty member and administrator, accreditation and primary orientation as a four-year liberal arts college." A reasonable expectation is that these institutions, and perhaps many others, strive toward academic excellence and spiritual approval in integrating the education of their students under the lordship of Jesus Christ.

Bible colleges are increasingly offering liberal arts majors, but their primary objective continues to be to prepare students for Christian ministries and church-related vocations. More than 90 (of an estimated total of 400) such institutions in the United States and Canada are members of the Accrediting Association of Bible Colleges, whose "Tenets of Faith" are closely parallel to the Apostles' Creed and the posture of many of the evangelical colleges. That position is also a summary of *The Fundamentals, a Testimony to the*

Truth, a series of books published between 1901 and 1915 and from which the word *fundamentalism* came.

Approximately one-half of the member colleges in AABC are also regionally accredited, a sign of significant academic progress. While their mean full-time enrollment is only 300, more than 75 percent of all Protestant missionaries in the world over the past 100 years have come from Bible colleges. Their work represents both the beginning and the continuation of evangelical revival so visible in many parts of the world today.

Although the Bible college understands itself to be career oriented, the very high level of student and faculty commitment to the lordship of Christ and the authority of Scripture forms a basis for mature understanding of God as Creator and Redeemer. Indeed, among the criteria for accreditation in AABC is this statement: "Students should not only gain a broad knowledge that will engender awe for the Creator but also be equipped with an understanding of the presuppositions which form the basis of the world view held by those to whom they are called to minister."

A third environment for evangelical higher education is graduate study in Christian institutions. Many of the colleges mentioned above have master's level programs, and some doctoral programs exist. But the dream of "a Christian university," nourished through recent decades, has not come to reality. Specifically evangelical graduate study is therefore scattered among many of these institutions.

Graduate study at evangelical theological seminaries must be recognized as an important factor. An informal list of seminaries whose executives have formed an "evangelical fellowship" includes 55 such institutions, with a total enrollment of 21,976; not included are many evangelical students who are preparing at other seminaries. The evangelical seminaries in view are graduate schools, offering a variety of master's level degrees and specialized doctoral study.

Fourthly, and importantly, Christian higher education is taking place on campuses where the atmosphere is hostile to the gospel cause. Christian professors at secular universities are bearing testimony in their fields of expertise, to whatever degree that is possible. Churches and parachurch organizations (like InterVarsity) help students to understand their education in the Christian context. Capable men and women are preparing themselves through graduate study to serve as faculty members in secular situations, in order to show that ultimately Jesus is wisdom. In these kinds of contexts, the Christian's vulnerability is obvious; that recognition can enhance his or her growth toward maturity.

Finally, the kind of higher education that was described above is being fostered and nourished in worship, in small groups, through personal study and through committed service. The ultimate goal is to understand and worship Jesus as Lord of all—all fields of study, all facts of knowledge, all believers' lives. So in their callings and careers, whether as clerks or corporate executives, or even as clergymen, Christians must always seek the implications of life under King Jesus, the wisdom of God.

Christian higher education has to do with priorities:

How much better to get wisdom than gold, to choose understanding rather than silver (Prov. 16:16 NIV).

You are in Christ Jesus, who has become for us wisdom from God—that is, our righteousness, holiness and redemption. Therefore, as it is written: 'Let him who boasts boast in the Lord' (1 Cor. 1:30–31 NIV).

The State of Catholic Higher Education

Russell A. Kirk

Writing in 1862, Orestes Brownson—the most eminent American Catholic layman of his day—expressed his dissatisfaction with Catholic colleges and schools. But he hoped strongly for widespread improvement, in the dawning age:

> Then our schools will send out living men, alive with the love of God and of man,—men of large minds, of liberal studies, and generous aims,—men inspired by faith and genius, who will take the command of their age, breath their whole souls into it, inform it with their own love of truth, and raise it to the level of their own high and noble aspirations. . . . Let us console ourselves for what Catholic education now is with what it may become, and with what we may by well-directed effort aid it in becoming.[1]

In 1862, there existed five Catholic universities in the United States—Georgetown, Fordham, Notre Dame, Villanova, and Holy Cross; only Georgetown had been founded before 1840. Catholic University of America would not be established until a quarter of a century after Brownson published his essay "Catholic Schools and Education," quoted above. Catholic colleges were growing in number, but Brownson had good reason for his strictures on the quality of the higher learning in its Catholic aspect.

In 1949, during a period of great apparent prosperity for Catholic universities and colleges in the United States, Father Leo R. Ward of the University of Notre Dame published his book *Blueprint for a Catholic University.* Father Ward, a learned and kindly professor of philosophy, was no more satisfied with such institutions than Orestes Brownson had been. In both secular and Catholic universities, he found methods had been emphasized, but ends had been forgotten. Catholic higher education had not escaped such confusion about goals and methods and materials. Why not? For two main reasons:

> First, they could not totally escape being influenced by the environment in which they lived. . . . Secondly, as a matter of fact they have in many matters been followers of non-Catholic schools, letting others set standards for them, and these lead-standards, amounting sometimes to ends and sometimes in sum to the formal principle of the educational order, have to some degree been un-Catholic and never, at their very best, genuinely and vitally Catholic.[2]

During the late forties and the fifties, Catholic universities and colleges grew tremendously in enrollments and benefactions. Many brand-new colleges sprang up, mushroomlike: in Erie, Pennsylvania, alone five Catholic colleges were created during this period, only one of them surviving to the present day. Enrollment of veterans of the Second World War accounted for part of this growth; also those years were a sanguine time, and the Catholic Church in the United States seemed confident and secure. But Father Ward perceived the weaknesses behind the handsome facade:

> The real problem of the Catholic schools comes from the fact that they have settled in many matters for the mediocre: merely trying to keep up, not to get behind, not to lapse from being accredited. . . . Sometimes even this is a great trial. Moreover, they have taken as end simply to keep the faith, not to build or rebuild kingdoms, but to hold on, to see themselves as frankly only in a state of siege, where defending the walls is the whole problem.[3]

Just so; yet in 1992 many Catholic scholars would rejoice if somehow it were possible to restore Catholic education to the condition, however imperfect, in which it stood during the late forties and the fifties. With vertiginous speed, the whole Catholic apparatus seems to have almost dissolved in America since Vatican II. A good many Catholic colleges have gone down to dusty death; many or most of the survivors—some 230 Catholic universities or colleges—have made such concessions to the world, flesh, and the Devil as to imperil their title of "Catholic" nowadays.

The Catholic college nearest to me is a sufficient example of this trend. Three decades ago this was a sound Dominican institution with a highly intelligent monsignor as president. When he left office, the order of nuns to whom the college belongs brought in a lay president, a boomer type, who literally cast out of doors the handsome statue of Saint Thomas Aquinas. (Some drunken students, coming upon this displaced personage, flung the statue into a stream, where it disintegrated.) After a few years in office, this progressive president chose as commencement speaker—over the protest of many members of the staff—a black female politician who ardently advocated abortion-on-demand. The bishop, although latitudinarian in much, resigned from the college's board in protest against this choice. When the black politician (non-Catholic) delivered her commencement address, she denounced the bishop. Since then, this college—now mostly a business school—has efficiently swept into the dustbin most vestiges of Catholic doctrine and practice. Nowadays Catholic students, in point of both intellect and moral teaching, would be prudent to attend not the decayed "Catholic" college but instead either the neighboring Calvinist college or state university.

Yet not all is lost at many of the long-established Catholic colleges in this land. Their campuses, by contrast with those of secular educational institutions, retain some degree of order; dignity lingers in their ceremonies; theology is not expelled, even if it often takes strange forms. Although many might like to ignore John Paul II, that Pope's influence begins to be felt at some of the better institutions.

The university is the home of the intellect, Father Ward tells us, "Otherwise it is every kind of hodge-podge and jumble and is properly nothing at all." What is the specific end of a Catholic university? he inquires. "Let us begin to reply by saying that only on one condition can Catholic higher learning ever be at all. It can be only on condition that Catholic theology be given the primacy and be allowed and encouraged to specify this university. Not Catholic religion as a praxis, but Catholic theology as a science is what makes the Catholic university to be."[4]

At the heart of the difficulty experienced by Catholic higher education in 1992, then, is the confused state of theology and moral philosophy in university and college. But before turning to that difficult subject, let us deal with certain other troubles. The problems of Catholic colleges today are grave, and to some of their difficulties no answers have been found that might satisfy everybody. One perplexity is the contest between quality and quantity.

Catholic colleges confront the question of how widely their doors ought to be opened; in this they are perplexed more severely than are state institutions, and perhaps more than the Protestant denominational college and other independent colleges. The Catholic colleges desire to receive so many students as they decently can so that in some degree they may counter the militant secularism, strong in state institutions, that weighs upon our time. It is not too much to say that Catholic colleges have been in the habit of snatching brands from the burning. That is a worthy undertaking. But is such "remedial" social work the true end of a college of arts and sciences?

Yet the problem is not merely one of what the Catholic colleges would like to do: it is one of what they *might* do, given their limited resources. It scarcely seems necessary to say that the typical Catholic college is short of money; and the odds remain that there never will be enough money. As things are moving, colleges will be fortunate if, like Alice, they contrive to run as fast as they can in order to remain where they are. Catholic colleges never will be able to increase infinitely in size or number, and simultaneously to improve, or even maintain, tolerable standards of scholarship. They might either give a great mass of students mediocre training in almost everything or give a reasonably select body of students a decent education in certain established disciplines. Certain Catholic women's colleges in or near great cities already have chosen the former alternative: they school principally "minority" girls, subsidized by public funds. They were once genuine liberal arts colleges.

It is hard and sometimes perilous to decline a mission to the masses. Yet, the means being limited, I believe that the Catholic colleges would be wiser to choose the latter alternative, that of the humane scale—offering serious intellectual disciplines, theology being the queen of them, to students who actually may condescend to study.

In short, to Catholic colleges I recommend raising all standards; and that upon the hard ground of necessity, without embarking upon higher arguments. For in quantity, the Catholic campuses already have lost the battle; they never will contrive to enroll one tenth—nay, one twentieth—so many students as do the secular institutions. Nor is it probable that many Catholic colleges will be able to afford, in the future, the costly race in "plant," "amenities," and "special facilities"—not if they are intent upon increased enrollments also. To be almost as good, in any endeavor, is to join the vanquished.

In the long run, the influence of educational establishments is measured not by how many graduates they turn out but by the mental and moral fibre of those graduates. Princeton, for instance, always will count for more than Behemoth State College, even though Behemoth, year upon year, has ten times the enrollment of Princeton. The interest of all Christians will be better served today by a reputation for intellectual power and moral worth than by mere numbers. In the long run intelligence will tell, even in a university.

What Christian faith and Christian learning mainly require today is a restoration of their intellectual respectability and their moral efficacy. If that reputation is restored, the influence upon the crowd—and upon secular institutions—will follow. That occurring, it will not be necessary to compete for funds and students, for even Behemoth State, to some degree, will be converted through example.

The task of restoring the reputation of Christian faith and learning—and that of Catholic colleges—is most urgent. Monsignor John Tracy Ellis, about twenty-seven years ago, did not exaggerate the prevalence of doubts of the intellectual respectability and moral efficacy of Catholic colleges—whether or not that reputation really has been justified. A soft impeachment admitted by the friends of Catholic higher education becomes a fierce defamation in the mouths of the ideologue and the secularist zealot. Even if Catholic colleges are no worse than other colleges—and I think they are not worse, but in some matters perceptibly better—still they must become *conspicuously* better in several things than are secular institutions if they are to restore the good repute of Christian learning and faith; for they labor under the handicap of prejudice.

Much more might be written about intellectual standards, but my theme is this: it seems that if the Catholic college must make a choice between quality and quantity, it ought to choose quality—not for scholarship alone but for the effectual defense of Christian faith and learning. To gain a high reputation in the liberal arts and the pure sciences, Catholic colleges enjoy a clear road, for few other colleges are treading that path nowadays. In the fullness of time, it is the theological and humane and scientific disciplines that will tell, not today's football victories or technological displays or malignant academic fads like Deconstructionism or Multiculturalism.

"What we want," Orestes Brownson wrote in 1873, near the end of his life, "is a high-toned Catholic public opinion, independent of the public opinion of the country at large, and in strict accordance with Catholic tradition and Catholic aspirations." Brownson saw even then the beginnings of such a Catholic public opinion in the young men issuing from the Catholic colleges. One hundred and nineteen years later, Brownson's aspiration remains to be realized.

Can the great intellectual tradition of the Catholic Church be renewed, here near the close of the twentieth century? Generally speaking, the administrators of Catholic universities and colleges seem incompetent to reinvigorate their institutions. One is tempted to suspect that morals, and even faith, are matters of almost indifference to many of them: they have been appointed to do a routine job.

Take faith, or at least its outward manifestations. In the state of New York, Christian universities and colleges are eligible for modest grants from state funds—if they virtually convert themselves into secular institutions. (These grants are called "the Bundy money.") In compliance, at Fordham University even crucifixes, images, and other religious symbols have been removed from buildings. This is true also of nearly all other Catholic universities and colleges in that state. Even their libraries must be subjected to the surveillance of inspectors who may determine whether the Catholic institution has "too many Catholic books." Have Catholic educational administrators heard of the man who sold his birthright for a mess of pottage?

Or turn to morals. Georgetown University, the oldest of Catholic universities in America (founded 1789), is badly infected with neoterism. Recently that university recognized and partially funded one student organization that militantly advocates abortion on demand, and another student organization for homosexuals. Students and others have petitioned the Archdiocese of Washington, under canon law, to intervene—if necessary, depriving Georgetown University of calling itself "Catholic". Many more instances of the decay of Catholic doctrine and custom on many campuses might be cited.

Yet it should be remembered that on every Catholic campus there remain some members, clerical and lay, of faculty and staff, who have kept the faith and also are able teachers. And the situation at Catholic University, across the city, is different from that at Georgetown University. At Catholic, a pontifical university, schools and departments usually are headed by scholars who accept the magisterium of the church. The University's dismissal of Professor Charles Curran, and several of its recent appointments to chairs, sufficiently indicate its fidelity to doctrine and dogmata.

Of course various other Catholic centers of higher education continue to function within the church's traditions. One of the better-known of these is the University of Dallas; and the University of Steubenville, where the charismatic movement is strong, has reinvigorated its theological and philosophical departments. Nevertheless, so widespread has been the decline of teaching of faith and morals in the Catholic colleges of America since Vatican II that many Catholic families have despaired of sending their sons and daughters to the nominally Catholic colleges and universities that the elder generation had attended.

In consequence, academic adherents of orthodoxy during the past quarter of a century have founded new Catholic colleges on a small scale. Some of these endeavors have collapsed within a few years. The earliest of them, however—Thomas Aquinas College, near Santa Paula, California, founded in 1971—enjoys a growing influence; it has a strong Great Books curriculum, in emulation of the program at St. John's College in Annapolis. Another recent, lively, quite small, and genuinely Catholic institution is Thomas More College of the Liberal Arts, at Merrimack, New Hampshire, emphasizing studies in humane letters and history. Such humane ventures are leavening the lump.

The confused state of theology and moral philosophy in Catholic universities and colleges of the present day, I remarked earlier, lies at the heart of the difficulty experienced by Catholic higher education. Do Catholic universities have an end, an object? For that matter, does human existence have an object? One might not so surmise from the courses of study pursued by a great many students at Catholic institutions. What Christopher Dawson called "secular humanism" has triumphed within various Catholic ivory towers.

To awake once more right reason and moral imagination among administrators and professors and in the Catholic higher learning generally, a sign may be required— say something like the vindication of the Shroud of Turin by men of science. Short of some such event, it is conceivable that an eloquent and intellectually gifted ecclesiastic (like Newman) or layman (like Brownson) might point the way to intellectual and moral restoration. Such a one is yet to appear.

Despite the present sunken state of Catholic educational institutions in America, one need not wholly despair of amendment. For those universities and colleges still possess certain advantages over the secular establishment of higher education.

First, the Catholic university is directly descended from the medieval universities of Europe and so can draw upon the deep well of intellectual experience and tradition.

Second, the Catholic university still enjoys independence of decision and action for the most part; so far, it has successfully repelled various endeavors of federal and state governmental agencies to dominate Christian educational policies. (The temptation to accept governmental grants, however, and to accede to the conditions attached, remains ominous.)

Third, all Catholic institutions pay at least lip service to belief in the existence of a transcendent order of being and in the cardinal and the theological virtues; thus they retain some affection for the permanent things.

Fourth, the Catholic university still recognizes principles of natural law, which provide an ethical footing for the civil social order. In an age dominated by American power and wealth, such an understanding of justice is more needed in the United States than ever before.

Fifth, the Catholic university is redeemed somewhat from the provinciality of place and the provinciality of time by its connection with a great international organization, the church, which has survived the tooth of time.

What with the decay of purpose and of standards in the typical state university and college, there exists at present some opportunity for Catholic higher education to become what Brownson and Father Ward hoped for. It cannot suffice merely to hold the walls in a state of siege, for the barbarians already are within the walls of academe. G. K. Chesterton's lines in *The Ballad of the White Horse* come to mind concerning the barbarians coming again:

> What though they come with scroll and pen,
> And grave as a shaven clerk,

By this sign you shall know them,
That they ruin and make dark.

When Catholic higher learning in America commences to cleanse its own stable by thrusting out those barbarians who have come with scroll and pen, the Catholic schools may again, in Brownson's words, "send out living men, alive with the love of God and man . . . who will take command of their age." John Paul II has breathed life into a stricken Church; and we may hope that some warm-hearted Catholic scholars will begin to work out the university's salvation with diligence.

Chapter

GOVERNMENT

William Bentley Ball

William Bentley Ball is a constitutional lawyer who has been lead counsel in First and Fourteenth Amendment litigations in 22 states and in 9 cases in Supreme Court of the United States, including the landmark decision in the Amish case *Wisconsin v. Yoder.* A member of the Christian Legal Society's Center for Law and Religious Freedom and of the Fellowship of Catholic Scholars, he also gives a seminar on religious liberty at Dickinson Law School. For the past quarter of a century he has been associated with the law firm of Ball, Skelly, Murren & Connell in Harrisburg, Pennsylvania.

Robert P. Dugan, Jr.

Robert P. Dugan, Jr., has directed the National Association of Evangelicals' Office of Public Affairs in the nation's capital since 1978. He edits the monthly newsletter *NAE Washington Insight*, and his first book, *Winning the New Civil War: Recapturing America's Values*, was published in 1991. He has served as president of the Conservative Baptist Association of America, received honorary degrees from Denver Seminary, Geneva College, and Roberts Wesleyan College, and is listed in *Who's Who in America*. He served eighteen years in pastoral ministry in New Jersey, New Hampshire, Illinois, and Colorado. He was educated at Wheaton College and Fuller Theological Seminary.

Intrusions upon the Sacred

William Bentley Ball

THE SECULARIST THRUST

The Catholic bishops of Pennsylvania, in November, 1978, published a statement condemning governmental intrusions upon religious ministries and religious life. In part, they said:

> ... under our American constitutional form of government the Church should not feel that it must live by sufferance but should instead insist that, as it commits itself to live according to the law, so must government. As the Church ought never seek or accept favors by grace of administrators, so it should be forceful in requiring governmental administrators to follow statutes and to observe the Constitution. Those individuals are public servants, and they have no power except that given them by constitutional statutes. . . . [1]

This declaration was at once portrayed as alarmist and as inappropriate for a society whose necessities, so it was claimed, call for socialization. The critics capsulized their point with the quip, "Christ came to save us, not to exempt us." [2] They sought to heighten the persuasiveness of their criticism by denying that churches were the victims of any governmental "conspiracy" (though the Pennsylvania bishops had made no such allegation). Much criticism of the bishops' position inferred a dual view of religious liberty: (1) religious liberty is by exemption, (2) the exemption is a gift of the state, whose domain is total (and whose giving of exemption is itself a manifestation of its total power). That, however, contradicts the concept of religious liberty given by the Free Exercise Clause of the First Amendment and misapprehends the proper nature of the state.

The Free Exercise Clause contains no exemptions; rather, it declares religious liberty a matter of fundamental right.[3] That right is limited, not by what government may at any time demand, but by something essentially different—the common good. The common good indeed embraces social justice (a point not merely admitted, but insisted upon, by the Pennsylvanians). But, as J. Maritain, the author of *Man and State*, has pointed out, there are "goods which transcend the political common good ... [T]he Christian knows that [the order of society] is a supernatural order, and that the ultimate end—the absolute ultimate end—of the human person is God."[4] The Pennsylvania bishops' declaration saw the free exercise of religion as therefore an essential of the common good. And from that flowed their positive conclusions that vigilance with respect to exercises of governmental power is imperative, and where the exercise of that power may be injurious to religion, resistance likewise is imperative.[5]

This view was thus opposite in emphasis to the views not only of the Pennsylvanians' critics but also of many large religious bodies having public affairs offices within the Beltway. With these, all too often political image-making, fear of the media, or (above all) a supine, uncritical willingness to accept injurious regulation of religion have resulted in the worsening of our laws and greater and greater disadvantage to religion.

The prediction of the Catholic historian, Christopher Dawson, more than half a century ago, is proving daily more correct:

> ... there will be no department of life in which the state will not intervene and which will not be obliged to conform to the mechanized order of the new society.
>
> This is the situation that Christians have got to face. The great danger that we have to meet is not the danger of violent persecution but rather that of the crushing out of religion from modern life by the sheer weight of state-inspired public opinion and by the mass organization of society on a purely secular basis.[6]

For us, today, Dawson's grim prediction is being borne out in ways all too evident. Out of many examples, it is in three areas that the threat of state-imposed secularism is especially ominous: the educating of children, taxation, and cultural control. These areas are, in obvious respects, interrelated.

THE EDUCATING OF CHILDREN

While great attention has been given to several nationally publicized criticisms of American education in the past two decades, one of the most revealing inventories of American education has consisted, not of publications, but of trial records. I refer to the records developed in a series of cases involving the new wave of Protestant schools established in the 1970s. These vividly illustrate governmental intrusions upon the sacred.

Each of the cases arose out of efforts made by state public school authorities either to shut these new schools down or to prosecute parents whose children were enrolled in them. In each case the state demanded that the Protestant school, as the price of its existence, or of the freedom of its parent supporters from jailing, become a carbon copy of the government schools and totally subject to government control. In several states the schools and parents, on grounds of religious liberty and parental rights, resisted. In four states—Vermont, Ohio, Kentucky, and Maine—their resistance in court was successful.[7] In each, the resistance began against seemingly insuperable odds. In each, the schools, pastors, and parents turned the odds about, with the public school establishment becoming the *de facto* defendant, and victory for religious and parental freedom being achieved.

The public education authorities, in each of these cases, had begun with the presumption that the state is not only a superior educator but really the *sole* educator—all private education existing by state sufferance. While private education enjoyed considerable freedom in some states, in many it was only freedom with a long leash. In Pennsylvania, for example, while private schools had long operated largely according to their own designs, the State Board of Education had reserved statutory power to prescribe all activities taking place in any school.[8] Alarmed at the appearance of the new Protestant schools after 1970 and the fact that these schools (and, in particular, the parents who chose them) insisted on independence from the state bureaucracy, the public school authorities in several states decided to crack down. Here were schools that would not brook government's dictating their curricula, their textbooks, their pedagogy, the teachers they would employ, and monitoring and surveillance by agents of the state. These schools correctly regarded the state not as the master it should not be but as the competitor it actually was.[9]

While it is to be hoped that some day the full story of these cases will be told, a glimpse at one of them shows the striking features of each of them. In the *Bangor Baptist School* case, Maine's education commission demanded that eighteen evangelical elementary schools be shut down unless they had certification of state approval, i.e., unless they were governmentally licensed. But, as they were to prove on trial, the schools were ministries. Supported solely by impecunious congregations, they accepted no form of public subsidy. They would not exist except for their religious purpose. They could not in conscience seek a government permit to carry out a ministry. The state's conditions for licensing included dictation of curriculum, state certification of teachers, and close state monitoring. Pastors of churches operating the nonapproved schools and parents of children enrolled there brought suit in federal court on religious freedom grounds to put a stop to the state's intrusion.

Maine is economically a poor state. But the Maine public school establishment, as though mortally threatened, decided that it must go all out to bring the Christian schools to heel. It was thus that the state felt that it had best afford the services of nationally famous out-of-state educational experts[10] as witnesses.

Prior to their appearance on the stand had been the schools' witnesses, especially parents—who, to the Deputy Attorney General's disappointment, turned out to be, not redneck fanatics, but intelligent and competent individuals pleased with the educational product they had freely chosen. Children testified and, under cross-examination by the state, proved literate and well-spoken. The schools put into evidence the records of good student performance on nationally standardized achievement tests. Then, however, came the state's retained experts. All testified that every child must have a "quality" education, and that Maine's program assured that. Maine, they said, had the right prescription; good education was sure to follow. These witnesses proved a cross-examiner's delight. None, it was admitted, had the slightest familiarity with the schools that were before the court. None could say that inferior education had resulted in any state that lacked regulations such as Maine's. None could point to the slightest proof that "good education" was in fact happening in Maine's public schools. All, in fact, had difficulty defining the goals of education. One testified that theories of education are in a constant "state of flux." Hence, he was forced to concede, Maine's "prescription" had no necessary validity.

The schools' expert witnesses, Dr. Russell Kirk and Dr. Donald Erickson, thereafter destroyed the last intellectual pretensions of the state's case, Kirk especially criticizing state teacher-certification schemes as largely worthless. Erickson, the nation's leading authority on educational effects, stated that no cause-effect relationship could be proved between Maine's regulations and the actual happening of education. He stated, however, that education was obviously "happening" in the Christian schools. Thus the case concluded, not with the showing that the state had anticipated. The trial instead held up to the public an unpleasant picture of the pretensions and failures of public education and the arrogant misuse of power by the state in its attempt to suppress the Christian schools. Victories such as that of the Catholic schools in the NLRB cases[11] and the Protestant schools in Maine have been encouraging to those who prize religious liberty and intellectual freedom. But the tide is still running in favor of the secularist educational monopoly both at the state and federal levels. The public schools possess the high majority of our children, awesome financial and lobbying powers supported by the public treasury, and the support of militant unions and of some religious pressure groups. In some states, religious schools, careless of their mission and rights, accede to unreasonable regulations. And even for those religious schools most faithful to their mission and courageous in defending it, economic pressures provide the temptation to seek public aid, even at the price of licensing.[12]

TAXATION

Perhaps no greater threatened intrusion upon religious liberty exists than in exercises of the power of taxation. Responsible religious bodies in our country have never held that any and all persons, institutions, or activities claiming to be "religious" should be free of the taxing power of the public. But the ever-broadening definition of "religion," not only as assumed by charlatans but even as given by our courts,[13] complicates the question of "religious" exemptions from our tax laws. This complication is made even more difficult by the clumsiness of our tax law drafters in creating language which, being utterly ambiguous, gives tax administrators

211

a free hand in interpreting the language (sometimes to the great disadvantage of true religious interests).[14]

This is not the place to attempt to define the proper metes and bounds of the taxing power or a definition of what religious interests should be free of that power. Bearing constantly in mind Chief Justice Marshall's warning in 1819 that the power to tax is the power to destroy, an examination of actual and potential intrusions by government today upon religious liberty should focus us closely upon the four most significant recent decisions of the Supreme Court on the taxation of religion.

In 1970, *in Walz v. Tax Commission*,[15] the Supreme Court held that exempting from taxation properties used exclusively for religious worship did not violate the First Amendment's Establishment Clause. It is disappointing that the Court did not state that houses of worship should be tax-free because they are *religious*.[16] Rather, the Court stressed a secular basis for exemption: churches are "beneficial and stabilizing influences in community life"—like libraries or playgrounds. It is true that the Court hedged this a bit by saying that using a "social welfare yardstick"[17] to measure qualifications of church properties for exemption could create unconstitutional entanglements with religion. In view of the later statements by the Court that we now look to, the *Walz* decision does not now appear to be a formidable barrier to tax-intrusion upon religious freedom.

In *United States v. Lee*,[18] in 1982, the Court moved drastically farther in confining religious exemption, stating that "[b]ecause the broad public interest in maintaining a sound tax system is of such a high order, religious belief in conflict with the payment of taxes affords no basis for resisting the tax." (*Id.* at 260.)

More ominous still came *Bob Jones University v. United States* in 1983.[19] The Supreme Court there held that a pervasively religious organization will lose its exemption from federal income taxation under Section 501(c)(3) of the Internal Revenue Code if, even though sincerely following out its clearly stated doctrine, it thereby offends "federal public policy." This was pure invention by the Supreme Court. Neither the Constitution nor any statute defines or contains that term. Justice Powell pointed to "the element of conformity" implicit in the Court's "federal public policy" standard. "Taken together," he said, "these passages, in the majority's opinion, suggest that the primary function of a tax-exempt organization is to act on behalf of the government in carrying out governmentally approved policies." Tax-exemption, he believed, is "one indispensable means of limiting the influence of governmental orthodoxy in important areas of community life." The "federal public policy" doctrine, the epicenter of the Court's ruling, was, in fact, but a restatement of the seventeenth century doctrine of Reason of State, whereby it was held that the prince could violate the common law and rights of citizens "for the end of public utility."[20] Nazi Germany expressed the principle as *Gleichshaltung*, or the universal coordination of belief and practice with the polity of the national state.[21]

The Court has left outstanding a blank check. The "federal public policy" against racial discrimination considered in *Bob Jones* may be succeeded by other federal public policies (e.g., against "sexual orientation" discrimination in hiring).

In *Texas Monthly v. Bullock*[22] in 1989 the Court, in what dissenting Justice Scalia called "a judicial demolition project," held unconstitutional the sales tax exemption granted to religious literature but not to other literature. This decision, stating that tax exemptions are, legally, "subsidies,"[23] at core attacks the concept of religious tax exemption. Religion, in the meaning of the Court, is not protectable from taxation just because it is religion. Only if it has secular justification may it qualify for exemption.

Thus, we are brought to a condition whereby the protection of religion from confiscation of its liberties through taxation is imperiled. As Dean Kelley has warned, much more than money or property is at stake in this circumstance.[24]

CULTURAL CONTROL

Secularism's voracious social appetite is not confined to the educating of the young. By other means, too, it seeks to transform our culture. Companion authors of this book well describe the moral transformation being sought. To that may be added many other manifestations of intended cultural change. Two occur to me as especially significant—one largely unobserved and the other widely observed (and managing to gain ground). Both constitute significant government intrusions upon religious freedom.

The first is the "landmarking" of houses of worship. Statutes and ordinances calling for the governmental designation of buildings having important historic or aesthetic significance have been widely enacted in the past decade. As in the religious school cases, the very vice of the law is that it is imposed indiscriminately on the

secular and the religious. This species of environmental law typically creates a secular commission that has power to adjudge
whether particular structures meet broadly stated historical or
aesthetic criteria. If so, they enter the confinement of the commission's jurisdiction. It is close confinement. The Philadelphia ordinance is typical: once a building is "designated," the owner has "an
affirmative duty to preserve the building, at the exclusive expense
of the owner, in the condition, configuration, style and appearance
mandated by the Commission."[25] If a church desires to alter its
building, it must submit detailed plans for a Commission review
that is independent of the usual reasonable requirements of building codes. Maintaining the building in the condition in which designation freezes it may be expensive. But if the church pleads
financial hardship, it must submit voluminous financial information
that may include matters involving confidentially entrusted stew-
ardship funds. The Philadelphia "landmark" ordinance, in the
words of the Pennsylvania Supreme Court, gives the Commission
"almost absolute control over the property, including the physical
details and uses to which it could be put."[26]

Irrespective of the desirability of such laws generally, when they
are applied to houses of worship[27] they are inherently injurious.
And houses of worship have an *organic* character. Changes in
liturgy may require alteration of worship space. Changes in the
population of a congregation may dictate a different *religious* use of
the premises, with such ministries created as a home for unwed
mothers, a retreat house, or a soup kitchen. It is essential that the
satisfaction of merely cultural presuppositions not be permitted to
fossilize houses of worship. Exteriors of many churches are
designed to convey religious messages. So it is with interiors. It is
utterly inappropriate for governmental bodies to attempt to require
those messages to be amended or to be frozen in a particular form.
Building codes and, in given circumstances, zoning regulations,
may be reasonable limitations on churches in respect to control of
their properties. But the basic right of churches to administer their
own temporal goods for the religious ends to which they are
dedicated rests upon different and far more important justifications
than historic or cultural preservation.

The costs to landmarked churches are often prohibitive and
thus confiscatory. The case of the United Methodist Church of St.
Paul and St. Andrew saw New York City's Landmark Preservation
Commission designate the church edifice as a sort of aesthetic

mongrel—"a brilliant exemplar of 19th century eclecticism representing a fusion of Early Christian, German Romanesque and Italian Renaissance styles." Located in a declining neighborhood, the church was to be maintained, at the congregation's expense, in the physical style it acquired when the neighborhood was affluent. Barred was its use for aid to the poor, which the church had determined was the present requirement of its religious ministry.[28] The landmarking ordinances, with their myopic concentration on the subjective cultural inclinations of the administrative commission members, are usually religion-blind. It is no exaggeration to say that their thrust in relation to churches is precisely the secularist thrust which, in the former Soviet Union, simply went the full length of the possibilities of state control of church edifices and converted them into museums.[29]

A second manifestation of secularist cultural imposition is found in some aspects of the now much bruited "political correctness" controversy. Cultural demands of the quasi-governmental bodies that are the chief regional accrediting agencies for institutions of higher education have proved extremely threatening not only to the academic freedom of secular institutions but, in particular, to the religious freedom of religious institutions. A case in point is that of Westminster Theological Seminary.

Sixty-year-old Westminster had been accredited by the Middle States Association of Colleges and Schools since 1975. Since that time the seminary's work had been monitored and evaluated by Middle States through a regular schedule of reports and visits. Throughout its life Westminster had been governed by a board of trustees composed of ordained elders. In the churches that share Westminster's commitments, that ordination is available only to men—a position based on Westminster's understanding of biblical teaching.

In the 1980s Middle States adopted the requirement that boards of trustees of all colleges be "representative" of "student constituencies" in "age, race, ethnicity, gender, points of view, interests and experiences." In pursuit of this, Middle States in March, 1990, demanded that women be appointed to Westminster's board. While recognition as an accredited institution is normally based on factors relating to academic excellence and financial stability, Westminster's failure to appoint women to its board, and that alone, caused Middle States to issue a "show cause order" giving the Seminary six months to show why its accreditation should not be revoked. Following review of Westminster's response to the "show cause" order, Middle States denied the seminary the "exemption" it had sought, refusing to revoke its order.

Westminster, after diligent efforts to inform Middle States that the Seminary dared not, in good conscience, fail to follow its religious convictions in its board appointments, filed a formal complaint against Middle States with the Council on Postsecondary Education (COPA, an agency that oversees accrediting agencies). Westminster's complaint centered upon the fact that compliance with Middle States' conditions would force it to violate its own religious integrity. It attacked the action of Middle States, an outside secular agency, in presuming to appropriate the inherent power of religious institutions to determine and observe their own doctrine. What, Westminster asked, had become of the established principle that the integrity of every educational institution (even secular) depends upon fidelity to its stated mission? Westminster showed that requiring its conformity to Middle States' "standards" injured not only its religious autonomy and freedom but also its academic freedom, its reputation, it finances, and the employment prospects of its graduates.

The Seminary's complaint raised a warning signal, not only to COPA but to all other schools within Middle States' seven-state region, by pointing to the infinitely wide reach of the vague regulations in question, or what Middle States chose to describe as its accreditation "eligibility criteria." These appeared, oddly enough, not in any volume entitled "Eligibility Criteria," or "Standards," or "Regulations," but in a pamphlet entitled *Characteristics of Excellence in Higher Education*. These regulations were plainly impossible to rationally apply.

"Diversity in gender" was, of course, the category for board membership for which Middle States had pressed for compliance (though the other categories were equally regulatory). Westminster, in its complaint, pointed out that it was in full compliance with all applicable federal and state sex discrimination laws. None of those dictated who might serve on its board. This but highlighted the totally arbitrary nature of Middle States' demands.

Thanks to Westminster's spirited resistance, the U.S. Secretary of Education, Lamar Alexander, suspended Middle States' federal accreditation. He expressed grave concern over the Federal government's lending its authority to "accrediting associations to impose their own views of social policy on schools that clearly provide a quality education." At once thereafter Middle States cancelled its revocation of Westminster's accreditation.

While this is the fortunate end of the Westminster story, it may not be the end of "political correctness" intrusions upon religious liberty since the forces that generate such "eligibility criteria" have by no means retired from the lists.

THE FUTURE

The Smith Decision

On April 17, 1990, the nation was brought to a new starting point in its contemplation of religious freedom. The decision in *Employment Division of Oregon v. Smith*,[30] announced by the Supreme Court on that day, obliterated the main defenses that religion in this country has had against governmental aggression. Involved in the case was the use of peyote by Native Americans in a religious ceremony. Fired from their jobs as public employees for use of a hallucinogenic drug (a criminal offense under Oregon law), they sought and were denied unemployment compensation. Claiming that this denied them the free exercise of their religion, they took their case to the Supreme Court. Ruling against them, the Court held that any "religiously neutral" law of "general application" (the Oregon law being an example) would be upheld even though injurious to religious liberty—even though *severely* injurious to religious liberty.

We have seen "laws of general application" in Pennsylvania's NLRB cases noted above. The National Labor Relations Act, in other words, did not single out religious employers. It applied to all employers. Granted that Congress so intended it (and that thus it was a law of "general application"), was it "religiously neutral"? That depends on whether you look merely at words and ignore their effects.[31] The Act said nothing about religion. It spoke of "employers" and "employees," and since the church-schools employed people, NLRB deemed them governed by the Act. But, with great good sense, the courts measured the devastating impact of NLRB jurisdiction on a religious ministry. Under the *Smith* case, all such impacts must be discounted. If your state legislature passes a law that "all" schools shall present a state-prepared course of sex instruction, your church school will not prevail in court on the ground of violation of its religious freedom—even though the course flagrantly attacks Christian morality. If the state, in spite of the school's plea, shows even minimal justification for the law (e.g., "safer sex"), the state wins.

This is a radical departure from the prior constitutional jurisprudence of religious liberty. Before *Smith*, the Free Exercise Clause had been interpreted to provide a very high hurdle that government would have to cross before it could impose upon religious freedom. Government would be required to show, not that its action was in the public interest, but that it was necessitated by a *supreme* societal interest (or what the Supreme Court called a "compelling state interest") and that it had no course of action less burdensome to religion. That hurdle was not a paper hurdle; rather, government was required to *prove* its claim of compelling state interest. In other words, where government would seek to limit religious freedom in a particular matter, government would have to go into court like any other litigant, come up with its evidence, try to make its case stick.[32] Putting government on its proof was obviously an important mandate of fairness. The power, prestige, and financial and attorney resources of government invariably give government an immense advantage over religious claimants in litigations. The advantage is sometimes prospectively so great that the latter are forced to bow without contest.

This advantage is made even more ominous by the fact that the Court in *Smith* has also made clear its view that, with minimum "public interest" justification, legislatures can override religious rights. It has always been held that legislative acts are presumed constitutional. But until *Smith* that presumption could be rebutted in cases involving religious liberty, by application of the "compelling state interest" test. All acts of legislatures are deemed in the public interest; they would not otherwise be enacted. But with what subject matter do legislatures today deal? The name is infinity. Almost no area of human life today can safely claim that it will be immune from regulation by legislatures. Since even a thin "public interest" justification will suffice to render legislative enactments enforceable against religious interests, religion is now broadly vulnerable to the power of the state. Religion should not have to engage in political endeavors for its protection, and individuals and small religious groups rarely have the means to.

A final aspect of *Smith* was the Court's further downgrading of the Free Exercise Clause by its assertion that its prior religious liberty decisions such as that upholding the Amish in the *Yoder* case, were basically "hybrid" cases in which *other* rights were primarily involved (in *Yoder*, parental rights as such). Religion, in this astonishing view, was but a vicarious, piggy-backed factor.

WHAT IS TO BE DONE?

The threat of governmental intrusions upon the sacred is now being addressed chiefly in terms of focus upon the *Smith* decision. Many remedies for the protection of religious liberty are being suggested. All state constitutions contain bills of rights that are aimed at that protection. At least three state supreme courts have recently held that, irrespective of *Smith*, religious liberty finds protection under such provisions.[33] Another avenue of relief may be found in the passing of state or federal legislation providing specific protections to religion. An example is the Pennsylvania statute to which we have referred in endnote 8. These sorts of efforts are, of course, fully in step with the philosophy of the Rehnquist Court with its emphasis on federalism and states' rightful powers. In addition there is now evident a groundswell of responsible scholarly criticism of *Smith*.[34] It is not beyond hope that the justices will, directly or by nuance, overrule *Smith*. The Court has overruled itself many times in the past,[35] and should come to see that *Smith* is in crying need of early correction.

The most dramatic effort to secure correction is the proposed "Religious Freedom Restoration Act," whereby courts would be required to apply the pre-*Smith* "compelling state interest" test in all Free Exercise cases. Whether or not this proposal is enacted into law, its very introduction must necessarily vividly dramatize to the Court the growing consensus that *Smith* is a reprehensibly bad decision.[36]

Helpful indeed though it would be to rid the law of *Smith* by whatever means, the ultimate protection of religious freedom will be found not in the law but in what we think of religion. The answer to the problem of governmental intrusion upon the sacred must begin with apprehension of the sacred. The problem here is one of *faith*. Only where faith is strong will that apprehension be clear. Are there things that are not Caesar's? In the matter at hand is one of them involved? To the extent that what is really sacred, what is really essential to ministry, is not appreciated and dearly prized, political or other pretexts for nonresistance will be reached for. Of course it must be determined whether an "intrusion" is actually presented. This depends upon finding out what the government action means legally and assessing the facts respecting its potential impact. The failure of major religious groups to perceive what the language of the 1989 Dodd child care bill really imported in terms of religious child care brought the nation perilously close to legislation that would have transferred child care totally to the state.[37]

Judgments as to appropriate action in response to threatened intrusions may involve pain. There may be the prospect of ultimate confrontations. There is often the lure of the assurances of political personages that fears of ill effects are exaggerated or that the effects are anyhow inevitable. Unhappily, for some the worst hazard to be faced is the prospect of loss of favorable image by the media and by others who "count." Madison had said that it is proper "to take alarm at the first experiment with our liberties." Ecclesiastical compromisers too often seem to say that it is proper to take flight at that point. Much is said these days (and properly) about the need for "understanding" and "compassion." But far too little is said about the importance of conviction and courage. That redoubtable fighter for religious liberty, Baptist Isaac Backus, said it all in 1773:

> We are not insensible that an open appearance against any part of the conduct of men in power is commonly attended with difficulty and danger. And could we have found any way wherein with clearness we could have avoided [it] we would gladly have taken it. But our blessed Lord and only Redeemer has commanded us to *stand fast in the liberty wherewith he has made us free*. And things appear so to us at present that we cannot see how we can fully obey this command without refusing any active compliance with some laws about religious affairs that are laid upon us. And as those who are interested against us often accuse us of complaining unreasonably, we are brought under a necessity of laying open particular facts which otherwise we would gladly have concealed. And all must be sensible that there is a vast difference between exposing the faults, either of individuals or communities when the cause of truth and equity would suffer without it and the doing of it without any such occasion. We view it to be our incumbent duty to render unto Caesar the things that are his but also that it is of as much importance not to render unto him anything that belongs only to God, who is to be obeyed rather than any man [italics in original].[38]

The Attack
on Ministries

Robert P. Dugan, Jr.

A specific threat of federal intrusion into the teaching ministry of churches, more than anything else, spawned unprecedented evangelical involvement in politics in the 1980s. Only part of that new enterprise became what is labeled "the new religious right." Internal Revenue Service officials from those days may now have adequate leisure to look back, either to lament or laud what they brought forth.

In considerably less than infinite wisdom, the IRS in August 1978 set forth proposed rules for private schools, sounding an alarm that would grow into a howl of outrage and protest. Private schools were to be presumed guilty of racial discrimination if their student bodies did not adequately reflect the minority population in their local communities. The high price of such supposed racism would be the loss of tax-exempt status—not ordered by a court of law, but by a decision of some anonymous IRS bureaucrat, looking solely at a mix of statistics.

Many evangelicals regarded the rules as a threat to the very existence of the Christian school movement. Pastors and religious broadcasters did not have to be highly trained lawyers to grasp the injustice of force on church-sponsored schools and the burden of proving their innocence against, say, a statistical charge of being a segregationist "white flight academy." Even the untaught realize that American justice is not supposed to work that way—with the accused having to prove the absence of wrong motivation. Further, while it may be admitted, to their shame, that a small number of

221

such schools were discriminatory, evangelicals sacrificially supported their schools because they were intended to teach a Christian world-and-life view, in a disciplined and demanding academic setting, to the glory of God—not to keep others out.

Less than a month after moving to the nation's capital in late 1978 to lead NAE's Office of Public Affairs, I found myself testifying before the Commissioner of the IRS on this matter. A December date had been scheduled for public comments on the rules, and dozens upon dozens of testimonies eventually filled four full days with stormy protests. I remember well one testimony that left the IRS's assumptions mortally wounded. A Hebrew school in a Miami neighborhood with fifty percent Hispanics had very few Latinos in its enrollment. Given that most of those Hispanics were Roman Catholic, how could the IRS fairly charge that Jewish school with segregation? While some Jewish parents may have chosen Catholic schools in preference to inferior public schools, Catholics were not likely to choose Jewish religious schools.

During the hearings it struck me that, should the IRS force Jews to recruit Hispanics in order to meet certain student percentage requirements, the federal government would indirectly have become an agent for Jewish proselytism. How ironic. Whenever such recruitment, for the saving of tax-exempt status, would be required, whether in a Hebrew school or a fundamentalist Baptist school, it could never square with the spirit of the First Amendment.

To this 1978 threat of governmental intrusion there was a happy ending. The weight of the collective testimony, buttressed by an outpouring of grass roots protest, crushed the IRS's desire to proceed. It postponed implementation of the Proposed Revenue Procedures. Then, in 1980, Congress nailed the lid to the coffin by passing the Ashbrook-Dornan amendments that prohibited the IRS from so withdrawing tax-exempt status from religious schools.

America's Founding Fathers foresaw that government might be inclined to arrogate power to itself and ride roughshod over fundamental rights of the people. So it was that Thomas Jefferson, serving then as ambassador to France, wrote to James Madison in December 1787 after studying the Constitution then pending ratification:

> I will now tell you what I do not like. First, the omission of a bill of rights, providing clearly, and without the aid of sophism, for

freedom of religion, freedom of the press, protection against standing armies, restriction of monopolies. . . .[1]

On July 31, 1788, Jefferson again addressed a missive to Madison from Paris, more precisely declaring his hopes for such a package of rights. He wanted to protect the practice of religion from the government—not the reverse:

I hope . . . a bill of rights will be formed to guard the people against the federal government, as they are already guarded against their State governments in most instances.[2]

The Free Exercise Clause of the First Amendment in that bill of Rights, in due course, has proven to be a bulwark against governmental intrusion into churches and other religious organizations—at least until an unfortunate 1990 Supreme Court decision eviscerated that clause. About that, more later.

Representatives of over ninety percent of organized religion in the United States leaned heavily on the Free Exercise Clause when they assembled in Washington, D.C. in February 1981 for a conference on Government Intervention in Religious Affairs. This impressively inclusive conclave was cosponsored by, among others, the U.S. Catholic Conference, The Synagogue Council of America, the National Association of Evangelicals, the Baptist Joint Committee on Public Affairs, the Lutheran Council in the U.S.A., and the General Conference of Seventh-day Adventists.

At the opening session, conference chair William P. Thompson listed seventeen actions by state and federal governmental agencies that were troubling the religious community. Let me list about half of them:[3]

- Efforts to regulate fund-raising solicitations by religious bodies.
- Efforts to require religious groups to register and report to governmental officials under "lobbying disclosure" laws.
- Attempts to collect unemployment compensation taxes from hitherto exempt church-related agencies.
- Imposition upon church-related colleges, by the then HEW Department, of certain requirements concerning mingling of the sexes to which they had religious objections.

223

- Efforts by several federal agencies to require church-related institutions to report employment and admissions statistics, even though they received no government funds, with threats to cut off such funds to students in such schools unless they hired faculty, for example, from other religious groups.
- Interrogation of church workers by grand juries about internal affairs of churches.
- Placing a church in receivership because of allegations of financial mismanagement made by dissident members.
- Withdrawal of tax exemption from various religious groups for failure to comply with "public policy."
- Determination by the IRS of what is "religious ministry" by clergy, in opposition to that religious body's own definition, to qualify for clergy housing allowance.

Thompson concluded by acknowledging that no one instance, taken by itself, would require such a gathering of religious leaders, but that the pattern they formed, when observed together, was distressing. Thus it was necessary to focus "on that portion of the church-state law of the United States where the activities of religious bodies intersect with the regulatory responsibility and authority of government."

Conference organizers entrusted the keynote address to the editor of this book, William Bentley Ball. He spoke about "Government as Big Brother to Religious Bodies,"[4] at the outset admitting that "Governmental intrusion upon religion is not always—or even usually—due to a conspiratorial design to put down religion. Frequently, it is due merely to inadvertence." In a summarizing paragraph, however, Ball stated:

> But always we must remember the great inherent weight of governmental action and the relative fragility of religious liberty. This should result, in all questionable cases, in *government's* being put upon its proof, in *government's* being restrained from all looseness in defining the reach of the public interest, and from all carelessness where religious interests are involved.

Within a few months of the conference, NAE's Washington office would have an opportunity walk through its door, allowing it to begin a process to restore the balance to which Ball referred. The "great inherent weight" of one of government's most powerful agencies, the IRS, threatened the activity of a southern church. Leaders from that Mobile, Alabama congregation visited us, complaining about an IRS investigation of their church. At first, the church felt that it should cooperate, given the biblical admonition to "submit yourselves for the Lord's sake to every authority instituted among men: whether to the king, as the supreme authority, or to governors, who are sent by him to punish those who do wrong and to commend those who do right"(1 Peter 2:13–14 NIV).

Their frustration was understandable, however, as the IRS persistently refused to divulge the reasons for its inquiry. Eventually the church drew the line, particularly when an incredibly audacious request was made—that an IRS official be permitted to examine the pastor's personal counseling notes. (Catholics, understanding the privacy of the confessional booth, would be highly indignant; so would Protestants, who believe in clergy confidentiality; and so even would secularists, who regard lawyer-client conversations as sacrosanct.)

A year later, the Gulf Coast Community Church at last cleared its name—but at a cost of more than $100,000 in legal and accounting fees, not to mention long months of frustration and aggravation. If the IRS had only explained its concerns at the outset, that time and money could have been saved. It was ultimately revealed that a disgruntled former church member had stolen documents from the church office and taken them to the IRS, alleging irregularities that proved to be totally unfounded.

In time, the church's Washington visits led to the drafting of legislation to prevent future harassment of churches, conventions, or associations of churches. In the summer of 1984, the resulting Church Audit Procedures Act was attached to the Senate's Deficit Reduction Act, and it became the law of the land. Unconstrained IRS "fishing expeditions" are happily a thing of the past, for Catholic, evangelical, or any other churches in the United States.

Over the years of my tenure in Washington, the people whom Mr. Ball calls "orthodox evangelicals" have often and gladly come to the side of those he labels "orthodox Catholics." We have fought together, for example, to assure that Congress would build neither a floor under nor a ceiling over charitable contributions, and we have from time to time tried to establish the deductibility of charitable contributions for non-itemizers.

In 1988, many evangelicals supported the U.S. Catholic Conference in its fight against a group called Abortion Rights Mobilization

(ARM). NAE joined in an *amicus curiae* brief to the Supreme Court, as ARM contended that the Catholic Church would have lost its tax-exempt status. It is evident to Catholics and evangelicals alike that churches should be able to speak out on issues without some third party threatening loss of tax-exemption. Such threats can easily chill the right of a church to address moral questions, for churches and religious organizations generally can ill afford to incur the enormous legal costs necessary to defend themselves.

Landmarking, of all things, can become a threat to the practice of religion. It may be difficult to believe, but landmark commissions have been known to deny to a "national historic site" church even the right to move an altar. Thus, NAE and the Christian Legal Society, with others, filed a friend-of-the-court brief in the 1990 case *Society of Jesus of New England v. Landmarks Commission*. Evangelicals would like to have that reciprocated the next time a shrunken inner-city Protestant congregation is forced to spend more than its annual budget—money it literally does not have—to repair the roof on its out-dated but expensive "historic" building. That congregation may need the liberty to sell its building to a developer, in turn securing space for worship and ministry and funds to carry on outside ministries to the disadvantaged for years to come.[5]

Beyond these above instances, successful evangelical efforts in correcting an injustice that had ensnared Geogetown University in a years-long legal contest over a District of Columbia human rights statute stand out in my mind as of critical importance. The eventual stance of the University in this struggle, however, remains a disappointment.

Geogetown was required to make facilities and finances available to campus gay right groups. Rather than continue appeals litigation, or pursue a legislative remedy, the University made a "face-saving" surrender, agreeing to provide to the homosexual advocacy groups the monetary and facilities benefits of sponsorship without the formal nomenclature of sponsorship.

In the summer of 1988, Senator William Armstrong read of the matter in *The Rocky Mountain News* and won a surprise Senate vote, which conditioned D.C. appropriations on the District's amending its statute so to excuse religious schools. The measure became law in 1988, was set aside in the courts, and later in 1989 was re-enacted by Congress with direct application, rather than as a condition on D.C. appropriations.

NAE led the contest for public support, rallying press conferences in both summers. We were joined by parachurch organizations and groups representing conservative sentiment in the Presbyterian, Methodist, and Roman Catholic denominations.

The issue was plainly religious liberty. Can government force a religious university to subsidize activism and advocacy contrary to its fundamental beliefs? As a Roman Catholic institution, Georgetown believes that homosexual behavior is sinful. It would make as much sense, we contended, if Hebrew Union College should be forced to fund a Campus Crusade for Christ group, or for Howard University, an African-American institution, to be compelled to subsidize a white supremacist group.

Yet we were unable to obtain support from the University. The University instead communicated to Congress that it did not seek correction of the law. The public press suggested that Georgetown was motivated by a desire to obtain District approval for a much needed floating of bonds. Thus Georgetown remains bound by a settlement of its choosing, while the rights of other religious schools in the District have been restored and Congress has established a favorable precedent.

Evangelicals have had other occasions to long for stronger support from their Catholic friends, though in the matter of the Civil Rights Restoration Act of 1988, commonly referred to as the "Grove City" bill, Catholics and evangelicals stood shoulder-to-shoulder for a period of time to assure that this non-discrimination legislation would be abortion-neutral. Evangelicals had other concerns about imposing moral constraints and preserving a Christian ethos at colleges, however, and about dealing with men and women according to distinct marital and parental roles, family status and the like. They sought to shore up defective religious exemption provisions. Once the abortion-neutral amendment prevailed, frankly, efforts of the Roman Catholic establishment faded, leaving evangelicals and orthodox Jewish organizations without their help.

It may be that Catholic educational circles have a more liberal perspective than the church itself, or it may be that the church, as part of the political establishment, was over-confident that it could always work something out with the authorities should discrimination charges arise. In any case, we fell just nine votes short of sustaining President Reagan's veto of the Grove City bill in the House of Representatives. It is painful for us to recall that if the

227

Catholic Church had remained with us, the veto would surely have been upheld.

Now, there is a dire need for Catholics to join with evangelicals and others to protect religious liberty. In April 1990, the Supreme Court in *Employment Division v. Smith* handed down a devastating decision that essentially nullifies the Free Exercise Clause protection of the First Amendment. Going beyond the immediate decision about the denial of unemployment benefits to Native Americans who had used the drug peyote as a sacrament in worship, Justice Scalia, speaking for the majority, announced a new rule of constitutional law. If prohibiting the exercise of religion is "merely the incidental effect of a generally applicable and otherwise valid provision, the First Amendment has not been offended." We were appalled enough to participate in a May 10 press conference petitioning the Supreme Court to rehear the case. It refused. Until then, it had been established law that government had to demonstrate a "compelling state interest"—such as public health or safety—to justify applying a law that would impinge an individual's free exercise of religion. The Court abandoned that standard, although neither party to the case argued for a new test. This judicial activism, ironically, was perpetrated by the conservative bloc on the High Court.

Evangelicals immediately joined a rapidly developing and broad-based religious and civil rights coalition, which began to draw up a piece of remedial legislation that would bear the title: The Religious Freedom Restoration Act (RFRA). Unhappily, expected Catholic support never fully materialized, either in Congress or in the religious community. National Right To Life attorneys felt they had discovered a fatal flaw in RFRA. Given the possible overturning of *Roe v. Wade*, they argued then and since that RFRA might possibly be employed to establish something not heretofore found in the law, to substitute a religious right for the present "privacy right" to abortion. There remains an impasse, as sponsors of the legislation insist they cannot add an amendment accommodating these interests as expressed by the U.S. Catholic Conference, or meeting their objections concerning possible abortion claims.

We cannot agree with the Catholic conference's position on RFRA. We can find no basis in law for any claim that RFRA is an "abortion bill." (That is also the opinion of the Congressional Research Service.) Needless to say, if we thought for a moment that RFRA could possibly be used to enhance abortion rights, evangelicals could not in good conscience support the bill, notwithstanding the ominous threat to religious liberty of *Employment Division v. Smith.*

RFRA would simply restore the compelling government interest test, nothing more, nothing less. That test was used for decades before *Smith* to strike sensible balances between religious liberty and competing governmental interests. RFRA is as neutral with respect to the abortion issue as the Free Exercise Clause itself.

Any claim under RFRA to a religious right of abortion, assuming it is found to be sincere, would face the government's claim of a compelling interest in unborn human life. That the Supreme Court would uphold the government's claim is assured for two reasons. First, the government's compelling interest in protecting the life of the unborn throughout pregnancy is self-evident. Second, Chief Justice Rehnquist and Justices White, O'Connor, and Kennedy have already taken a firm stand that government has a compelling interest in protecting unborn life throughout pregnancy. (Cf. the 1989 *Webster,* 1986 *Thornburgh,* and 1983 *Akron* cases.) Justice Scalia has indicated general agreement with Justice White's view on abortion and is the most adamant Justice for overruling *Roe v. Wade.*

Are these five Justices, who have been waiting for years to overturn the Court's holding that a woman has a constitutional right to abortion, apt to find a free exercise right to abortion? Never. How could they possibly conclude that government does not have a compelling interest in unborn children throughout pregnancy when they have expressly said it does? Moreover, Justices Souter and Thomas will likely create a majority of seven in any such case. Thus it is extremely disheartening to see Catholic opposition threaten passage of legislation absolutely essential to protect our First Liberty and to feel that this important constitutional dialogue has been stymied.

It seems providential to me that I have been asked to write a chapter about Catholic-evangelical cooperation at this time when our relations are highly strained on this issue. Evangelicals view religious freedom as the keystone in their pantheon of political values. Not incidentally, I observe that passage of RFRA would restore a constitutional guarantee of free exercise rights so that we may battle, together, for the protection of unborn human beings.

These words of Abraham Lincoln in his "First Inaugural Address," while in a different context, are very applicable here: "We are not enemies, but friends. We must not be enemies. Though passion may have stained, it must not break our bonds of affection." Indeed.

Especially now, in the last decade of the twentieth century, Roman Catholics and evangelicals must together contend for religious liberty and for Judeo-Christian values. We are in the midst of a raging *Kulturkampf*, a culture war to determine the ways of thinking, living, and behaving that define our society. My new book, *Winning the New Civil War: Recapturing America's Values*, sketches some of the conflict between cultural conservatives and cultural radicals.

Perhaps no issue better encapsulates the culture war than that of abortion. No matter what one thinks of the tactics of Operation Rescue in Wichita in the summer of 1991, the issue of women securing late, third trimester abortions in Kansas is quite abhorrent to millions of Catholics and evangelicals—and to the Almighty God. Columnist Joseph Sobran has caustically observed: "Killing and dismembering a fetus in its ninth month is, one would think, an activity worthy of Jeffrey Dahmer, the Milwaukee madman. But the major media, which have given us graphic descriptions of Dahmer's crimes, have avoided even mentioning (let alone describing) what goes on at Women's Health Care Services in Wichita."

Governmental intrusion into religious organizations diminishes the religious freedom essential to struggle for the "righteousness that exalts a nation" and against the abominations that would warrant God's wrath. Catholics and evangelicals absolutely must defend each other's religious liberty—and that of all Americans, including those of no faith. One recalls Benjamin Franklin's comment at the signing of the Declaration of Independence: "We must all hang together, or assuredly we shall all hang separately."

All of us must look beyond our self-interests and be prepared to defend to the death each other's religious liberty. Let an evangelical German Lutheran pastor, imprisoned for eight years by the Nazi regime, have the last word. He observed the days when Hitler was coming to power, in the thirties:

First they came for the communists, but we were not communists, so we said nothing. Then they came for the trade unionists, but we were not trade unionists, so we said nothing. Then they came for the Jews, but we were not Jews, so we said nothing. Then they came for the mentally deficient, but we were not mentally deficient, so we said nothing. Then they came for me, and no one bothered to say anything either. We did not know what was going on. Maybe we did not want to know.

Chapter

RIGHTS

John A. Lapp

John A. Lapp is executive secretary of Mennonite Central Committee. After earning his Ph.D. in history at the University of Pennsylvania, he taught at Eastern Mennonite and Goshen colleges. Lapp became dean of Goshen College and later provost. He has published articles in the denominational journals *Mennonite Quarterly Review*, *Christian Century*, and *Christianity and Crisis*. He has written *The Mennonite Church in India, 1897–1962*, and *The View from East Jerusalem*.

John P. Hittinger

John P. Hittinger is an associate professor of philosophy at the College of St. Francis, Joliet, Ill. In 1990 he was a research fellow at the Jacques Maritain Center, the University of Notre Dame. He graduated from Notre Dame, then earned his Ph.D. from the Catholic University of America.

Human Rights: An Agenda for the Church

John A. Lapp

One of the most powerful moral and political forces of recent decades has been the global campaign for human rights. As this is being written, the Nobel Peace Prize has been awarded to Aung San Sun Kyi of Burma who is under house arrest for heroically calling for a new political system committed to protecting human rights. Yelena Bonner, widow of a previous Nobel Peace Prize Winner, Andre Sakharov, wrote in the October 1991 *Independent* from Moscow that "history demands a new approach to human rights protection: not only the rights of individuals but of entire nations."

Churches have not been oblivious to these concerns. The 1989 Manila Conference of the Lausanne Committee for World Evangelism called the global church to "earnestly desire freedom of religion as defined by the Universal Declaration of Human Rights." Then they added: "The proclamation of God's Kingdom necessarily demands the prophetic denunciation of all that is incompatible with it. Among the evils we deplore are destructive violence, including . . . the abuse of human rights." They called on Christians to "repent for the narrowness of our concerns and vision."

A year later at the Seoul Convocation on Justice, Peace and Integrity of Creation (JPIC), sponsored by the World Council of Churches, the 10th affirmation noted that "human rights come from God." Then they noted: "The term 'human rights' must be clearly understood to refer not only to individual rights but also to the collective social, economic and cultural rights of peoples (including those with disabilities) such as the right to land and its resources, to one's own ethnic and racial identity and to the exercise of religious and political freedom."

In light of these strong statements from Manila and Seoul we might well ask why it is necessary to identify human rights as an agenda for the church. One obvious reason is that statements in denominational or interchurch assemblies do not mean that local congregations or individual believers feel the same way. More significantly, most rationales for human rights are largely cast in secular terms. Yet there has been a rich Christian history of concern for human rights. And if the church today is to bear a wholistic witness, human rights will surely be one concern.

THE ENTHRONEMENT OF HUMAN RIGHTS

It was Winston Churchill at the end of World War II who said that the first and most important task of the United Nations was "the enthronement of human rights." It is no accident that from the Charter of 1945 to more recent General Assembly discussions, human rights and the U.N. have gone hand in hand.

This enthronement, however, is the result of 300 years of widening and intensifying discussion by statesmen and philosophers as well as the realization of some human rights in the political structures of the modern world. Human rights would appear to be one of the essential ingredients of modernity in politics. As Kenneth Minoque, a political scientist, put it in a historical overview, "The idea of human rights is as modern as the internal combustion engine, and from one point of view, it is no less a technological device for achieving a common human purpose."[1]

The term "human rights" is a twentieth century rendition of such concepts as "natural rights" or "the rights of man," which became commonplace in Western language during the eighteenth century. The Bill of Rights enacted in the English Parliament in 1689, the first ten amendments to the Constitution of the United States, and the Declaration of the Rights of Man and the Citizen by French revolutionaries in 1789 are the forerunners of rights *language* now found in the fundamental documents of virtually every state around the world.

Though legally established, the concept of human rights is less rooted in positive or enacted law than in the notion that the person, himself or herself as part of essential humanness, deserves dignity and respect. Jesus of Nazareth didn't use rights language but surely represented human rights at its fullest when he summarized the gospel for the wealthy young man: "Love your neighbor as yourself" (Matt. 19:19 NIV).

Rights language became common parlance through the writings, teaching, and ideals of the European and American Enlightenments. It was John Locke, Baron Montesquieu, Thomas Jefferson, Immanuel Kant, John Stuart Mill, and their popularizers who translated notions of human dignity into "natural rights," which in turn led to the rich interest in human rights in today's world.

Before the twentieth century the familiar phrases of the American Declaration of Independence set the parameter of rights language. Equality, liberty, happiness, property, and security were the moral rights that undergird positive rights such as freedom of speech, religion, and press; freedom from unreasonable search, seizure, and arbitrary arrest; and guarantees to trial by jury and the right to vote.

The fullest statements regarding human rights today are found in the United Nations Charter (1945), the U.N. Universal Declaration of Human Rights (1948), the U.N. International Covenant on Economic, Social and Cultural Rights (1966), and U.N. International Covenant on Civil and Political Rights (1966). A simple catalog of all the "human rights and fundamental freedoms" expressed in these documents would take pages. In addition to the rights stated above, these documents create definitions of "human rights" to include such social and economic values as the right to a nationality, to self-determination, to marry and found a family, to equal access to public services, to work and to exercise free choice of employment, to just and favorable remuneration, "to a standard of living adequate for the health and well-being" of an individual and his family, "including food, clothing, housing and medical care," the right to education, to rest and leisure, to participate in the cultural life of the community, to social and international order, to leave any country, to enjoy in other countries asylum from persecution, to equal status of all races, tribes, minorities, and sexes as well as for differently abled individuals.

These and other statements on human rights usually include a set of philosophic affirmations, guarantees of both positive freedoms and protections against the arbitrary abuse of such freedoms, all as part of the rule of law.

"Human rights" are part of the contemporary scene in other ways. Former President Carter called human rights "the soul of our foreign policy." Amnesty International performs a heroic service in making concrete the rights of individuals which have been violated in countries on every continent. The Civil Rights movement in the U.S., the Native Peoples movement in Canada, and the campaigns for social and political justice around the world truly suggest that Winston Churchill's vision, if not reality, is firmly established.

This quick overview might suggest that human rights are the growing edge of a humanizing vision promulgated by the philosophers and that they have been gradually realized. That would overlook two additional reasons why human rights are at the center of recent discussions: a growing understanding of its meaning and an increasing awareness of rights violations. Modern communications highlights repression of civil liberties when they occur as in Vietnam, pre-Gorbachev Soviet Union, and Pinochet's Chile; as in discrimination and harassment of Jews in most Western countries; as among Palestinians in Israel and the occupied territories; as in restrictions on the church in El Salvador, Iran, and Indonesia; as in proscriptions against minority people in the United States, Canada, and India. We are concerned because of the precarious status of rights almost everywhere.

THE COMPLEXITIES OF HUMAN RIGHTS

There are problematic dimensions to human rights. The most obvious problem is the realization of human rights. Any person involved in the realities of institutions soon becomes aware of the rights of workers, teachers, students, patients, clients, buyers, sellers, and property owners. Translating a multitude of often competing rights into reality for the international and cross– cultural scene should provide both perspective and humility. Anyone involved in community and institutional structures soon realizes his or her role in the treatment of people and human rights questions and hence, the difficulty of finding a neutral place to stand.

Although the process is difficult, there are also difficulties with the terminology itself.

First, what do we include as human rights? The catalog list above ties together broad political right economic considerations, and familial and societal concerns. If everything is a right, how do we deal with contradictory demands? Do we begin with the right to life or the right to a certain style of life?

Answering these questions requires a serious attention to our presuppositions and values. The U.N. declaration says there is a right to marriage and to raise a family. But marriage at what age and what kind of family? Western bloc nations have focused on political rights; Eastern bloc countries have emphasized economic rights. Hence the anecdote of a decade ago describing the two dogs passing on the bridge between Poland and Czechoslovakia going in opposite directions. The one going to Poland needs freedom to bark; the other going to Czechoslovakia needs food to eat!

In an effort to cope with these dilemmas some theorists have emphasized "human needs" rather than "human rights." The Overseas Development Council (ODC) has developed the "PQLI"—Physical Quality of Life Index, which uses infant mortality, life expectancy, and literacy rates to measure how basic needs are being met. The ODC suggests that justice, freedom, happiness, and a sense of participation, though important, are not basic. What may be considered a need today may not have been a need in an earlier epoch and may not be so in another environment. We know enough about the complex inter-relationships of body and spirit to know that food affects the extent and dynamic of literacy. Frederick Herzog rather shockingly noted that "Not all people are in a physical condition to grasp the Gospel. They are too poor."[2]

A second problem has to do with the nature of rights and the language of rights. Are we dealing with universal absolutes, revealed truth, or legal enactments?

Maurice Cranston has classified human rights as "a form of moral right . . . [that differs] from other moral rights in being the rights of all people at all times and in all situations." As moral rights they are not earned, bought, given, or inherited. They belong to man "simply because he is man."[3]

Richard Niebanck helpfully observed that "the specification of human rights stands midway between the articulation of general principles of justice and the actual conversion of those principles into legislation." Rights should be viewed within the moral and philosophical matrix that gives rise to law rather than from within formal law itself. As such, rights are part of a value system that stands in judgment over all legal systems and requires modesty in any claims of achievement. Rights have always been historically conditioned. Well into the eighteenth century, rights were perceived more as limitations on princes and governments, only gradually becoming "claims to protection against [or] liberation from perceived oppression." With the coming of the social question in the nineteenth century, rights became "claims to a just share of wealth or opportunity." Third world theorists have emphasized survival needs and rights to cultural authenticity. Because of this contextualizing of rights, Niebanck calls them "a provisional specification of justice within a socio-historical context."[4]

That leads to a third problem, namely the interconnection of human rights with all sorts of other social and political justice issues.

It can be argued that a particular style of government is necessary to guarantee or promote human rights. While the historical record is not totally convincing, it does suggest that constitutional foundations of authority and widespread participation in the political process prevent human rights guarantees from being arbitrary and limited.

Similarly, some limits on the power and influence of the military seem necessary if a broad spectrum of rights is to be achieved and extended. The very nature of militarism with its command structure and authoritarian order contradicts a wholesome regard for fundamental freedoms. Today with humanity hostage to the threat of a nuclear holocaust, the most fundamental right of all—to life itself—is jeopardized.

Some dialectic between individual freedom and public order has to pervade any understanding of rights. Indeed, until survival is no longer a daily concern and a community has some sense of security, it is doubtful that the struggle for individual political rights will be meaningful or successful.

A fourth problem with rights language is the ease with which this concern can become a slogan or shibboleth. Noam Chomsky said "human rights have only an instrumental function in the political culture, serving as a weapon against adversaries and a device to mobilize the domestic public behind the banner of our nobility."[5] This is perhaps unduly harsh, but certainly much of the use of rights language during the Cold War debates was in this form. Human rights have indeed been used to score points or upstage the opposition.

HUMAN RIGHTS: AN ISSUE FOR THE CHURCH

In light of these problems, rights terminology should be used with considerable care. The context is important, for recognition of rights is seen in historical development and is embedded in a cultural tradition. Rights must be seen within a moral as well as a socio-political framework, which is exactly why human rights are an issue for the church.

Up to this point we have described and analyzed the phenomenon of human rights. We are looking at an ideal. Specifically, there are certain prerogatives, such as protection and respect, that human beings ought to have as humans. Such prerogatives have been part of our history for a relatively short time. There is considerable disagreement over what precisely constitutes these prerogatives, partially because of historical conditioning. Yet rights belong to a moral realm of what ought to be rather than a legal realm of what is.

The connections to religion, specifically Protestant Christianity, are not obvious. Rights are not an explicit concept found in the Bible or in the history of the church. Indeed, the claim is widely made that rights develop out of eighteenth century deism that hardly represented traditional Christianity, either in its view of God or man.

The terminology of rights is not very biblical, although one could find proof texts. Nevertheless, the notion of individual prerogative is found both in the Old and New Testament. The Mosaic law frequently talks of the dignity of strangers, the poor, widows, neighbors. Both Moses and the prophets emphasized justice and love, not only in the treatments of individual people but also in the social solidarity and integrity of corporate life. Biblical accounts are much more concerned for the well-being of the other than for oneself or one's group.

The concern for justice and righteousness found in the law was built on an understanding of God as justice, which is to be reflected in the quality of being human. Men and women created in God's image reflect this right of God. As the Chilean Catholic bishops put it in 1977, "Man is God's creature, God's child, God's collaborator, and God's heir. We can indeed assert that man's rights were promulgated by God even before they were promulgated by man himself."[6] God as ruler includes the notion of judgment on injustice and the abuse of people.

The concepts of creation and providence similarly help us see a common creatureliness under the beneficence of a God of justice. The implications of faith in this kind of God kept expanding the horizons of the covenant people and critiquing their own failures

241

to be compassionate toward the poor and the outsiders. To use the words of Jürgen Moltmann: "It is the duty of Christian faith beyond human rights and duties to stand for the dignity of human beings in their life with God and for God."[7]

Recent campaigns for human rights can be seen as flowing from the biblical tradition.

Similarly, the New Testament shows in Jesus, God's interest in all kinds and classes of people. The Magnificat of Mary eloquently points to a Messiah who cares for the downtrodden and unpopular, including harlots, tax collectors, and Samaritans. Jesus demonstrated the respect due people even in their sin and alienation. Salvation becomes a dramatic redirection of all people and inclusion in a fellowship, overcoming barriers of nationality, class, and sex. The fullest realization of the Kingdom of God proclaimed by Jesus will be a universal society of justice and the full realization of humanity.

It is also clear from biblical teaching that the abuse of people and the denial of rights is characteristic of the human situation. Any natural state of innocence is long gone. Rights and justice are not viewed as being part of the given social order but rather represent a new beginning, a conscious change. As Richard Neuhaus put it, "Far from being natural (biblically speaking), respect for human rights represents human victory over the apparent laws of nature"[8]

The World Alliance of Reformed Churches study document provides a convenient summary of why and how human rights are an issue of the church. Human rights, they say, are grounded in "God's right to, that is, his claim on human beings." This claim "commits us to a view of human life in its wholeness expressed in three basic complementaries: male and female, the individual and society, human life and its ecological context." Such a view has a negative dimension. It "warns us about the destroying powers we face in the struggle for the realization of human rights." Finally, they "confess the liberating power of Jesus Christ and affirm the church's ministry of reconciliation and grace."[9]

While it is not difficult to demonstrate the moral basis of human rights in the Judeo-Christian tradition, we should not avoid the hard question of why there has been so little discussion over rights during the past several hundred years within the church. Or even more critically, the way this tradition has been implicated in violation and sometimes sanctioning the violating of rights.

From the eighteenth century to the present, churches have fitfully moved from a concern for prisoners and slaves to contemporary statements on minorities, women, and refugees. The best statements by the church such as "Common Ground on Human Rights" from the Commission of the Churches on International Affairs at St. Polten in 1977 identify six critical issues for the church's agenda: the basic right to life amidst unjust socio-political systems; the right to enjoy and maintain cultural identity; the right to participate in communal decision-making processes; the right to dissent; the right to personal dignity and the condemnation of torture; the right to choose and express faith and a religion.[10]

HUMAN RIGHTS AND THE CHURCH'S WITNESS

Frederick Herzog asserted that "justice is human rights attained on the basis of God's rights." Based on this, "The church has nothing more to contribute to the human endeavor than God . . . [who provides the] criterion of human need."[11] One can almost say that for the church human rights are intrinsic to its faith but have been incidental in its witness.

Long before the emergence of rights language, the struggle of godly people created the foundation for this fundamental human concern. The struggle between the faithful and wayward kings in ancient Israel and between the several faiths of New Testament times established the parameters of what William Lee Miller called the "first freedom." The Apostolic declaration, "We must obey God rather than man" is at the root of the quest for religious freedom. The struggle for religious freedom by continental sectarians and English nonconformists generated both reflection on rights and a secular search for political guarantees. This struggle is not yet over. Minorities struggle for freedom in religiously defined states— Islamic, Jewish, Hindu, Shinto, Christian, Buddhist. Politically prophetic minorities in Africa and Latin America—Protestant and Catholic—question the alliance of hierarchies with landed and military power. Peace churches in all continents continue to strive for the recognition of conscience as a means of expressing opposition to war.

The church does have some unique resources to bring to the struggle. The first of these is the rootedness of these convictions in a long tradition. Interest in human rights tends to fluctuate from year to year, from place to place. Furthermore, the fragility of the human condition is a reminder that humanity and humanism alone are insufficient bulwarks. Rights are rights only if they are cherished and promoted in the most difficult circumstances. Hence Neuhaus said, "Our commitment to human rights, if it is to be sustained, must depend not on practice, law or the passing policies of governments (though we must be earnestly concerned about these), but rather on a promise that bestows dignity upon every person and demands of every person a respect."[12]

A second resource for the church is its realism. The enthronement of human rights will never be total. If one is really committed to human dignity, then we need to be completely realistic about the extent of horror and barbarity in our world. Indeed, it is doubtful that one should ever put much confidence in the political order to gain or protect human rights. The temptations to compromise and the pressure of other interests mean most human rights initiatives in the public order are motivated by pragmatic political needs rather than a commitment to dignity and personality. For this reason, highly committed independent agencies like Amnesty International appear to be the most effective form of international intervention in support of human rights today.

A third resource for the church's witness is its understanding that human rights never stand alone. They are part of the religious search for a just society. They grow out of such fundamental concerns as human survival and well-being. Rights for concerned Christians can never be only a slogan or a partisan club. Meeting needs for food, shelter, health, and education are as essential to human rights as is freedom of religion, speech, association, and movement. For the Christian, the first concern is not for oneself but for the disadvantaged. Rights will not stand the test of time or equality without a commensurate commitment to duty.

Fourth, the church is a special resource because it is rooted in specific places but universal in its relationships. Being on location and involved gives to its witness authenticity and realism. The grass-roots character of the local church helps people to perceive true needs and provides a community of support in the struggle for human dignity. By transcending boundaries of nationality and class, the church provides a worldwide network of support and correction. When one part of the body suffers there will be resonating voices of support. When another part of the body becomes too comfortable with status and power, the word of admonition can be forthcoming.

Hence, the church will be most effective when it demonstrates in its own life the meaning of justice and human dignity. This ennobling and empowering of the oppressed will be a far more effective means for realizing human rights than any governmental action. The practice of human rights comes long before their enthronement. Adolfo Perez Esquivel, the Nobel prize-winning Argentine defender of human rights puts it in a classic way:

> I, as a Christian, find all [human rights] values in the Gospel. I believe that every man, as an individual, must make these his own values, recognizing in the other his own brother. We say simply that the first liberation every man experiences is to become conscious that he is a person. From that point on, he begins to have a critical awareness of his own situation and a recognition of others as his equals. I believe that this is how we're going to find solutions. It will not be putting our interests before man himself.[13]

Three Philosophies
of Human Rights

John P. Hittinger

INTRODUCTION

The moral and political landscape of America today is dominated by a single feature: the discourse of rights. What began as a
matter of carefully delimited political prerogatives and protections
in Anglo-American jurisprudence has become a wild free-for-all of
personal and collective claims and counterclaims. Serious matters
such as questions of life and death or fair participation in the
political order as well as frivolous matters such as the legitimation
of any felt need have been enveloped in a disputation concerning
rights. The proliferation of rights claims is a concern not simply
because of the sheer number of things to which people now claim
rights but especially because of the unmanageable conflicts
between those claims. As is known too well, the right to life of the
unborn is in conflict with the "right to choose" of the woman; the
right to hire and fire is in conflict with the right to equal opportunity
for minorities; the right of citizens to safety in a drug-free environment is in conflict with the right to privacy of workers; and so forth
and so on. In the United States the courts are swamped with
conflicts that they must adjucate. And in personal life, the claims
of rights are frequently used to justify any course of action that an
individual has chosen, at least if accompanied with the proviso that
it does not harm anyone. A subjectivist situation ethic has taken to
itself the discourse of rights to conceal its confusion and disorder.

All citizens, including those who are Christian, cannot help but be perplexed by this state of affairs. There is the obvious benefit of employing rights language. It is needed to protect the claims of religion from unwarranted state intrusion, to protect vulnerable members of society, and in general to influence public policy. On the other hand, the rights discourse carries with it many assumptions about human nature and the moral order that run contrary to the very things to be protected; assumptions involving unbounded freedom or an individualist conception of political order.[1]

In light of this confusion in theory and practice in politics and ethics today, there is a pressing need for a sound philosophy of human rights. In addition to the careful work of jurisprudence and political science in analysis of rights claims and the strategic planning for political action, there is the need for an ultimate rationale or account of the nature of and foundation for rights. This would provide us with a point of reference or orientation for assessing the spirit, and in some way the letter, of rights claims. This essay will discuss three philosophies of human rights in order to explore the question whether a doctrine of rights should be derived from a thesis concerning the autonomy of the human being from any constraint such as a divine or natural order, or whether human rights are to be construed precisely as an element or part of an objective moral order. The three areas of inquiry are the modern liberal philosophy of John Locke, the contemporary jurisprudence of David A. Richards, and the Thomistic philosophy of Jacques Maritain.

HOBBES, LOCKE, AND THE ORIGIN OF MODERN PHILOSOPHIES OF HUMAN RIGHTS

There is scholarly dispute over the historical origin of moral and political discourse involving rights. Richard Tuck, for example, traced the origin back to the late medieval ages and the theology of Jean Gerson, who in a work published in 1402 first assimilated the term *ius*, that is justice or right, to the term *libertas* or freedom.[2] As Tuck explained, this is one of the first appearances of the idea of an active right, a right that does not have a strict correlative duty, thereby implying that right is a dominion over something to use as one pleases. Human freedom becomes the fundamental moral fact, not virtue or divine command. The development of such a notion wound its way through late medieval nominalism and became a major theme in the works of Hugo Grotius, John Seldon, and Thomas Hobbes. Hobbes' work, especially *Leviathan*, is usually marked as the turning point from the ancient natural right or natural law to the modern account of natural rights.[3]

Hobbes most articulately challenged the fundamental presuppositions of the Thomistic synthesis of biblical theology and Aristotelian philosophy—such as the sociability of man and the possibility of a common good, the existence of a highest good in virtue and contemplation, and the natural law derived from such human teleology. Hobbes, rather, began with a state of nature as a state of war, the futility of seeking a good higher than the pleasant preservation of the individual. "Hobbes' philosophy is based upon a view of human nature as selfish and contentious; he denied that there exists any good higher than comfortable self-preservation. As a result, he derived the natural law from a more fundamental right of self-preservation."

Following the early lead of Gerson, Hobbes defined "right of nature" (*jus naturale*) as "the liberty each man hath, to use his own power, as he will himself, for the preservation of his own nature."[4] Hobbes clearly distinguished right (*jus*) from law (*lex*)—"right, consisteth in liberty to do, or forbeare; whereas Law, determineth, and bindeth to one of them; so that Law, and Right, differ as much, as Obligation, and Liberty." For Hobbes right, i.e., liberty, clearly takes precedent over law, i.e., obligation. The fundamental right or liberty of the self is unbounded or unlimited by anything; by the fundamental right of preservation, each man has a right to everything and anything done in the pursuit of preservation and is without blame. The intolerable conflicts between individuals, however, amount to a state of war. It is reasonable, therefore, to limit one's claim to things for the sake of self-protection. Morality exists by way of contract. Morality is a rational deduction of moral rules from the right of self-preservation.[5]

Hobbes's defense of individual rights required the existence of an absolute power in society to keep all potential wrongdoers in such a state of awe that they would obey the law. Hobbes's account was shocking in so many ways, not the least of which was its implicit anti-theistic philosophy, that it was frequently decried and banned. The direct contrast between Hobbes and the biblical and philosophical accounts of moral and political order would in many ways be the easiest approach to take to the philosophical questions about rights.

However, the philosophy of John Locke presents a more instructive case. Locke transformed the Hobbesian philosophy into a more palatable and balanced philosophy of natural rights. It is in the Lockean form that many Americans came to know about rights. And Locke's philosophy contains a fundamental ambiguity that pertains to the alternatives mentioned above. That is, the very tension over the autonomy of the person and the workmanship of God is played out in the writing and interpretation of Locke.

Locke sought to find a solution to the problem of politics that would restore peace to a country divided by wars of religion. The tolerance of religious belief required, in his mind, the lowering of the goal and mission of the temporal order, away from the inculcation of virtue and the defense of the faith to the protection of the temporal welfare of its citizens—rights to life, liberty, and property.[6] By removing the matter of religious contention from the civil sphere Locke hoped to quell the disturbances inflicted upon Europe because of intolerance. Hobbes, however, removed contentious matters by making the sovereign absolute over the determination of the beliefs of citizens. It was Locke who overcame the inconsistencies in this account and sought to place structural and formal limits upon the sovereign political power and to bind the sovereign to the respect of rights to life, liberty, and property. The division of powers, taxation with representation, and limited prerogatives of the state power balanced by a "right to revolution" are all part of the Lockean system. For Hobbes rights are fundamental moral claims against others; Locke adds to this the claim of the individual against the state, at least when a "long train of abuses" is perceived by a majority and rouses it to act. Locke's more moderate and reasonable account of human rights has appealed to generations of political statesmen and thinkers. However, the seed of radical autonomy as the basis for human rights blooms fully in subsequent philosophers in the natural rights tradition.

Like Hobbes, Locke derived the principles of limited government from a hypothetical state of nature.[7] This original state of nature is said to be a state of "perfect freedom." By freedom Locke meant no more than an absence of restraint. Locke mentioned the bounds of a natural law in the same passage with perfect freedom. This is to distinguish "liberty" from "license." The natural law initially guides men in the state of nature to refrain from harm: "The State of Nature has a Law of Nature to govern it, which obliges every one; and Reason, which is that Law, teaches all Mankind, who will but consult it, that being all equal and independent, no one ought to harm another in his Life, Health, Liberty, or Possessions." The restraint demanded by natural law derives from an additional characteristic of the state of nature: in the state of nature men are equal, in addition to being free.[8] Locke made clear that equality means equal jurisdiction, or the absence of subordination and subjection. The basis for this mutual respect and recognition is the fundamental problem, since it is the basis for natural law.

The key difficulty in interpreting the philosophy of John Locke pertains to the foundation of natural rights and the rationale for mutual restraint. Locke in fact gives a twofold rationale and foundation. On the one hand, he spoke of man as God's workmanship and from this axiom derived the right to life, liberty, and property as essential to the divine moral order; on other occasions he simply appeals to the primacy of self-preservation and unfolds from radical autonomy the list of rights and the self-interested basis for mutual respect.

In the first model, the basis for equal respect is divine workmanship and the order of creation. Locke argued that all creatures are equal under God and occupy the same rank or status as "creature."[9] Thus, no one can assume to take the position of God and rule over others. This argument from the order of creation reflects a premodern understanding of equality. Men are neither beasts nor gods but occupy equally a ground midway between.[10] It is neither appropriate to act as a god nor to treat others as beasts or inferior creatures. Locke explicitly used this pre-modern image. In light of this order of creation, man can make no claim to absolute dominion over his fellow creatures. Mutual respect depends upon the recognition of one's status as a creature, along with others, before the Creator. That is, a human being cannot claim the type of superiority that would authorize the destruction or arbitrary use of another human being, and rights protect this status.

But Locke said that the grasp of "natural law" did not depend on divine revelation, nor did it depend on knowledge of God's promulgated law and sanctions. This content can be appreciated independently of the workmanship model. For to deny the mutuality of equal right is to propel oneself into a state of war with others. And by such a declaration one has "exposed his Life to the others Power to be taken away by him." To put oneself in such an insecure state is most unreasonable and dangerous. One is open to being treated like a noxious beast.[11] It is more safe, more reasonable, to acknowledge the equality of rights. Thus, mere self-interest would counsel mutuality and restraint. Locke referred to the law of nature as simply the law of reason and common equity: the law of nature is the reasonable restraint of common equity that will establish mutual security. It is discovered through the person's own desire for safety and security. The basis for restraint is fear of harm and self-interest. According to this model of rights, selfish interest, or comfortable preservation, is the basis for one's claims. Enlightened self-interest leads one to recognize the equal right of others to their life, liberty, and property.[12]

The legacy of Locke is therefore ambivalent. The advocate of limited government and an apparent friend of the theistic tradition, Locke nevertheless underwrote a model of radical human autonomy in which freedom dominates the moral order. Locke's philosophy of human rights was derived from a subjectivist account of the good; it lowers the goal of the state to a supposedly neutral position; it imposes a minimal obligation of nonharm; and ultimately it does encourage self-interest. The minimal obligations embodied in civil law become the extent of morality; the wide sphere of private life must come to occupy the bulk of human energies. With Locke, such freedom was aimed at unlimited acquisition of property and the self found its affirmation in labor and the "work ethic." But such terms as equal freedom and mutual respect came to be transformed under the inspiration of Rousseau and Kant to mean much more than civic liberty and protection of private property. In contemporary American jurisprudence they have come to promote the existence of what University of Illinois Professor Gerard Bradley has recently referred to as the "erotic self."[13]

CONTEMPORARY DEVELOPMENTS BY DAVID A. RICHARDS

David A. J. Richards is Professor of Law at New York University and Director of N.Y.U.'s Program for the Study of Law, Philosophy, and Social Theory. His publications cover constitutional and criminal law, political philosophy, and ethics. One of his works is entitled *Sex, Drugs, Death and the Law*.[14] It is a treatise that follows the logic of the right to privacy to the point of decriminalizing all consensual sex acts, including prostitution, as well as drug use and euthanasia. Richards stressed the radical departure in ethics and politics characteristic of the modern theory of rights elaborated by Locke.[15] He sought to purge American thought and culture of its religious influence; this included what Richards called its Calvinistic public morality and also natural law principles derived from Catholic morality and tradition.[16] Richards' work is animated by a grand democratic vision of a "national community of principle," based upon human autonomy and human rights; such a vision demands the radical critique and elimination of pre-modern communities and traditions that have practiced "majoritarian tyranny" and "degradation of persons."[17] Richards accused the pre-moderns of being defined by an externally imposed system of appropriate roles. This degradation lies at the heart of alternatives to liberalism, he supposed, whether it be ancient Greek, medieval Christian, or contemporary conservatism. Indeed, the bible or Thomistic natural law must be considered degrading because they attempt to guide or otherwise restrict the creative freedom of individual persons.

Richards adopted a Lockean view on the legitimate scope of governmental interference with human freedom. The only grounds for interference are the protection of "general goods" such as life, liberty, health, and property. He described the general goods as those goods "that rational and reasonable people would want protected as conditions of whatever else they want."[18] This has been called a "thin theory of the good" because of its minimal elaboration of what constitutes a good human life.[19] The government cannot impose a substantive way of life upon the citizens nor act in behalf of such a vision; the government must be properly "neutral among diverse ways people may interpretively weigh the pursuit of those goods in their vision of a good and decent life."[20] Autonomy is precisely the ability to form a plan of life; for the government to act on behalf of a distinctive conception of the good life would be to violate the equal respect for persons, many of whom choose diverse ways of life. "Fundamental political morality rests upon a neutral theory of the good for persons, which is compatible with broadly pluralistic life-styles and forms, and the most fundamental right of persons is their right to equal concern and respect, compatible with a like respect for all, in defining their own visions of the good life."[21]

Richards thus construed the First Amendment as an attempt to "guarantee and secure to a person the greatest equal respect for the rational and reasonable capacities of persons themselves to originate, exercise and express and change theories of life and how to live it well."[22]

The deepest value-protection therefore is not religion per se but the higher powers of the person, the capacity for critical reflection as a rational and reasonable person and creative expression of oneself.

The right of conscience is the primary right and the paradigm for all others. Expanded to include any conscientious belief or actions derived therefrom, so too other rights are similarly expanded and developed in light of the principle of autonomy and respect for persons. Pornography is extolled as the higher option against the repressed Catholic and puritan public morality.[23] Sexuality is a core value for Richards because through it "we express and realize a wholeness of emotion, intellect and self image guided by the just play of the self-determining powers of a free person."[24] As a good liberal he wished to demonstrate the constitutional legitimacy of the right to privacy, its rightful application in such cases involving contraceptive use in marriage, nonmarital contraceptive use, pornography in the home, and abortion services. In addition he criticized the Supreme Court for its failure to apply privacy rights to consensual homosexual acts.[25] Homosexuals ought to be afforded the same rights to privacy, family, adoption and so on as heterosexuals.[26] Such would forward the "great work of collective democratic decency that is the Constitution of the United States."[27]

In the work of David Richards the seed of radical autonomy planted by Hobbes and Locke for the sake of acquisition of property and comfortable self-preservation has matured to become the fruit of a full moral subjectivism and the clear abandonment of and attack upon any shred of classical natural law and virtue. How can a Christian philosopher or theologian meet the challenge of this philosophy of human rights?

JACQUES MARITAIN AND A
THOMISTIC PHILOSOPHY OF RIGHTS

The philosophy of Jacques Maritain is very important in the development of Thomistic social and political philosophy. Maritain's work has influenced the writings of both Pope Paul VI and Pope John Paul II. Maritain was a man of the world who actively participated in the United Nations drafting of a Charter of Human Rights. He was very interested in incorporating a sound philosophy of human rights into Christian social doctrine. Maritain insisted that we must face the difference between two philosophies of rights, which must be traced back to fundamental differences in philosophy of God. He distinguished the underlying philosophies as theocentric humanism and anthropocentric humanism: "the first kind of humanism recognizes that God is the center of man; it implies the Christian conception of man, sinner and redeemed, and the Christian conception of grace and freedom. The second kind of humanism believes that man himself is the center of man and implies a naturalistic conception of man and of freedom."[28] According to the philosophy of theocentric humanism, human rights rest upon a natural and divine order, according to which human beings possess a dignity in virtue of their nature and destiny as creatures before God. The rights are limited in scope and are designed to assist persons in attaining their full stature as human beings. According to anthropocentric humanism, rights are based upon "the claim that man is subject to no law other than that of his will and freedom" and as a result has become "infinite, escaping every objective measure, denying every limitation imposed upon the claims of the ego."[29] In his philosophy Maritain sought to rescue the notion of human rights from philosophical errors.

Maritain sets himself to the larger task of harmonizing Christianity and the democratic ideal, which includes human rights. The tragedy of the modern age is "the motivating forces in modern democracies repudiating the Gospel and Christianity in the name of human liberty, while motivating forces in the Christian social strata were combatting the democratic aspirations in the name of religion." It is the burden of his *Christianity and Democracy* to have "Christian inspiration and the democratic inspiration recognize each other and become reconciled." Maritain believed that modern democracy transcends aristocracy and monarchy, somehow preserving the best of both. Maritain did not envision the degree to which "democratic inspiration" would far outstrip "evangelical inspiration," thereby creating forms of conflict. Consumerism and gay rights can both claim "democratic inspiration," whereas their "evangelical inspiration" is unfounded. Still, Maritain's praise of democracy was always qualified and critical as he wished Christianity to serve as a check on the base tendencies of the democratic impulse, which culminate in "bourgeois liberalism."[30]

Maritain believed that Christianity was actually the historical condition necessary for the emergence of a philosophy of human rights. The historical adequacy of this claim may be questionable;

yet it is a great and salutary truth. Human dignity, the value of labor, the rights of conscience, the relativity of earthly authority are but a few of the truths elaborated by Maritain as due to Christian inspiration. The problem is that "democratic impulse" is not a single force. As Maritain knows, its origins also lie in ancient republicanism and in the modern turn to mastery of nature and worldly satisfaction. Both movements bear some antagonism towards Christianity, even if the latter movement often masks itself in Christian phraseology. Maritain hoped to purge the democratic movement of its errors and rest it on a Christian footing. But perhaps the modern project is now purging itself of its Christian trappings. Maritain equated the "pursuit of happiness" with the cultivation of the mind and self-sacrificial love. More generally, Maritain identified freedom with moral mastery and virtue. Maritain is thus truly premodern in outlook. Those democratic theories proposing a "thin theory of the good" would not find in Maritain the true essence of democracy. Although the Christian theorist may appropriate the terms of democracy, and even show origins in Christianity, the fact that those terms have developed a life of their own makes the prospects for reconciling Christianity and contemporary democratic ethos very problematic. Maritain has high hopes that Christians may be in the vanguard of democratic reform; but we cannot now fail to see that Christians may be called to resist its destructive excesses.

Whereas *Christianity and Democracy* outlined the spirit of Maritain's task, his *Rights of Man and Natural Law* outlined the basic concepts of his political philosophy. Maritain has given a masterful and lucid account of human rights, beginning with the philosophical notion of person as a being with intellect and will, in virtue of which he is oriented towards the realm of being, truth, and goodness. Therein resides human dignity: the person possesses some measure of wholeness and independence and cannot live as a mere part of a social organism or in a state of total servility. The freedom of human beings is intimately connected to truth and objective moral good.[31] Moreover, the person is social by nature in function of both his needs and perfections, that is, in virtue of human indigence and human generosity. The personalist basis for politics demands a communal correlative; the good of persons is a communion in the good life. The individualism of modern philosophies of human rights must be challenged by a more adequate appreciation of the social nature of the person. Maritain used the dignity of

255

the person to resist all forms of totalitarianism; man is more than a part of a temporal society. The person as such aspires to a supratemporal good. Maritain often cited the words of Thomas Aquinas, "Man is not ordered to political society by reason of himself as a whole and by reason of all that is in him." Human rights protect this human dignity against the onslaught of totalitarian power. But the liberal interpretation of rights also is premised upon the denial of transcendence; thus we are faced with the question whether a project such as Professor Richards's enhances or ultimately degrades the human person.

The philosophy of human rights must address the issue of the human good and the human perfection. According to Maritain human rights flow from the divine order reflected in human nature; it is the "right possessed by God to see the order of His Wisdom in beings respected, obeyed and loved by every intelligence." He does not give a Kantian type of account based upon human autonomy. From a definite conception of the good life Maritain derived human rights. He defined the key modern notion of freedom in terms of virtue, which he called liberty of expansion: it is "the flowering of moral and rational life, and of those interior activities which are the intellectual and moral virtues." But the modern philosophy of human rights "believes in liberty without mastery of self or moral responsibility."[32] For Maritain, therefore, the essential political task is "a task of civilization and culture." The rights of man follow from this goal—they represent the conditions necessary for the full flowering of human perfection in the multitude. Maritain expounded upon personal, civic, and economic rights in light of this concrete human good. For the precise enumeration one may consult *The Rights of Man and Natural Law*, including a resumé of rights provided at its end.[33] The rights protect and provide the material and legal conditions for human perfection. Suffice it to say that Maritain expected the slow but steady emancipation of man from the conditions that thwart his aspirations to truth and virtue. Liberation is for the sake of human perfection, not an end in itself, nor a freedom without terminus or measure. This account of freedom would appear to preserve what is best in a theory of rights by joining it to a notion of virtue. Rights are not a claim of subjectivity or a liberty free of obligation but conditions for human excellence, challenging political prudence in its task to achieve a common good and a decent human life for all.

CONCLUSION: THE CHALLENGE OF RIGHTS DISCOURSE

There is an obvious need for the understanding of and the use of rights discourse today. It is necessary for the very protection of the claims of religion and religious activity in a secular state. Rights language helps to explain the advocacy for the vulnerable members of society that Christian conscience demands. Thus, to influence public policy in a salutary way, rights discourse is inevitable. But the basis for and purpose of human rights discourse must be clearly understood if we are to avoid the confusion and equivocations of the present day. We must engage in a serious reading of modern philosophers such as Hobbes and Lockes; in addition, the contemporary developments of Rawls, Dworkin and Richards must be squarely faced; finally, Christian thinkers like Maritain and John Paul II have opened up horizons for a sound philosophy of human rights.[34]

The use of rights discourse is fraught with difficulties, not the least of which is sheer equivocation when engaged in discourse with the dominant liberal culture. The philosophy of human rights underlying such accounts—the radical autonomy of the human person—must be challenged and redefined. A sound philosophy of rights must make it clear that freedom is not an absolute, that rights are imbedded in an objective moral order that is accessible by reason (natural law) and revelation (divine law), and finally that rights are correlated with duties to the community, to others, and ultimately to God.

Notes

Legal citation form has been followed in several chapters except for some general references. All court cases have been set in italics for the sake of consistency.

Preface: William Bentley Ball

1. Alexander Pope, "An Essay on Man."
2. William Ball, "Why Can't We Work Together?" *Christianity Today*, July 16, 1990. I had earlier pursued the theme of this article in the Catholic lay magazine *Crisis* under the title "We'd Better Hang Together," Oct. 1989.

Chapter 1: Carl F. H. Henry

1. Willis B. Glover, *Biblical Origins of Modern Secular Culture,* (Macon, Ga.: Mercer Univ. Press, 1984), 140.
2. Ibid.
3. Ibid., 239.
4. Lesslie Newbiggin, *The Gospel in a Pluralist Society* (Grand Rapids, Mich.: Eerdmans, 1989), 1.
5. Ibid., 14.
6. Ibid., 4.
7. Ibid., 10.
8. Huston Smith, *Beyond the Post-Modern Mind* (New York: Crossroad, 1982), 134.
9. Jacques Ellul, *Living Faith: Belief and Doubt in a Perilous World* (San Francisco: Harper and Row, 1983), 193 ff.
10. Alasdair MacIntyre, *After Virtue* (South Bend, Ind.: Notre Dame Univ. Press, 1981).
11. Pitirim A. Sorokin, *The Crisis of Our Age* (New York: Dutton, 1942).
12. Ibid., 225.
13. Cf. Frederick Case, "Minds at Risk," *Washington Post,* July 29, 1991, C5.
14. Cf. H. Wayne House, *Restoring the Constitution* (Dallas, Tex.: Probe, 1987), 114.
15. David A. Noebel, *Understanding the Times* (Manitou Springs, Col.: Summit Press, 1991), 541.
16. Glover, 130.

Chapter 1 : James Hitchcock

1. "Religion in America," *The Gallup Report* 222 (Mar. 1984).
2. For a summary of such theories see David Martin, *A General Theory of Secularization* (New York: Harper and Row, 1978), 3.
3. Peter L. Berger, *A Rumor of Angels* (New York: Doubleday, 1969), 7.
4. Ibid., 41.

Chapter 2: Paul C. Vitz

1. This work was supported by a contract from the Department of Education, "Toward a Psychology of Character Education" and by an NIE Grant: NIE–G–84–0012 (Project No. 2–0099), "Equity in Values Education." This material will be part of a forthcoming book on moral education by the author.
2. S. B. Simon, L. W. Howe, H. Kirschenbaum, *Values Clarification*, rev. ed. (New York: Hart, 1978), 18–22.
3. Ibid., 15.
4. Ibid., 16.
5. Ibid., 18–22
6. Ibid., 18–19.
7. Ibid. For reasons that are not clear, Simon, Howe, and Kirschenbaum, in their very popular book *Values Clarification*, propose a different order: prizing, then choosing, then acting. (This order is no accident or error since it is stated with emphasis on page 19 and later in connection with one of the strategies on page 36.) Here there is little attention paid to what the students' initial values are or where they come from, since the first emphasis is on prizing their already existing values. Nor is there concern with whether the values of these young students are *worth* prizing. For these prominent Values Clarification theorists (Simon et al.) the process begins with the irrational, emotional prizing of whatever students already happen to have as values or goals and the secondary purpose of evaluation of consequences is overshadowed by the initial prizing and by the emphasis on self-acceptance.
8. L. E. Raths, M. Harmin, and S. B. Simon, *Values and Teaching*, 2nd ed. (Columbus, Ohio: Merrill, 1978), 30.
9. N. Wolterstorff, *Education for Responsible Action* (Grand Rapids, Mich.: Eerdmans, 1980), 17–18.
10. For critiques of this strongly narcissistic position, see D. T. Campbell, "On the Conflicts between Biological and Social Evolution and between Psychology and Moral Tradition," *American Psychologist* 30 (1975), 1103–26; W. K. Kilpatrick, *Psychological Seduction* (Nashville, Tenn.: Nelson, 1983); Christopher Lasch, *The Culture of Narcissism* (New York: Norton, 1979); Paul C. Vitz, "Psychology as Religion," *The Cult of Self Worship* (Grand

Rapids, Mich.: Eerdmans, 1977); M. Wallach and L. Wallach, *Psychology's Sanction for Selfishness* (San Francisco, Calif.: Freeman, 1983).

11. Raths, 9.

12. Konrad Lorenz, *On Aggression* (New York: Harcourt, Brace World, 1966); Niko Tinbergen, "On War and Peace in Animals and Man," *Science* CLX (1968) 1411–18.

13. E. O. Wilson, *Sociobiology, the New Synthesis* (Cambridge, Mass.: Harvard , 1975); D. T. Campbell, "On the Conflicts between Biological and Social Evolution and between Psychology and Moral Tradition," *American Psychologist* 30 (1975): 1103–26; D. T. Campbell, "Comments on the Sociobiology of Ethics and Moralizing," *Behavioral Science* 24 (1979): 37–45.

14. See writings of Edward Wynne, professor, College of Education, University of Illinois–Chicago.

15. E.g., Raths, 41.

16. Wolterstorff, 111–31.

17. Raths.

18. Wolterstorff, 127.

19. Raths, 114–15.

20. For a critique of Values Clarification procedures as well as other aspects since, see R. A. Baer, Jr., "Values Clarification as Indoctrination," *The Educational Forum* 41 (1977):155–65; Baer, "A Critique of the Use of Values Clarification in Environmental Education," *The Journal of Environmental Education* 12 (1980): 13–16; Baer, "Teaching Values in the Schools," *Principal* (Jan. 1982): 17–21, 36; W. J. Bennett and E. J. Delattre, "Moral Education in the Schools," *Public Interest* 50 (1978): 81–98; Paul C. Vitz, "Values Clarification in the Schools," *New Oxford Review* 48 (June 1981): 15–20.

21. Simon, (1978).

22. Baer, (1977), 155–65.

23. Bennett and DeLattre, 86.

24. Simon, 49–53.

25. Bennett and Delattre, 84.

26. Ibid., 86.

27. A. L. Lockwood, "Values Education and the Right to Privacy," *Journal of Moral Education* (Oct. 1977): 9–26.

28. Ibid., 10.

29. Ibid., 11.

30. Ibid.

31. Ibid., 19

32. Ibid., 20.

33. M. Eger, "The Conflict in Moral Education, *The Public Interest* (Spring 1981): 62–80.

34. E.g., see Vitz, "The Use of Stories in Moral Devlopment: New Psycho-

logical Reasons for an Old Education Method," *American Psychologist* 45 (1990): 709–20.

35. E.g., see S. L. Hanson and A. L. Ginsburg, "Gaining Ground: Values and High School Success, " *American Education Research Journal* 25 (1988): 344–65; D. Solomon, M. Watson, K. Delucchi, E. Schaps, and V. Battistich, "Enhancing Children's Prosocial Behavior in the Classroom," *American Educational Research Journal* 25 (1988): 527–54. Also contact Kevin Ryan, professor, School of Education, Boston University, or Edward Wynne, professor, College of Education, University of Illinois–Chicago.

Chapter 2: Harold O. J. Brown

1. Margaret Thatcher, "Unfinished Business, New Challenges," The Clare Boothe Luce Lecture for 1991 (Washington, D.C., Heritage Foundation, 1991), 8.
2. Pitirim A. Sorokin, *Social and Cultural Dynamics*, rev. one-vol. ed. (Boston: Porter Sargent, 1957), 494.
3. Ibid.
4. *Chicago Tribune*, Oct. 31, 1991, sec. 2., 1.
5. Sorokin, 494.
6. Raffaleo Balestrini, *Aborto, Infanticido, ed Espositione d'Infante* (Torino, Italy: Bocca, 1888), 141.
7. Edgar Bodenheimer, *Jurisprudence: The Philosophy and Method of the Law*, rev. ed. (Cambridge, Mass: Harvard, 1974).
8. Magda Denes, *In Necessity and Sorrow: Life and Death in an Abortion Hospital* (New York: Basic Books, 1976).
9. Lawrence Lader, *Abortion II: Making the Revolution* (Boston: Beacon, 1973), 225.
10. Beverly Wildung Harrison, *Our Right to Choose: Toward a New Ethic of Abortion* (Boston: Beacon, 1983).
11. *Chicago Tribune*, Sept. 29, 1991, op–ed page.

Chapter 3: Richard D. Land

1. "But our citizenship is in heaven" (Phil. 3:20 NIV).
2. Thomas Jefferson, "Notes on Virginia," Query 18, in *The Complete Jefferson*, ed. Saul K. Padover (New York: Duell, Sloan and Pearce, Inc., 1943), 676.
3. George Washington, "Farewell Address," Sept. 19, 1796, in *The Basic Writings of George Washington*, ed. Saxe Cummins (New York: Random House, 1948), 637.
4. Ibid., 638.
5. John Adams, Address to the Officers of the 1st Brigade, 3rd Division, Massachusetts Militia, Oct. 11, 1798.

6. Quoted in Adrienne Koch, ed., *The American Enlightenment: The Shaping of the American Experiment and a Free Society* (New York: George Braziller, 1965), 228–29.

7. Robert A. Baker, *A Baptist Source Book* (Nashville: Broadman, 1966), 43.

8. Robert Allen Rutland, *The Birth of the Bill of Rights, 1776–1791*, rev. ed. (Boston: Northeastern Univ. Press, 1983), 196.

9. Quoted in Lynn R. Buzzard and Samuel Ericsson, *The Battle for Religious Liberty* (Elgin, Ill: Cook, 1982), 45–46.

10. Ibid., 46.

11. James E. Tull, *Shapers of Baptist Thought* (Valley Forge, Penn.: Judson Press, 1972), citing *Irwin H. Polishook, Roger Williams, John Cotton and Religious Freedom* (Englewood Cliffs, N.J.: Prentice Hall, 1967), 46.

12. Roger Williams to Daniel Abbot, Jan. 15, 1681, in Edmund S. Morgan, ed. *Puritan Political Ideas* (Indianapolis, Ind.: Bobbs-Merrill, 1965), 224.

13. Daniel Webster, Discourse delivered at Plymouth, Massachusetts, Dec. 22, 1820.

14. Alexis de Tocqueville, *Democracy in America*, vol. 1, the Henry Reeve text as revised by Francis Bowen now further corrected and edited with a historical essay, editorial notes, and bibliographies by Phillips Bradley (New York: Vintage, 1945), 319.

15. Ibid., 311.

16. Ibid., vol. 2, 6.

17. Ibid., 152.

18. Ibid., vol. 1, 314.

19. Richard John Neuhaus, "What the Fundamentalists Want," *Commentary* 43 (Washington, D.C.: reprinted by Ethics and Public Policy Center, Washington, D. C., May 1985).

20. Dwight D. Eisenhower, quoted in Will Herbert, *Protestant-Catholic-Jew* (Garden City, N.Y.: Doubleday, 1955), 97.

21. *Zorach v. Clauson*, 343 U.S. 306 (1952).

22. Ibid.

23. *Abington School District v. Schempp*, 374 U.S. 203 (1963).

24. Richard John Neuhaus, *The Naked Public Square, Religion and Democracy in America* (Grand Rapids, Mich.: Eerdmans, 1964), 97–98.

25. Ibid., 98.

Chapter 3: Henry J. Hyde

1. William Lee Miller, *The First Liberty: Religion and the American Republic* (New York: Knopf, 1986), 145–46.

2. Cf. George Weigel, "A Grammar for the Debate—The Return of Natural Law," in *Catholicism and the Renewal of American Democracy* (Mahwah, N.J.: Paulist, 1989), 191–203.

Chapter 4: William E. May

1. Pope John Paul II, "'Stand Up' for Human Life," *Origins: NC Documentation Service* 9.18 (Oct. 18, 1979), 279.
2. See Vatican Council II, *Gaudium et spes*, n. 24.
3. Karol Wojtyla, *Love and Responsibility*, trans. H. Willetts (New York: Farrar, Straus, Giroux, 1981), 41.
4. Human beings are radically different in kind from other animals precisely because their ability to know the truth and make free choices can be explained only if there is present, within their makeup as human *beings*, entitative components entirely lacking to other animals. For an excellent philosophical consideration of this important subject see Mortimer Adler, *The Difference of Man and the Difference It Makes* (New York: Meridian, 1968).
5. The immortality of the soul was solemnly defined at the eighth session of the Fifth Lateran Council in 1513. See text in *Enchiridion Symbolorum Definitionum et Declarationum de rebus fidei et morum*, ed. Henricus Denzinger and Adolphus Schönmetzer, 33rd ed. (Romae: Herder, 1975), n. 1440.
6. E.g., see Vatican Council II, *Gaudium et spes*, nn. 3 and 14.
7. See St. Thomas Aquinas, *Summa Theologiae*, 1, 78.
8. It is for this reason that St. Thomas could write, "anima mea non est ego." See his *Super primam epistolam ad Corinthios lectura*, XV, lec. ii.
9. Germain Grisez, "Dualism and the New Morality," in *Atti del Congresso Internazionale (Roma-Napoli, 17–24 Aprile 1974) Tommaso D'Aquino nel Suo Settimo Centenario*, Vol. 5, *L'Agir Morale*, ed. Marcellino Zalba (Napoli: Editioni Dominicane Italiane, 1977), 275.
10. See Pope John Paul II, Apostolic Exhortation *Familiaris Consortio*, n. 30.
11. See Michael Tooley, "Abortion and Infanticide," *Philosophy and Public Affairs* 2 (1972): 44, 48, 55. Tooley later developed this theme more extensively in his *Abortion and Infanticide* (New York: Oxford , 1983), 50–86.
12. E.g., see Daniel Callahan, *Abortion: Law, Choice, and Morality* (New York: Macmillan, 1970), 497.
13. For further theological reflection on relevant texts of Scripture, see Augustine Regan, "The Worth of Human Life," *Studia Moralia* 6 (1968): 215–25.
14. *Catechismus ex decreto Ss. Concilii Tridentini ad Parochos, Pii V, Pont. Max., iussu editus* (Rome: Propagandae Fidei, 1839), 2:125–31 (on the fifth commandment). A recent English translation by Robert I. Bradley and Eugene Kevane has been published under the title *The Roman Catechism* (Boston: St. Paul Editions, 1985), 409–19. In the text I use the translation provided by Bradley and Kevane. A new catechism for the Universal Church is being prepared. One can be certain that this

new catechism will reaffirm the teaching of the *Catechism of the Council of Trent* on the absolute immorality of the intentional killing of the innocent.

15. Pius XII, "Address to the St. Luke Union of Italian Physicians," *Discorsi e Radio-messaggi* 6 (Nov. 12, 1944): 191. Cited in the Congregation for the Doctrine of the Faith's *Declaration on Procured Abortion, Acta Apostolicae Sedis* 66 (Nov. 18, 1974): 735, n. 15; trans. Austin Flannery, *Vatican Council II: More Post-Counciliar Documents* (Northport, N.Y.: Costello, 1982), 452.
16. The sources for this concept of *innocent* have recently been analyzed by John Finnis, Germain Grisez, and Joseph Boyle in their *Nuclear Deterrence, Morality and Realism* (New York: Oxford , 1987), 87–88.
17. Pope Pius XII, "Address to the St. Luke Union of Italian Physicians," 191–92.
18. The "direct"–"indirect" terminology in the sense used by Pope Pius XII and the modern magisterium emerged after Aquinas, who conveys the same meaning with terms such as *per se* (=direct) as opposed to *per accidens, praeter intentionem*, etc.
19. St. Thomas Aquinas, *Summa Theologiae*, 49, 2; cf. *In 2 Sent.*, d. 32, q. 2, a. 1; *Summa Contra Gentiles*, 2, 41; *De malo*, 1, 5; *De veritate*, 5, 4, ad 1.
20. John Finnis, "The Consistent Ethic—A Philosophical Critique," in *Consistent Ethic of Life*, ed. Thomas G. Fuechtmann (Kansas City, Mo.: Sheed and Ward, 1988), 148–49.
21. Vatican Council II, *Gaudium et spes*, n. 27; emphasis added.
22. For an extended treatment of the reasons why contraception is an *anti-life* choice see Germain Grisez, Joseph Boyle, John Finnis, and William E. May, "'Every Marital Act Ought to Be Open to New Life': Toward a Clearer Understanding," *Thomist* 52 (1988): 365–426; reprinted in Germain Grisez et al., *The Teaching of Humanae Vitae: A Defense* (San Francisco: Ignatius, 1988).

Chapter 4: Norman L. Geisler

1. Paul Kurtz, ed., *Humanist Manifestos One and Two* (Buffalo, N.Y.: Prometheus, 1973), 8.
2. Ibid., 17.
3. Joseph Fletcher, *Situation Ethics: The New Morality* (Philadelphia: Westminster, 1966), 120.
4. Ibid., 134
5. Ibid., 43–44
6. See Kurtz, *Humanist Manifestos One and Two*, 18–19.
7. Kurtz, 6.
8. Fletcher, 43–44
9. C. S. Lewis, *The Abolition of Man* (New York: Macmillan, 1973), 56.

10. Ibid.
11. Greg Bahnsen, *Theonomy in Christian Ethics*, (Phillipsburg, NJ: Presbyterian and Reformed, 1977), 445.
12. See essay by Micheal Kinsley, "Judges, Democracy and Natural Law," *Time*, Aug. 12, 1991, 68.
13. Natural law is described in the Bible as that which human beings "do by nature" (Rom. 2:14 KJV). It is the law "written in the hearts" of all men (v. 15 NASB). Those who disobey it go contrary to nature (Rom. 1:27). The natural law condemns such things as "wickedness, evil, greed, and depravity." The actions opposed to it are "envy, murder, strife, deceit, and malice" (Rom. 1:29–31 NASB).
14. Heraclitus, *"Fragments 197-201"* trans. G. S. Kirk and J. E. Raven, *The Presocratic Philosophers: A Critical History with a Selection of Texts* (New York: Cambridge, 1964), 188–89.
15. See Plato, *Republic* (New York: Pantheon, 1964), Books IV–VI.
16. Cicero stated that "there is a true law, right reason in accord with nature; it is of universal application, unchanging and everlasting. . . . There is one law . . . binding at all times upon all peoples." Cicero, *The Republic* 3.22, cited in Paul E. Sigmund, *Natural Law in Political Thought* (Cambridge, Mass.: Winthrop, 1971), 22.
17. Philip Schaff, ed., *A Select Library of the Nicene and Post-Nicene Fathers of the Christian Church*, vol 5. (Grand Rapids, Mich.: Eerdmans, 1956), *On the Spirit and the Letter*, by Augustine, 48.
18. Schaff, vol. 3, *On the Good of Marriage*, by Augustine, 203, 407.
19. Schaff, *On the Spirit and the Letter*, by Augustine, 48.
20. Ibid., 5.103.
21. Schaff, *Reply to Faustus the Manichean*, 19.1, by Augustine, 239.
22. Thomas Aquinas, 1–2 *Summa Theologica* 91.2, in *Basic Writings of Saint Thomas Aquinas*, ed. Anton Pegis (New York: Random House, 1944), 750.
23. Aquinas, 1–2 *Summa Theologica* 90.4, in *Basic Writings*, 747.
24. Ibid., 90.1, 743.
25. Ibid., 91.1, 748.
26. For further discussion see *Thomas Aquinas: An Evangelical Appraisal* (Grand Rapids, Mich.: Baker, 1991).
27. Aquinas, 91.4, 753.
28. John Calvin, *Institutes of the Christian Religion* 2.2.22 , vol. I, 241.
29. Ibid., 241.
30. Ibid., 242.
31. Ibid., 1.5.1., 51.
32. John Calvin, *The Epistles of Paul the Apostle to the Romans and to the Thessalonians (2:14)*, vol. 8, eds. David W. Torrance and Thomas F. Torrance (Grand Rapids, Mich.: Eerdmans, 1979), 48.
33. Ibid.

34. Ibid.
35. Ibid., 49.
36. John Locke, *An Essay*, 2.6, in *The Great Books*, vol. 35 (Chicago: Encyclopedia Britannica, 1952), 26.
37. Richard Hooker, *Of the Laws of Ecclesiastical Polity*, 4 vols. (1594, 1597). Available in a reprint edition from Harvard University Press, Cambridge, Mass.
38. Locke, 26.
39. A strong religious argument for natural law is presented by St. Paul in Romans 1–2 where the justice of God in condemning the unbelieving Gentiles was based on the fact that God had clearly (1:19 NASB) revealed himself through nature to all men and that his law was "written in their hearts" (2:15 NASB). It certainly would be contradictory to divine justice to condemn people for not living according to a standard they never had and never knew. So the fact of natural law seems absolutely indispensable to the belief in divine justice.
40. C. S. Lewis, 95–121.
41. See Rom. 2:14 NASB.
42. Confucius, *Analects of Confucius*, trans. Arthur Waley (New York: Random, 1966), 25:23; cf. 12:2.
43. Seneca, as cited by John T. Noonan, Jr., ed., *The Morality of Abortion: Legal and Historical Perspectives* (Cambridge, Mass.: Harvard, 1970), 7, footnote.
44. Ibid.
45. The biblical support that a human embryo is fully human is very strong:

    1. Unborn babies are called *children*, the same word used of infants and young children (Luke 1:41–44, cf. 2:12–16; Ex. 21:22), and sometimes even of adults (1 Kings 3:17).

    2. The unborn are *created* by God (Ps. 139:13), just as God created Adam and Eve in his image (Gen. 1:27).

    3. The life of the unborn is protected by the same punishment for injury or death (Ex. 21:22) as that of an adult (Gen. 9:6).

    4. Christ was human (the God-man) from the time he was *conceived* in Mary's womb (Matt. 1:20–21; Luke 1:26f.).

    5. The image of God includes *male and female* (Gen. 1:27), but it is a scientific fact that maleness or femaleness (i.e., gender) is determined at the moment of conception.

    6. Unborn children possess personal characteristics such as *sin* (Ps. 51:5) and *joy* that are distinctive of human persons.

7. Personal pronouns are used to describe unborn children (Gen. 25:22–23; Jer. 15) just as they are of any other human being.

8. The unborn are said to be *known* intimately and personally by God as he would know any other person (Job 10:2–7; Ps. 139:15–16; Jer. 1:5).

9. The unborn are even *called* by God before birth (Gen. 25:22–23; Judg. 13:2–7; Isa. 49:1, 5; Gal. 1:15).

46. See my "The Beginning of Individual Life" in Francis Beckwith and Norman L. Geisler, *Matters of Life and Death* (Grand Rapids, Mich.: Baker, 1991).
47. See Jewish Torah, Ex. 21:22–23.
48. See Frank Beckwith, ch. 5.
49. Mark Twain, *Christian Science* (New York: Harper and Brothers, 1907), 359–361.
50. Ibid.

Chapter 5: Randall J. Hekman

1. George Barna, *What Americans Believe* (Ventura, Calif.: Regal, 1991), 157.
2. E.g., see "Putting Children First: A Progressive Family Policy for the 1990's" (Washington, D.C.: Progressive Policy Institute, 1991).
3. Barna, 85.
4. In this discussion I acknowledge my indebtedness to Kevin Campbell of Focus on the Family.
5. E.g. , see comments, Blackstone's Commentaries, ed. B. C. Gavit, 193.

Chapter 5: Carl A. Anderson

1. John Paul II, Apostolic Exhortation, *Familiaris Consortio* Nov. 2, 1981, para. 13.
2. Ibid., para. 3.
3. Ibid. , para. 17.
4. Paul Johnson, "The Family as an Emblem of Freedom," in *Emblem of Freedom: The American Family in the 1980s*, eds. Carl Anderson and William Gribbin (Durham, N.C.: Carolina Academic Press, 1981), 25.
5. Max Rheinstein, *Marriage Stability, Divorce and the Law* (Chicago: Univ. of Chicago Press, 1972), 267.
6. Ibid., 200.
7. Quoted in Paul Hazard, *European Thought in the Eighteenth Century: From Montesquieu to Lessing* (Cleveland, Ohio: Meridian, 1963), 208.
8. Ibid., 165.
9. Ibid., 169.

10. Rheinstein, 25.
11. Carl Becker, *The Heavenly City of the Eighteenth Century Philosophers* (New Haven, Conn.: Yale, 1932), 66.
12. Robert Nisbet, *The Quest for Community* (New York: Oxford, 1953), 140.
13. Rheinstein, 202.
14. Mary Ann Glendon, "The French Divorce Reform Law of 1976," *American Journal of Comparative Law* 24 (1976): 199–200.
15. Karl Marx and Frederick Engels, *Selected Works* (New York: International Publishers, 1968), 468. See also, Jean Bethke Elshtain, *Public Man, Private Woman: Women in Social and Political Thought* (Princeton, N.J.: Princeton Univ. Press, 1981), ch. 4.
16. Ibid., 502–03.
17. Ibid., 503.
18. Ibid., 510.
19. Ibid.
20. Murray Feshbach, "The Soviet Union: Population Trends and Dilemmas," *Population Bulletin* 37 (1982): 5. See also, Paul Sachdev, ed., *International Handbook on Abortion* (New York: Greenwood, 1988) and Allan Carlson, *The Swedish Experiment in Family Politics: The Myrdals and the Interwar Population Crisis* (New Brunswick, Canada: Transaction Publishers, 1990).
21. Jan Gorecki, "Communist Family Pattern: Law as an Instrument of Change," University of Illinois Law Forum 1972 (1972): 121, 124; see also Harold Berman, "Soviet Family Law in Light of Russian History and Marxist Theory," *Yale Law Journal* 56 (1946): 26.
22. Quoted in Igor Shafarevich, *The Socialist Phenomenon* (New York: Harper and Row, 1980), 245.
23. Ibid.
24. Ibid., 261.
25. Jerome Shestack, "The Jurisprudence of Human Rights," in *Human Rights in International Law: Legal and Policy Issues*, vol.1, ed. Theodor Meron (New York: Oxford, 1984), 83.
26. *L'Osservatore Romano*, Feb. 13, 1982, English edition.
27. The following references present "conscience" in a variety of contexts: Acts 23:1, 24:16; Rom. 2:15, 9:1, 13:5; 1 Cor. 8:7, 10, 12, 10:25, 27–29; 2 Cor. 1:12, 4:2, 5:11; 1 Tim. 1:5, 19, 3:9, 4:2; 2 Tim. 1:3; Titus 1:15; Heb. 9:9, 14, 10:2, 22, 13:18; 1 Peter 2:19, 3:16, 21. See Gerhard Friedrich, *Theological Dictionary of the New Testament*, VII, trans. and ed. Geoffrey Bromiley (Grand Rapids, Mich.: Eerdmans, 1971), 899–919.
28. George Parkin Grant, *English-Speaking Justice* (South Bend, Ind.: Univ. of Notre Dame Press, 1985), 16.
29. Ibid., 28.
30. Ibid.
31. 420 U.S. 113 (1973); see especially Charles Rice, *Beyond Abortion: The*

Theory and Practice of the Secular State (Chicago: Franciscan Herald Press, 1979) and John T. Noonan, Jr., *A Private Choice: Abortion in America in the Seventies* (New York: Free Press, 1979).

32. *Byrn v. New York City Health and Hospital Corp.,* 286 N.E. 2d 887 (1972).

33. Ibid., 889.

34. 381 U.S. 479 (1965). For an analysis of the *Griswold* case, see Robert Bork, "Neutral Principles and Some First Amendment Problems," *Indiana Law Journal* 47 (1971): 1; and Louis Henkin, "Privacy and Autonomy," *Columbia Law Review* 74 (1974): 1410.

35. Ibid., 486.

36. 495 U.S. 438 (1972).

37. Ibid., 453.

38. Ibid.

39. Mary Ann Glendon, "Marriage and the State: The Withering Away of Marriage," *Virginia Law Review* 62 (1976): 699.

40. Lenore Wietzman, *The Divorce Revolution: The Unexpected Social and Economic Consequences for Women and Children in America* (New York: The Free Press, 1985), 357–78.

41. U.S. Congress, Senate, Committee on the Judiciary, *Hearings on the Nomination of Robert H. Bork to be Associate Justice of the Supreme Court of the United States*, 100th Cong., 1st sess., 1987.

42. William May, *Sex, Marriage, and Chastity* (Chicago: Franciscan Herald Press, 1981), 77–79.

Chapter 6: Robert A. Destro

1. D. H. Oakes, *The Wall Between Church and State* (Univ. of Chicago Press, 1963), 41 and n.

2. E.g., see Ohio Rev. Code §3321.38 (Baldwin, 1991).

3. See Social Studies Review and Development Committee, *One Nation, Many Peoples: A Declaration of Cultural Interdependence: The Report of the New York State Social Studies Review and Development Committee* (Albany, N.Y.: New York State Education Dept., June 1991).

4. J. Berger, "Parents v. Condom Plan: New York Schools Face Legal Wilderness in Giving Condoms With No Parental Say," *New York Times*, Oct. 1, 1991 (Final Late ed.), A1, col. 5. Condom program enrollment will proceed without either parental consent or knowledge. Compare *West Virginia State Board of Education v. Barnette*, 319 U.S. 624 (1943).

5. *Accord, Brown v. Board of Education*, 347 U.S. 483 (1954). [segregation as a barrier to choice in education; black children could not "choose" to attend school nearest their home, much less to an integrated one.]

6. *1990 Statistical Abstract of the United States*, Table 209, 129.

7. Id. Total spending in all sectors amounted to $161.8 billion, or $3572.61 per child in both public and private schools.

8. See A. Thernstrom, *School Choice in Massachusetts* (Boston: Pioneer Institute for Public Policy Research, 1991), 100, quoting Chubb and Moe, *Politics, Markets and America's Schools* (Washington, D.C.: The Brookings Institution, 1990), 38.

9. E.g., see D. C. Rudd, "Kimbrough's Plan Unifying Its Opposition," *Chicago Tribune*, July 7, 1991, Final ed., Chicagoland Section, at 1, col. c. [recounting the political turmoil surrounding the recent reform efforts and its impact on school councils.]

10. See *Chaney v. Grover*, 159 Wis.2d 150, 464 N. W. 2d 220 (Wis. App. 1990), *review granted*, No. 90–807 (Wisconsin Supreme Court, pending). [coalition of education and civil rights organizations seeking to invalidate the program and a companion case brought by a coalition of parents and children enrolled in nonsectarian private schools seeking to invalidate regulations of the Superintendent of Public Instructions that would effectively turn private schools into carbon copies of the public schools.]

11. National Catholic Education Assn., *Catholic Schools for the 21st Century: The Catholic School and Society* (Washington, D.C, 1991), 7, quoting National Center for Education Statistics, *Projections of Education Statistics to 2000*, 12 [hereafter NCEA 2000].

12. There were 25,616 nonpublic schools operating during 1985–86. 38.6 percent (9,911) of those schools were affiliated with the Catholic Church, 42 percent were affiliated with other religious groups, and 19.3 percent had no religious affiliation. The mean enrollment for all nonpublic schools during that period was 234. See Id. at 8, quoting United States Dept. of Education, Office of Educational Research and Improvement, *Digest of Education Statistics*, 1989, 66.

13. The briefs of the parties in the litigation over the Milwaukee Parental Choice Program are quite instructive, even to the well-informed student of educational choice issues.

14. E.g., Ohio Constitution, Art. VI, §2 (Baldwin, 1991); Wisconsin Constitution, Art. X, §3 (1991).

15. U.S. Const. Amend. XIV (1868). *Pierce v. Society of Sisters,* 268 U.S. 466 (1925).

16. A third alternative, cross-registration or "shared time," is not widely available and it is opposed for the same reasons that any aid might be available for children attending nonpublic schools. See note 19 *post.*

17. See generally, A. Thernstrom, note 8, op cit. (and sources collected there); D. J. Monti, *A Semblance of Justices* (Univ. of Mo. Press, 1985). Noting that one of the few ways in which one can make sense of the contradictory findings about the promise of structural and institutional reform in the public school system and its effects after *Brown v. Board of Education* and the mandate to desegregate in the 1970s is to admit the "heretical" possibility that "[p]erhaps . . . such fights

merely purchased the illusion of change, while providing a medium through which the legitimacy of old boundaries and institutions could be reaffirmed by virtue of having been tested so severely."

18. There have been a whole series of cases raising the issue of the fairness of various state education funding mechanisms. The federal courts generally do not get involved absent proof of intentional discrimination on the basis of a prohibited classification such as race or national origin. See *San Antonio School District v. Rodriguez*, 411 U.S. 1 (1973). The State courts have not been so timid. See generally J. K. Underwood and W. E. Sparkman, *School Finance Litigation: A New Wave of Reform*, 14 Harv. J. Law Pub. Pol. 517 (1991).

19. E.g., see *Lanner v. Wimmer*, 662 F.2d 1349 (10th Cir. 1981); *Thomas v. Allegany County Board Of Education*, 51 Md. App. 312; 443 A.2d 622 (1982); *Snyder v. Charlotte Public School Dist.*, 421 Mich. 517; 365 N.W.2d 151 (1985); *Traverse City School District v. Attorney General*, 384 Mich. 390, 185 N.W.2d 9 (1971); State ex rel *School Dist of Hartington v. Nebraska Bd. of Ed.*, 188 Neb. 1, 195 N.W. 2d 161 (1972), *cert denied* 409 U.S. 921 (1972).

20. See generally B. C. Hafen, *The Constitutional Status of Marriage, Kinship, and Sexual Privacy — Balancing the Individual and Social Interests*, 81 Mich. L. Rev. 463 (1983).

21. *Pierce v. Society of Sisters*, 268 U.S. 510, 535 (1925).

22. The degree to which government education policy affects families is debatable, but the fact that there is some effect is not seriously disputed. The task here is to explore the assumptions concerning private and, in particular, Catholic schools, and to attempt to discern the basis upon which current policies penalize choice.

23. The number of non-Catholic, poor, minority, inner-city children attending Catholic schools in their own neighborhoods, even though the tuition is clearly a burden on the family, is a good example of such a rational trade-off. James Coleman, for example, found that such enrollment provides disadvantaged youth with a marked advantage. See generally A. Thernstrom, note 8, op. cit.; J. S. Coleman and T. Hoffer, *Public and Private High Schools: The Impact on Communities* (New York: Basic Books, 1987), ch. 1; A. Thernstrom, "Outclassed: Why Parochial Schools Beat Public Ones," *The New Republic*, May 13, 1991, 12–14.

24. See M. Levinson, "Living on the Edge," *Newsweek*, Nov. 4, 1991, at 23, col. 3. Recounts the story of a lower-middle class minority parent who pulled her child from a church-related school and enrolled him in a public school due to lack of funds, notwithstanding the increased physical danger to her child.

25. *Wisconsin v. Yoder*, 406 U.S. 205, 233 (1972). The state courts have also recognized the sensitivity of this concern. In *re Rose Child Dependency Case*, 161 Pa. Super. 204, 208, 54 A. 2d 297 (1947), for example, the court

discussed the policy behind involuntary deprivation of child custody for neglect and stated:

> It is a serious matter for the long arm of the state to reach into a home and snatch a child from its mother. It is a power which a government dedicated to freedom for the individual should exercise with extreme care, and only where the evidence clearly establishes its necessity. . . . Under our system of government children are not the property of the state to be reared only where and under such conditions as officials deem best.

> The power of the juvenile court is not to adjudicate what is for the best interests of a child but to adjudicate whether or not the child is neglected.

In re Rinker, 117 A. 2d 780 (Pa. Super. 1955). Accord Petition of Kauch, 358 Mass. 327, 264 N. E. 2d 371 (1970).

26. See generally J. K. Underwood and W. E. Sparkman, op. cit., n. 18.
27. See Harris v. McRae, 448 U.S. 297, 318 (1980).
28. Allan Bloom, The Closing of the American Mind (New York: Simon Schuster, 1987), 26.
29. Such "public" choices include not only those made by state and local educational authorities but also those made by federal authorities (including judges), whose authority exists because the public schools are agencies of the states.
30. James M. O'Neill, Catholicism and American Freedom (New York: Harper Bros, 1952), 6.
31. See M. DeWolf Howe, The Garden and the Wilderness (Chicago: Univ. of Chicago Press, 1965), 11. "The evangelical principle of separation endorsed a host of favoring tributes to faith— tributes so substantial that they have produced in the aggregate what may fairly be described as a de facto establishment of religion." See generally D. Boles, The Bible, Religion, and the Public Schools (Ames, Iowa: Iowa State Univ. Press,1961), 35; Utter Larson, Church and State on the Frontier: The History of the Establishment Clauses in the Washington State Constitution, 15 Hastings Const. L.Q. 451, 458-67 (1988). In Witters v. Washington Department of Services for the Blind, 112 Wash. 2d 363; 771 P. 2d 1119 (1989), reaffirming on state constitutional grounds, 102 Wash. 2d 624, 689 P. 2d 53 (1984), rev'd, 474 U.S. 481 (1986), Justice Utter of the Washington Supreme Court has noted that "Such practices were particularly offensive to the recent waves of Catholic and Jewish immigrants who objected to their children receiving compulsory instruction in the majority Protestant faith." See B. Parkany, "Religious Instruction in the Washington Constitution" (thesis, Washington State Lib., 1965); D. Boles, supra. Id. (Utter, Dolliver, Durham JJ. dissenting).
32. J. Madison, "Memorial and Remonstrance Against Religious Assess-

ments" (1785), quoted in *Everson v. Board of Education*, 330 U.S. 1, 63–72 (1947) (Rutledge, J., dissenting).

33. C. Beals, *Brass-Knuckle Crusade* (New York: Hastings House, 1960), 45–77, quoted in P. A. Fisher, *Behind the Lodge Door: Church, State and Freemasonry in America* (Washington, D.C.: Shield, 1988).

34. H. A. Buetow, "A History of United States Catholic Schooling" (National Catholic Education Assn., Keynote Series #2, 1985), 13.

35. Lyman Beecher, *A Plea For the West*, 2d ed. (Cincinnati: Truman Smith, 1835), 20.

36. Sr. M. E. Thomas, "Nativism in the Old Northwest" (doctoral diss., Catholic Univ. of America, Washington, D.C., 1936), 53.

37. Id. at 182.

38. W. G. Katz, *Religion and the American Constitutions* (Chicago:Northwestern Univ. Press, 1964), 63.

39. W. O. Bourne, *History of the Public School Society of the City of New York*, (1870), 7, 31, 45, quoted in P. A. Fisher, op. cit., note 33.

40. Northwest Ordinance of 1787, as adopted by Congress, Statutes of 1789, c. 8 (Aug. 7, 1789) ["Religion, morality, and knowledge being necessary to good government and the happiness of mankind, schools and the means of education shall be forever encouraged"].

41. See *Board of Education v. Minor,* 23 Ohio St. 211 (1872). [attempt to compel the Cincinnati Board of Education to mandate reading of the King James Bible over the objection of Catholic parents].

42. P. Blanshard, *American Freedom and Catholic Power* (Boston: Beacon Press, 1949), 74–85.

43. See generally, People ex rel *Ring v. Board of Education* of District 24, 245 Ill. 334, 92 N.E. 251 (1910) [school prayers: objection of Catholic parents]; *Board of Education v. Minor*, 23 Ohio St. 211 (1872) [Bible reading: objection of Catholic parents to use of King James Version].

44. P. Blanshard, note 42, op. cit., 80.

45. O'Neill, op. cit., note 30, 7–8.

46. S. F. B. Morse, *Imminent Dangers to the Free Institutions of the United States through Foreign Immigration and the Present State of the Naturalization Laws: A Series of Numbers Originally Published in the New York Journal of Commerce by AN AMERICAN* (New York: E. B. Clayton, 1835) [*The American Immigration Collection* (New York: Arno Press and *New York Times*, 1969], 8–9 (emphasis in the original).

> Yes; these Foreign despots are suddenly stirred up to combine and promote the greater activity of Popery in this country; and this too, just after they had been convinced of the truth, . . . that Popery is utterly opposed to Republican liberty. These are the facts in the case. Americans, explain them in your own way . . . . [T]hese crowned heads have . . . sent Jesuits as their almoners, and ship-loads of Roman Catholic emigrants, and for the sole purpose of converting us

to the religion of Popery, and without political design, credat Judaeus Appella, non ego.

47. E.g., see *Wisconsin v. Yoder*, 406 U.S. 205 (1972); *Pierce v. Society of Sisters*, 268 U.S. 466 (1925): *Meyer v. Nebraska*, 262 U.S. 390 (1923).

48. Brief of Appellee, *Pierce v. Society of Sisters*, 286 U.S. 466 (1925) at 97, quoting the Official Oregon Ballot Summary.

49. Compare J. M. Cuddihy, *No Offense: Civil Religion and Protestant Taste* (New York: Seabury Press, 1978).

50. 286 U.S. 466 (1925).

51. E.g., see *Aguilar v. Felton*, 473 U.S. 402 (1985); *Meek v. Pittenger*, 421 U.S. 349 (1975).

52. *Aguilar v. Felton*, 473 U.S. 402 (1985); *Lemon v. Kurtzman*, 403 U.S. 602 (1971).

53. *Ball v. School District of Grand Rapids*, 473 U.S. 373 (1985); *Aguilar v. Felton*, 473 U.S. 402 (1985).

54. The "political divisiveness" argument had its genesis in *Walz v. Tax Comm'n*, 397 U.S. 664 (1970), when the late Justice John Harlan cited one sentence in Professor Paul Freund's article, "Public Aid to Parochial Schools," 82 Harv. L. Rev 1680 (1969), to support the idea that highly charged political controversies such as debates over the funding for church-related schools "engender a risk of politicizing religion" and that "history cautions that political fragmentation on sectarian lines must be guarded against." 397 U.S. at 695. See generally E. M. Gaffney, Jr., *Political Divisiveness Along Religious Lines: The Entanglement of the Court in Sloppy History and Bad Public Policy*, 24 L. Rev. (St. Louis Univ., 1980) 205, 223.

55. Compare *United States v. Lee*, 455 U.S. 252 (1982) and *Allen v. Wright*, 468 U.S. 737 (1984) with *Aguilar v. Felton*, 473 U.S. 402 (1985) and *Flast v. Cohen*, 392 U.S. 83 (1968). But see *Valley Forge Christian College v. Americans United for Separation of Church and State*, 454 U.S. 464 (1982).

56. In *County of Allegheny v. American Civil Liberties Union Greater Pittsburgh Chapter*, 109 S.Ct. 3086, 3119 (1989), the Court appears to have adopted Justice Sandra Day O'Connor's "endorsement" analysis as a component of the Establishment Clause standard of review. It provides:

> As a theoretical matter, the endorsement test captures the essential command of the Establishment Clause, namely, that government must not make a person's religious beliefs relevant to their standing in the political community by conveying a message "that religion or a particular religious belief is favored or preferred."

The test also holds that "Disparagement sends the opposite message," but the Court has yet to deal with such a case directly. But see *Edwards v. Aguillard*, 107 S.Ct. 2573 (1987); *Aguilar v. Felton*, 473 U.S. 402 (1985); *Meek v. Pittenger*, 421 U.S. 349 (1975).

57. E.g., see *Board of Education v. Mergens*, 110 S.Ct. 2356 (1990); *Board of Education of Island Trees Union School Dist. v. Pico*, 457 U.S. 853 (1982); *Mozert v. Hawkins County Board of Education*, 827 F.2d 1058 (6th Cir., 1987), rev'g 647 F. Supp. 1194 (E.D. Tenn. 1986); *Brandon v. Board of Education of Guilderland Central School Dist.*, 635 F.2d 971 (2d Cir. 1981), *cert denied*, 454 U.S. 1123 (1981).

58. E.g., see *State of Michigan v. Emmanuel Baptist Preschool,* 434 Mich. 380, 455 N.W. 2d 1 (1990).

59. *Wisconsin v. Yoder,* 406 U.S. 205 (1972).

60. E.g., see *Florey v. Sioux Falls School Dist.*, 619 F.2d 1311 (8th Cir. 1980) [holiday programs].

61. Bloom, op. cit., note 28.

62. E. Flax, "New Guide Calls for Broad Approach to Sex Education," *Education Week*, Oct. 23, 1991, 12, col. 1 [SIECUS suggesting that sex education "should have the same prominence in the curriculum as more traditional subject areas, such as mathematics"].

63. L. Tribe, *American Constitutional Law*, §14–13, 2d ed. (Westbury, N.Y.: Foundation Press, 1988) 1274–75 nn.

64. Id. §14-8, 1204.

65. L. H. Tribe, *Constitutional Law* , 2d ed. (Westbur, N.Y.: Foundation Press, 1988), 1154–1301. For an illuminating discussion of this topic, see G. V. Bradley, "Church Autonomy in the Constitutional Order: The End of Church and State," *La. L. Rev.* 49 (1989): 1057, 1086.

66. J. P. Dolan, *The American Catholic Experience: A History from Colonial Times to the Present* (Garden City, N.J.: Doubleday, 1985) ch. 11, noted in A. Thernstrom, op. cit. note 8, 98 and n. 9.

Chapter 6: James W. Skillen

1. For background here, see Rockne M. McCarthy, James W. Skillen, and William A. Harper, *Disestablishment a Second Time: Genuine Pluralism for American Schools* (Grand Rapids, Mich.: Eerdmans and the Christian Univ. Press, 1982), 30–51; Charles L. Glenn, Jr., *The Myth of the Common School* (Amherst, Mass.: Univ. of Massachusetts Press, 1988), 86–178; James W. Skillen, "Thomas Jefferson and the Religious Character of Education," *Religion and Public Education* 14 (Winter 1987): 379–87; David Little, "Thomas Jefferson's Religious Views and their Influence on the Supreme Court's Interpretation of the First Amendment," *Catholic University Law Review* 56 (1976): 56ff.; Lawrence Cremin, ed., *The Republic and the School: Horace Mann on the Education of Free Men* (New York: Teachers College Press, 1957);

Jonathan Messerli, *Horace Mann: A Biography* (New York: Knopf, 1972).

2. See Diane Ravitch, *The Great School Wars: New York City, 1805–1973* (New York: Basic Books, 1974), 3–104; Glenn, 63–85, 115–78, 207–34; McCarthy, Skillen, Harper, 52–90; Rockne M. McCarthy, "Public Schools and Public Justice: the Past, the Present, and the Future," in Richard John Neuhaus, ed., *Democracy and the Renewal of Public Education* (Grand Rapids, Mich.: Eerdmans, 1987), 57–75; Michael B. Katz, *Class, Bureaucracy, and Schools: The Illusion of Educational Change in America* (New York: Praeger, 1975), 56–104; and Laurence Iannaccone, "Changing Political Patterns and Governmental Regulations," in Robert B. Everhart, ed., *The Public School Monopoly: A Critical Analysis of Education and the State in American Society* (San Francisco: Pacific Institute for Public Policy Research, 1982), 295–324.

3. See Ravitch, 33–76; Glenn, 73–84, 196–206; Vincent Lannie, *Public Money and Parochial Education: Bishop Hughes, Governor Seward, and the New York School Controversy* (Cleveland, Ohio: Case Western Reserve Univ. Press, 1968); Stanley K. Schultz, *The Culture Factory; Boston Public Schools, 1789–1860* (New York: Oxford, 1973); Edward G. Hartmann, *The Movement to Americanize the Immigrant* (New York: Columbia, 1948); Ray Allen Billington, *The Protestant Crusade, 1800– 1860: A Study of the Origins of American Nativism* (Chicago: Quadrangle Paperbacks, 1964 [1938]); Herman Eschenbacher, "Education and Social Unity in the Ante-bellum Period," *Harvard Educational Review* 30 (Spring 1960); C. H. Edson, "Schooling for Work and Working at School: Perspectives on Immigrant and Working-Class Education in Urban America, 1880–1920," in Everhart, 145–87; Charles L. Glenn, Jr., "'Molding Citizens,'" in Neuhaus, 25–56.

4. There is, of course, the question of whether anything educational can be "nonsectarian." The claim of neutrality is made by those who assume that "nonsectarian" means "neutral." All the evidence points to the impossibility of neutrality in any form of education. See Richard A. Baer, Jr., "American Public Education and the Myth of Value Neutrality," in Neuhaus, 1–24; Richard A. Baer, Jr., "The Myth of Neutrality," in Ken Sidey, ed., *The Blackboard Fumble* (Wheaton, Ill.: Victor, 1989); and Richard A. Baer, Jr., "The Supreme Court's Discriminatory Use of the Term 'Sectarian,'" *The Journal of Law and Politics* 6 (Spring 1990): 449–68.

5. Historical development of the argument here and below can be found in James W. Skillen, "Religion and Education Policy: Where Do We Go From Here?" *The Journal of Law and Politics* 6 (Spring 1990): 503–29; McCarthy, Skillen, Harper, 15–72; Skillen, "Thomas Jefferson and the Religious Character of Education."

6. For a historical and documentary introduction to the tradition of

pluralist or pluriform political philosophy, see James W. Skillen and Rockne M. McCarthy, eds., *Political Order and the Plural Structure of Society* (Atlanta, Ga.: Scholars Press, 1991), esp. the Introduction. For background on different approaches to the ordering of pluriform societies, see Kenneth McRae, ed., *Consociational Democracy: Political Accommodation in Segmented Societies* (Toronto: McClelland and Stewart, 1974), particularly Jurg Steiner, "The Principles of Majority and Proportionality," 98–106. With regard to schooling and the plural structure of society, see Charles L. Glenn, Jr., *Choice of Schools in Six Nations* (Washington, D.C.: U.S. Department of Education, 1989).

7. The argument that follows is detailed in Skillen, "Religion and Education Policy," 519–29; McCarthy, Skillen, Harper, 124–36; McCarthy, et al., *Society, State and Schools*, 169–208; and Rockne M. McCarthy, "A New Definition of 'Public' Education," in Sidey, 77–88.

8. For background on this point, see William Lee Miller, *The First Liberty: Religion and the American Republic* (New York: Knopf, 1986); James Davison Hunter and Os Guinness, eds., *Articles of Faith, Articles of Peace: The Religious Liberty Clauses and the American Public Philosophy* (Washington, D.C.: The Brookings Institution, 1990), 17–39; Bernard J. Zylstra, "Using the Constitution to Defend Religious Rights," in Lynn R. Buzzard, ed., *Freedom and Faith: The Impact of Law on Religious Liberty* (Westchester, Ill.: Crossway, 1981), 106–15; Carl Esbeck, "Establishment Clause Limits on Governmental Interference with Religious Organizations," *Washington and Lee Law Review* 41 (1984): 347–420, and Carl Esbeck, "Religion and a Neutral State: Imperative or Impossibility," *Cumberland Law Review* 15 (1984–85): 74ff.

9. See Stephen Arons, *Compelling Belief: The Culture of American Schooling* (Amherst: Univ. of Massachusetts Press, 1986); Stephen Arons, "Separation of School and State: Pierce Reconsidered," *Harvard Educational Review* 46: 77–104; John E. Coons, "Intellectual Liberty and the Schools," *Journal of Law, Ethics, and Public Policy* 1 (1985): 495–533; John E. Coons and Stephen D. Sugarman, *Education by Choice: The Case for Family Control* (Berkeley, Calif.: Univ. of California Press, 1978); Michael E. Manley-Casimir, ed., *Family Choice in Schooling* (Lexington, Mass.: Heath, 1982); Tyll van Geel, "The Search for Constitutional Limits on Governmental Authority to Inculcate Youth," *Texas Law Review* 62 (1983): 199–297. For comparisons with other countries, see Thomas J. La Belle, "A Comparative and International Perspective on the Prospects for Family and Community Control of Schooling," in Everhart, 269–93, and Dennis Doyle, "Family Choice in Education: The Case of Denmark, Holland, and Australia," (National Institute of Education Contract no. EPA 30032, 1984). For a variety of views, both pro and con, on "educational choice," see the special issue of *Educational Leadership* 48 (Dec. 1990–Jan. 1991) on the subject. For background

on the question of taxation, see Thomas W. Vitullo-Martin, "The Impact of Taxation Policy on Public and Private Schools," in Everhart, 423–469.

10. See the *amicus curiae* brief of the Association for Public Justice on the Mobile, Alabama case (*Smith v. Board of School Commissioners of Mobile County*, case No. 87–7216) before the U.S. Court of Appeals for the Eleventh Circuit, May 1987.

11. The importance of parental choice amounts to much more than its enhancement of "market freedom." See Stephen Arons, "Out of the Fire and into the Frying Pan," *First Things* (Jan. 1991): 48–52, a critique of John E. Chubb and Terry M. Moe, *Politics, Markets, and American Schools* (Washington, D.C.: The Brookings Institution, 1990).

12. With respect to the important question of racial justice, see Stephen Sugarman, "Part of the Solution Rather than Part of the Problem: A Role for American Private Elementary and Secondary Schools," *William and Mary Law Review* 31 (1990): 681–93; Stephen Arons, "Educational Choice as a Civil Rights Strategy," in N. Devins, ed., *Public Values, Private Schools* (London: Falmer, 1989), 63–80; Stephen Arons and Charles R. Lawrence III, "The Manipulation of Consciousness: A First Amendment Critique of Schooling," in Everhart, 225–68; Charles R. Lawrence III, "Segregation 'Misunderstood': The *Milliken* Decision Revisited," *University of San Francisco Law Review* 12 (Fall 1977): 16–38; Coons and Sugarman, 109–24; James W. Skillen, *The Scattered Voice: Christians at Odds in the Public Square* (Grand Rapids, Mich.: Zondervan, 1990), 119–39, 203–05.

Chapter 7: George C. Fuller

1. John Henry Newman, *The Idea of a University*, ed. Martin J. Svaglic (New York: Holt, Rinehart and Winston, 1960), 139. Robert T. Sandin, *The Search for Excellence: The Christian College in an Age of Educational Competition* (Macon, Ga.: Mercer Univ. Press, 1982), 26, directs attention to these words of John Calvin: "Not all the articles of true doctrine are of the same sort. Some are so necessary to know that they should be certain and unquestioned by all men as the proper principle of religion. Such are: God is one; Christ is God and the Son of God; our salvation rests on God's mercy; and the like. Among the churches there are other articles of doctrine disputed which still do not break the unity of faith. . . . A difference of opinion over these nonessential matters should in no wise be the basis of schism among the churches" (*Institutes of the Christian Religion*, IV, 1, 12). Roman Catholic and evangelical education may differ in important apologetic and epistemological formulations, but points of contact seem apparent today among those who cherish the best in each heritage.

2. Newman, 335.
3. Ibid., 331.
4. Aurelius Augustine, *The Works of Aurelius Augustine*, trans. and ed. Marcus Dods, vol. 2 (Edinburgh: T. and T. Clark, 1871), 49.
5. Cornelius van Til, *Essays on Christian Education* (Nutley, N.J.: Presbyterian and Reformed, 1977), 8. Van Til affirmed, "If the facts of the world are not created and redeemed by God in Christ, then they are like beads that have no holes in them and therefore cannot be strung into a string of beads. If the laws of the world are not what they are as relating the facts that are created and redeemed by Christ, these laws are like a string of infinite length, neither end of which can be found. Seeking to string beads that cannot be strung because they have no holes in them, with the task of the educator who seeks to educate without presupposing the truth of what the self-attesting Christ has spoken in the Scriptures" (p. 16). Van Til further stated, "Non-Christians believe that the Universe has created God. They have a finite god. Christians believe that God has created the universe. They have a finite universe. Non-Christians therefore are not concerned with bringing the [student] face to face with God. They want to bring the [student] face to face with the Universe" (p. 185).
6. Vern S. Poythress, "Mathematics," in *Foundations of Christian Scholarship*, ed. Gary North (Vallecito, Calif.: Ross House Books, 1976), 188.
7. Arthur F. Holmes, *Shaping Character: Moral Education in the Christian College* (Grand Rapids, Mich.:Eerdmans, 1991), 4.
8. van Til, 1.
9. Sandin, 75.
10. Newman, 330.
11. van Til, 81.
12. Newman, 19–20.
13. C. Robert Pace, *Education and Evangelism: A Profile of Protestant Colleges*, Profiles Sponsored by The Carnegie Commission on Higher Education, vol. 11 (New York: McGraw-Hill, 1972), 1.
14. Ibid.

Chapter 7: Russell A. Kirk

1. Orestes Brownson, "Catholic Schools and Education," reprinted in Alvan S. Ryan, ed., *The Brownson Reader* (New York: P. J. Kennedy and Sons, 1955), 144.
2. Leo R. Ward, *Blueprint for a Catholic University* (St. Louis, Mo.: B. Herder, 1949), 7.
3. Ibid.
4. Ibid., 96–7.

Chapter 8: William Bentley Ball

1. *Catholic Standard and Times*, Nov. 30, 1978.
2. NC News Service, Nov. 15, 1978.
3. That right is a separately stated free-standing right, not an adjunct to other First Amendment rights (freedom of speech, press, assembly, or petition).
4. Jacques Maritain, *Man and the State* (Chicago: Univ. of Chicago Press), 149. Closely linked to the concept of the common good is the principle of subsidiarity. The encyclical of Pius XI, *Quadragesimo anno*, stated the principle: "Of its very nature, the true aim of all social activity should be to help individual members of the social body, but never to destroy or absorb them." Consequently "it is wrong to withdraw from the individual and commit to the community at large what private enterprise and industry can accomplish." Thus "it is a disturbance of right order for a larger and higher organization to arrogate to itself functions which can be performed efficiently by smaller and lower bodies."
5. Today they have not departed from that view but have successfully supported laws in their state protecting the freedom of all religious schools from undue regulation, rights of the unborn and the terminally ill, and freedom of school choice for all parents.
6. C. Dawson, *Religion and The Totalitarian State*, quoted in R. Kirk, *The Portable Conservative Reader*, 494.
7. *State of Vermont v. LaBarge*, 357 A. 2d 121 (1976); *State of Ohio v. Whisner*, 47 Ohio St. 2d 181 (1976); *Kentucky State Board of Education v. Rudasill*, 589 S.W. 2d 877 (1979); *Bangor Baptist School v. State of Maine*, 576 F. Supp. 1299 (D.Me. 1983).
8. Through the efforts of the evangelical Keystone Christian Education Association, aided by the Pennsylvania Catholic Conference, this power was taken away. In 1988, Pennsylvania adopted a statute, which some have rightly called "Magna Carta for religious schools," depriving the State Board of its prior regulatory powers. P.L. 1321, 24 P.S. 13–1327.
9. The schools did not believe that they were a law unto themselves, free to disregard the common good. They hence made clear the fact that they did not resist laws prescribing a curriculum of the traditional basic branches of learning, reasonable health, safety and building codes, laws against fraudulent solicitation, etc. Also they were amenable to self-administering, value-free, nationally standardized achievement tests and to providing parents with the results of these.
10. They were Dr. John Cronin, President, Massachusetts Higher Education Assistance Corporation; Dr. George Madaus, Director, Center for

the Study of Testing; Evaluation and Educational Policy; and Dr. Kevin Ryan, Professor of Education, Brown University.

11. In 1977, the National Labor Relations Board sought to exercise its jurisdiction over Catholic schools in Scranton and Chicago. Federal courts in the Pennsylvania cases held that the imposition of NLRB jurisdiction would violate both the Free Exercise and Establishment Clauses of the First Amendment. *Caulfield v. Hirsch*, E.D. Pa. No. 76–279 (Civ. 1977); *McCormick v. Hirsch*, 460 F. Supp. 1337 (1978). In a sequel to the Pennsylvania cases, *NLRB v. Catholic Bishop of Chicago*, 440 U.S. 490 (1979), the Supreme Court held that the Congress had not actually intended church-operated schools to be within NLRB jurisdiction. Thus the Court avoided the question of whether, if Congress *had* so intended (as the Pennsylvania federal judges had assumed), applying the Act to such schools would have been unconstitutional. It nevertheless gave strong indication that it would.

12. But public aid to parents in, for example, the form of vouchers, should not provide any such danger where, as in Pennsylvania and California currently, voucher proposals have been made which are workable, beneficial, and devoid of unacceptable state educational controls.

13. In *Torcaso v. Watkins*, 367 U.S. 488 (1961) the Supreme Court held nontheistic belief-groupings such as Secular Humanism and Ethical Culture (capitalization by the Court) to be "religions" within the meaning of the Religion Clauses, protected though they had already been under the other clauses of the First Amendment. This radical departure, while necessarily subjecting secular humanism, for example, to the prohibitions of the Establishment Clause, also gave it Free Exercise status.

14. Section 501 (c) (3) of the Internal Revenue Code, under which religious bodies may seek income tax-exempt status, while of dubious constitutionality, is also unclear in its language. It provides, for example, that "no substantial part" of the activities of an organization within its terms shall consist of attempting to influence legislation. Under this broad language, IRS has issued complex regulations which have proved greatly limiting to the rights of religious bodies to act with freedom in the public forum.

15. 397 U.S. 664 (1976).

16. Nor did the Court, in *Walz*, hold that there is a Free Exercise right of churches to tax-exemption. The Free Exercise Clause was not addressed by the Court in that case.

17. But in 1989, the Court brandished that yardstick, saying that the exemption recognized in *Walz* "presented the legitimate purpose and effect of contributing to the community's moral and intellectual diversity and encouraging private groups to undertake projects that advance the community's well-being and that would otherwise have

to be funded by tax revenues or left undone." *Texas Monthly v. Bullock*, U.S.,109 S. Ct. 890 (1989).

18. 455 U.S. 252 (1982).

19. 461 U.S. 574 (1983). The bizarre *political* story of this case I have related in my chapter in *The Assault on Religion*, ed. R. Kirk (Center For Judicial Studies, 1986).

20. See C. J. Friedrich, *The Age of the Baroque*, Reprint of 1952 edition (Westport, Conn.: Greenwood, 1983) 15–17.

21. See R. Grunberger, *The Twelve-Year Reich* (New York: 1979), 481–501.

22. 455 U.S. 252 (1989).

23. The Court had already indicated this in *Bob Jones* and *Regan v. Taxation With Representation*, 411 U.S. 540, 544 (1983).

24. D. Kelley, *Why Churches Should Not Pay Taxes*.

25. The Philadelphia Code, §14-2007 (7) (i).

26. *United States Artists Theater Circuit, Inc. v. City of Philadelphia, Philadelphia Historical Commission*, 595 A.2d 6, 11 (Pa. 1991).

27. I make the assumption that a house of worship is a building considered by its religious owner as impressed with a sacred character. Under the law of the Catholic Church, for example, it is called a "sacred building," "destined for divine worship" (Coriden, Green and Heintschel, *The Code of Canon Law* [Mawwah, N.J.: Paulist,1985]), only if it "can in no way be employed for divine worship and is impossible to repair it," can it be "relegated to profane but not sordid use by the diocesan bishop." Code, 1277.

28. See *Church of St. Paul and St. Andrew v. Barwick*, 67 NY2d 510 (1986), *cert denied* 479 U.S. 985 (1986).

29. In two recent cases, state courts have held landmarking of churches violative of religious liberty: *Society of Jesus of New England v. Boston Landmark Commission*, 564 N.E. 2d 571 (Mass., 1990) and *First Covenant Church of Seattle v. City of Seattle*, 787 P.2d 1352 (WA, 1990). In *Society of Jesus* the court relied upon religious liberty provisions of the state constitution. The U.S. Supreme Court refused to review *First Covenant* and remanded the case to the state courts where a second ruling under the state consitution pends.

30. 494 U.S. 872 (1990).

31. What is *not* a religiously "neutral" law? The Court meant a law which either names some religion or its representative or which expressly bars some religious physical act or religious abstention. The Court gave examples: assembling for worship, the sacramental use of bread and wine, abstaining from certain foods or modes of transportation. A nonreligiously "neutral" law would also be one which bans the casting of "statues that are to be used for worship purposes," or prohibits "bowing down before a golden calf." The Court seemed unaware of two obvious facts. First, no such laws exist or have not

existed in this country in this century. Second, legislators (politicians) are utterly unlikely to enact prohibitory laws naming Methodists, Catholics, Waldensians, or any religious group, or to bar religious services, attack dietary laws, or to legislate about golden calves. This short list of what legislatures are forbidden to do would amount to nonsense were it not for its implication of what they are allowed to do.

32. *Wisconsin v. Yoder*, 406 U.S. 205, 215 (1972).

33. While many state constitutions embody provisions reflecting so extreme a view of church-state separation as to invalidate, for example, freedom of parental choice of religious education [see my article as to the origins of these, "The Blaine Amendment: New Look and Old Bugaboo," 165 *N.Y. Law Journal*, Nos. 64–67 (1970)], in these recent cases state bills of rights have been utilized to protect religious liberty where the Free Exercise Clause would be held not to under *Smith*. See *Hershberger v. Minnesota*, 462 N.W.2d 393 (MN 1990), *First Covenant Church of Seattle, supra*, and *Society of Jesus of New England, supra*.

34. E.g., see D. Laycock, "The Remnants of Free Exercise," *1990 Supreme Court Review*, 1.

35. See *Minersville v. Gobitis*, 310 U.S. 586 (1940) (public school children of Jehovah's Witnesses must salute flag); *West Virginia State Board of Education v. Barnette*, 319 U.S. 624 (1943) (such a requirement unconstitutional).

36. Supporters of the view that a Congressional act is needed for the overcoming of *Smith* are divided over whether such an act should, in some way, assure that it cannot be availed of in challenges to abortion-restrictive laws. My own answer has been that it should be amended solely to provide that the term "compelling state interest" would include the supreme interest of society in preventing the taking of innocent human life through abortion.

37. See my article "Giving Our Kids to the Feds," *Human Life Review*, Fall, 1989, 61.

38. From Backus's "An Appeal to the Public for Religious Liberty" in W. G. McLoughlin, *Isaac Backus on Church, State and Calvinism*, 316–317.

Chapter 8: Robert P. Dugan, Jr.

1. Robert L. Cord, *Separation of Church and State: Historical Fact and Current Fiction* (New York: Lambeth Press, 1982), 86.
2. Ibid.
3. Dean M. Kelley, ed., *Government Intervention in Religious Affairs* (New York: The Pilgrim Press, 1982), 17f.
4. Ibid., 20ff.
5. Exactly such a case was that of *Church of St. Paul and St. Andrew v. Barwick*, 496 N.E. 2d 183, 479 U.S. 985 (1986). This book's editor

represented this Methodist church in its effort to secure Supreme Court review of the New York Court of Appeals decision aimed at making a museum out of a house of worship—at the Church's expense. The Supreme Court refused review. (Editor's note).

Chapter 9: John A. Lapp

1. Laquer and Rubin, ed., *The Human Rights Reader* (New York: New American Library, 1979), 3.
2. Frederick Herzog, *Justice Church* (Maryknoll, N.Y.: Orbis, 1980), 26.
3. Maurice Cranston, *What Are Human Rights* (New York: Taplinger, 1973), 21, 24.
4. George W. Forell and Wm. H. Lazareth, eds., *Human Rights: Rhetoric or Reality?* (Philadelphia: Fortress, 1978), 38–9.
5. Noam Chomsky, *Deterring Democracy* (New York : Verso, 1991), 130.
6. Walter Laqueur and Barry Rubin, eds., *The Human Rights Reader,* (New York: New American Library, 1979), 317.
7. Jurgen Moltmann, *On Human Dignity: Political Theology and Ethics* (Philadelphia: Fortress, 1984), 20.
8. Richard John Neuhaus, "What We Mean By Human Rights and Why," *Christian Century,* Dec. 6, 1978, 977.
9. Allen O. Miller, ed., *A Christian Declaration on Human Rights* (Grand Rapids, Mich.: Eerdmans, 1977), 144–46.
10. Ibid., 17
11. Herzog, 111, 124.
12. Neuhaus, 1177.
13. Quoted in *Context*, Apr. 1, 1981.

Chapter 9: John P. Hittinger

1. See Stanley Hauerwas, "The Church and Liberal Democracy: The Moral Limits of a Secular Polity," in Hauerwas, *A Community of Character* (South Bend, Ind.: Univ. of Notre Dame Press, 1981), 72–88.
2. Richard Tuck, *Natural Rights Theories: Their Origin and Development* (New York: Cambridge, 1979), 24–31.
3. See Leo Strauss, *Natural Right and History* (Chicago: Univ. of Chicago Press, 1952); *What is Political Philosophy?* (New York: Free Press, 1959); Richard Tuck, *Hobbes* (New York: Oxford, 1989); C. B. MacPherson, *The Political Theory of Possessive Individualism* (New York: Oxford, 1962); David Johnson, *The Rhetoric of Leviathan* (Princeton, N.J.: Princeton Univ. Press, 1986); Ian Shapiro, *The Evolution of Rights in Liberal Theory* (New York: Cambridge, 1986).
4. Thomas Hobbes, *Leviathan*, ed. C. B. MacPherson (New York: Penguin, 1968), 189.

5. See Hobbes, *Leviathan;* see also Tuck, *Hobbes,* and Strauss, *Natural Right and History.*

6. John Locke, *Letter concerning Toleration* (Indianapolis, Ind.: Hackett, 1983).

7. "To understand Political Power right, and derive it from its Original, we must consider what state all Men are naturally in, and that is a state of perfect Freedom to order their Actions, and dispose of their Possessions, and Persons, as they think fit, within the bounds of the Law of Nature, without asking leave or depending on the Will of any other Man." In John Locke, *Two Treatises of Government*, ed. Peter Laslett, (New York: Cambridge, 1968), 2.4.

8. Ibid.: "A State also of Equality, wherein all Power and Jurisdiction is reciprocal, no one having more than another: there being nothing more evident, than that Creatures of the same species and rank promiscuously born to all the same advantages of Nature, and the use of the same faculties, should also be equal one amongst another without Subordination or Subjection, unless the Lord and Master of them all, should by any manifest declaration of his Will set one above another, and confer on him by an evident and clear appointment an undoubted Right to Dominion and Sovereignty."

9. Ibid., 2.6: "For Men being all the Workmanship of one Omnipotent, and infinitely wise Maker; All the Servants of one Sovereign Master, sent into the World by his order and about his business, they are his Property, whose Workmanship they are, made to last during his, not another's Pleasure. And being furnished with like Faculties, sharing all in one Community of Nature, there cannot be supposed any such Subordination among us, that may authorize us to destroy one another, as if we were made for one another's uses, as the inferior ranks of Creatures are for ours."

10. See Harry Jaffa, "Equality as a Conservative Principle," in Jaffa, *How to Think about the American Revolution*, (Durham, N.C.: Carolina Academic Press, 1978), 13–48.

11. Locke, *Two Treatises,* 2.16: "One may destroy a Man who makes War upon him, or has discovered an Enmity to his being, for the same Reason, that he may kill a Wolf or a Lyon; because such men are not under the ties of the Common Law of Reason, have no other Rule, but that of Force and Violence, and so may be treated as Beasts of Prey, those dangerous and noxious Creatures, that will be sure to destroy him, whenever he falls into their Power."

12. See also John Locke, *Essay Concerning Human Understanding*, ed. Peter Niditch (Oxford: Clarendon, 1975), I.3.6: "It is no wonder, that every one should, not only allow, but recommend, and magnifie those Rules to others, from whose observance of them, he is sure to reap Advantage to himself. He may, out of Interest, as well as Conviction, cry up

that for Sacred; which if once trampled on, and prophaned, he himself cannot be safe nor secure."

13. Gerard V. Bradley, "The Constitution and the Erotic Self," *First Things* 16 (Oct. 1991): 28–32.

14. David A. Richards, *Toleration and the Constitution* (New York: Oxford, 1986); David A. Richards, *Sex, Drugs, Death, and the Law*, (Totowa, N.J.: Rowman and Littlefield, 1982); David A. Richards, *Foundations of American Constitutionalism* (New York: Oxford, 1989); "Human Rights and Moral Ideals: An Essay on the Moral Theory of Liberalism," *Social Theory and Practice* 5 (1980): 461; "Rights and Autonomy," *Ethics* 92 (1981): 3.

15. *Sex, Drugs,* 1; "Rights and Autonomy," 3.

16. On Calvinism see *Sex, Drugs*, 2, 14, 90, 126, 194; *Foundations*, 25, 54; *Toleration*, 235, 240. On Catholicism see *Sex, Drugs*, 52; *Foundations*, 217; *Toleration*, 207, 259–60, 277–78.

17. On the community of principle, see *Foundations*, 295–99. On the degradation of traditional communities, see *Foundations*, 277; "Human Rights and Moral Ideals," 485–86: "The detailed casuistry of one's personal life, typical of older moral traditions, imposes unreal and factitious constraints which deny and disfigure the moral freedom that we, as persons, possess. To deny such freedom is to impose a false passivity and resignation, a slavery of the spirit which is neither natural nor humane."

18. *Toleration*, 245. See *Sex, Drugs*, 12–13.

19. See Michael Sandel, *Liberalism and the Limits of Justice* (New York: Cambridge, 1982), 25–28; see also John Finnis, *Fundamentals of Ethics* (Washington, D.C.: Georgetown Univ. Press, 1983), 48–53.

20. *Toleration*, 246.

21. "Human Rights and Moral Ideals," 461.

22. *Toleration*, 136.

23. *Toleration*, 206–10.

24. *Toleration*, 255–58.

25. *Sex, Drugs*, 63. "Certain of the traditional moral condemnations of homosexuals, appear, on analysis, to be vicious forms of social and legal persecution." See also "Human Rights and Moral Ideals," 479.

26. See *Foundations*, 246–247.

27. Ibid.

28. Jacques Maritain, *Integral Humanism* (South Bend, Ind.: Univ. of Notre Dame Press, 1973), 27–30; *The Range of Reason* (New York: Scribner's, 1952), chapters 7, 8, 14.

29. Jacques Maritain, *Christianity and Democracy and Rights of Man and Natural Law*, trans. Doris C. Anson (San Francisco: Ignatius, 1986), 145–47.

30. See John Hittinger, "Maritain and America," *This World*, vol. 8.

31. See also, John Paul II, "Rediscover the Relationship of Truth, Goodness and Freedom," *L'Osservatore Romano* 28 (Apr. 1986): 12. *Redemptor Hominis*, sec. 12.
32. *Range of Reason*, 187; see also, Jacques Maritain's *Freedom in the Modern World* (New York: Scribner's, 1936); and a collection of essays on Maritain: Simon and Adler, *Freedom in the Modern World*, ed. Michael D. Torre (South Bend, Ind.: Univ. of Notre Dame Press, 1989).
33. See 152–89, *The Rights of Man and Natural Law*; this list may also be found in *The Social and Political . . . of Jacques Maritain*, eds. Joseph Evans and Leo R. Ward, recently reissued by University of Notre Dame Press.
34. See James V. Schall, *The Church, the State and Society in the Thought of John Paul II* (Chicago: Franciscan Herald Press, 1982).

General Index

A

Abortion   22, 27, 37, 39, 51, 63, 66–73, 77, 92–3, 98, 110–1, 113, 118–9, 121–8, 135, 137, 140, 148–52, 197, 200, 227, 229–30, 253, 284
Abortion Rights Mobilization   225
Abortion, flaws in arguments for   124
Abortion, pro-choice   22, 63, 70, 72
Absolutes, denial of   135, 191
Absolutism   40, 113
Accrediting Association of Bible Colleges   193
Achievement tests   210
Adams, John Quincy   25
Adams, Samuel   81
AIDS   63, 71–2, 141, 158
Alcohol   142
Alexander, Lamar   216
American Revolution   25, 83, 87
Americans, religious nature of   96
Amnesty International   238, 244
Anarchy, social   57
Anderson, Carl A.   129, 144
Antinomianism   115
Apology   73
Apostolic declaration   243
Aquinas, Thomas   101, 116, 124, 145, 197, 201, 256
Aristotelian philosophy   248
Aristotle   49
Armstrong, William   226
Aruelius, Marcus   73
Ashbrook-Dornan amendments   222
Asia   40, 180
Augustine   116, 124, 145, 187

B

Backus, Isaac   220, 284
Baelstrini, Raffaelo   69
Ball, William Bentley   7, 9, 205, 207, 224
Ballad of the White Horse, The   202
Bangor Baptist School   210, 281

Baptists   30–1, 77, 83–4, 88, 90, 95, 205, 210, 220, 222–3,
Beecher, Lyman   164–5
Bennett   50, 52
Berger, Peter   35, 40
Bill of Rights   83, 122, 151, 236
Black, Hugo   84
Blanshard, Paul   165
Bloom, Allan   114, 168
Bob Jones University   212
Bob Jones University v. United States   212–3
Bodenheimer, Edgar   69
Bonner, Yelena   235
Bork, Robert   69, 270
Bourbon Restoration   147
Bradley, Gerard   251
Brownson, Orestes   195–6, 200, 202–3
Burnham, James   64

C

Carter, Jimmy   91
Chaney v. Grover   271
Change, differing views of   60
Chapman, Steven   70
Charter of Human Rights   253
Chesterton, G. K.   202
Children
   custody of   273
   gift of God   139
   value of   139
Christian College Coalition   192
Christian Legal Society   205, 226
Christian school movement   221
Christianity and Democracy   254–5
Church and state   218–9, 228, 284
Church and state, conflicts   88
Church and state, separation of   25, 80–1, 85, 87, 90, 284
Church and state, the public debate   80–1, 92, 97–8
Church Audit Procedures Act   225
Churches, liberal   34–5
Churchill, Winston   236, 238

289

General Index

General Index

Scripture Index

Scripture Index